ALMART
SIDE OUT

Enter

D1532321

from stockboy
to stockholder
RON LOVELESS
with anna morter

It's a Numbers Game

200 million — *The number of customers and members Walmart serves each week*

2.2 million — *The number of "associates" currently employed by Walmart*

30,000 — *The number of suppliers that sell to Walmart*

2 — *The number of books written by authors who were there from the beginning – Sam Walton and Ron Loveless*

When you're the largest and most successful company in the world, you've got a big "target" on your back.

Critics hate it. Shoppers love it. Is Walmart the evil empire or low-price savior?

There's never been a book uniquely-positioned to answer that question. Until now.

Author Ron Loveless was there from the start. Actually, before the start. Born to a welfare-supported family in Hiwassee, Arkansas (population 98), Ron and Walmart are inextricably joined at the hip. His mother cleaned house for the man everyone called "Mr. Sam" long before the first Walmart opened its doors. Sam Walton himself watched Ron play Little League baseball and hired him away from his $1.50 per hour service station job when only one Walmart store existed.

Chronicling Ron's rise from stock boy to senior vice president (or in Ron's words, from "outhouse to penthouse"), *Walmart Inside Out* gives readers a rare, behind-the-scenes look at the corporate giant from a uniquely-balanced perspective. By turns enlightening, entertaining and endearing, *Walmart Inside Out* is written in an amiable, down-home style that feels like you're sitting on the author's porch, sharing stories and a cool drink on a gentle Arkansas night.

WALMART
INSIDE OUT

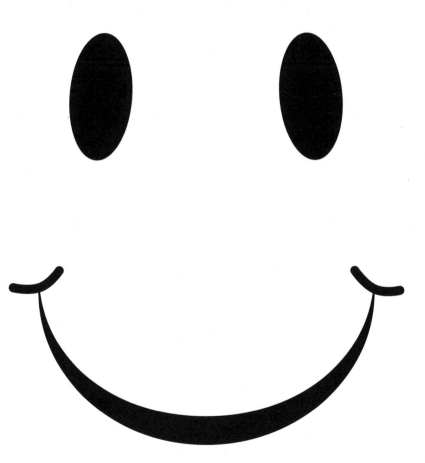

WALMART
INSIDE OUT

from stockboy
to stockholder

RON LOVELESS
with anna morter

Stephens Press ☺ Las Vegas, Nevada

Editor: Brian Rouff
Copy Editor: Jami Carpenter
Book Designer, Cover photos: Sue Campbell
Publishing Coordinator: Stacey Fott

First Printing

Cataloging-in-Publication

Loveless, Ronald L.
Walmart Inside Out : Stockboy to Stockholder / Ronald L. Loveless.
336 p. : photos ; 23 cm.

ISBN: 1-935043-41-2
ISBN-13: 978-1-935043-41-6
ISBN (ebook): 978-1-935043-42-3

Contents: Part one. Humble beginnings – Part two. My Career – Part three. Understanding Walmart's success – Part four. Lessons for suppliers, associates, and life. 1. Loveless, Ronald L. 2. Walmart (Firm)—Employees--Biography. 3. Walmart (Firm)—Management. 4. Retail trade—United States—Management. I. Title.

658.87'02 dc22   2011   2010937622

STEPHENS PRESS, LLC
A Stephens Media Company

Post Office Box 1600
Las Vegas, NV 89125-1600
www.stephenspress.com

Printed in United States of America

To the memory of my mother, Angie Ritchie,
and my sister, Patricia Musteen.

"I miss you both so much."

Contents

PART FOUR
LESSONS FOR SUPPLIERS, ASSOCIATES AND LIFE

Acknowledgments

This book would never have been written were it not for people in my life who pushed, begged, threatened, and encouraged me to stop "talking about" the lessons I had learned through my career and life and put them "to paper." The original thought of doing a book came to my mind twenty years ago. But as most first-time authors no doubt find out, it is truly a tough thing to do. As I learned from self-help books, I had to begin by simply sitting in front of the computer and putting my thoughts on paper. That was the beginning. The book you are about to read is the end result, for which I owe a great deal to the following people.

I finally sat down and began the process simply to get my wife, Robin, to stop heckling me about it. After starting it, I began to enjoy the writing, but not necessarily Robin's critiques. What she enjoyed in reading a book was in most cases considerably different from what I was writing and envisioning. Therefore, it is a minor miracle our marriage survived the process. I say this in jest, because I truly owe Robin a debt of gratitude for driving me to complete this book, putting up with my rebuttals to her suggestions, and loving me enough to stay through its completion. Robin, I love you for it.

As much of a renegade as I've been through my career and life, my family could have, and probably should have at times, given up on me. But the love I felt from my mom, Angie Ritchey, my sisters Connie and Pat, my first wife, Cindy, my kids, Ronnie II and Kim, stepdaughter April and grandson, Kody, in spite of my weaknesses, encouraged me to keep going on this project. My family was more proud of my accomplishments than I ever was. Thank you from the bottom of my heart for what each of you have meant to me. In Chapter Two, I refer to the untold number of possible "cousins" I have in my extended family, and at last I have found the benefit to having a huge family. It will increase the sales of this book. Ronnie, my son, helped remove the doubts daily as the project went forward. I may only sell fifty books, but he has personally solicited that many sales (signed). Thank you, Son.

My colleagues, too numerous to mention individually, have all been supportive and encouraging. My fellow Walmart associates and many northwest Arkansas friends also encouraged me to write this book. "Larry Robertson, I still have the two $10 bills you gave me with your note committing to the purchase of the first book off the press." Larry gave me this in 1998, showing a lot of trust that I would get it done. The purchase is finally coming to pass. Bob Wilkerson, at my golf club, Lost Springs Golf and Country Club, in Rogers, please stop asking me about the book. You're getting one of the first copies. Maybe I can concentrate on my game now.

Anna Morter ... what can I say? Anna and Tom Morter have been neighbors and friends of mine for many years here in Rogers, Arkansas. With a successful health clinic and healthcare organization called Morter HealthSystem, they are pioneers in the field of chiropractic and alternative applications for better health. Bio Energetic Synchronization Technique (BEST) was founded by Tom's father, Ted Morter, Jr. They have authored many books and hundreds of articles, newsletters, and educational materials for the healthcare industry as well as for the public. Knowing I needed help in making my manuscript professional enough that the publishers wouldn't just throw it into their trash cans, I solicited Anna to edit the initial writings. It is a testament to her ability that all the publishers I submitted the manuscript to — though often turned down — complimented us on the writing. She put in long hours (sorry Tom) at the computer even after warning me that her daughter's wedding was coming up, and she wasn't sure she could meet my deadlines (sorry Sarah). But she certainly did.

And last, but certainly not least, this book came to be a reality because of Stephens Press, LLC, my publisher. There is a story here also. Stephens, Inc., in Little Rock, Arkansas is a highly respected investment firm. In the early years of Walmart's growth I came to know Mike Smith and J.D. Simpson, two of their key folks. The Stephens people were involved with the initial public offering of Walmart stock in 1970. Stephens also owns a number of newspapers under the Stephens Media Group. As I sought a publishing company for my book, I noticed a newspaper ad for a book published by Stephens Press in Las Vegas.

I called Mike Smith at Stephens, whom I hadn't spoken to in years. He happened to be returning from a turkey hunt, being an avid outdoorsman, and after exchanging greetings, he asked me, "Ronnie, how is the Chicken Report doing?" Once again, the first thing anyone remembers me for is the darn LEIR. Thus, chapter one of this book explains the Chicken Report. Mike, that one is for you. Mike informed me that Stephens, indeed, did own a publishing company out in Las Vegas, and promised to have someone call me.

Thus began one of the most rewarding experiences of this entire project. I believe in divine intervention and that some things are meant to be. From the first phone call with Carolyn Hayes Uber, president of Stephens Press, LLC, and throughout this process, I feel fortunate to have met and worked with her. She is one of the most professional, talented, warm, and friendly people I've ever worked with. Recognized by her peers as one of the best in the business, she has done everything she has promised, and done so while contending with a tremendous personal health challenge. She is my publisher, but my hope is that, regardless of any success or failure of this book, I can count her as a friend when it's all said and done. Carolyn is one of those rare people you meet in life with true "heart" for others.

Carolyn suggested an editor to work with me, Brian Rouff. Brian is, himself, a successful businessman, author, and editor, residing in Las Vegas. His efforts made the book read and flow much better than I thought possible, and he worked long and late hours in helping get it done in record time. Brian, thank you for all your hard work and helping me complete my dream.

And I owe a big "thank you" to the entire Stephens Press, LLC team. It is a relatively small group with the abilities of a large one. Sue Campbell, book designer, is a master at her craft and her work in your hands speaks for itself. Stacey Fott, publishing coordinator, is responsible for the endless myriad of details from distributor snafus to social media promotions. Jami Carpenter, copyeditor, makes sure every apostrophe is correct. Joe da Costa, publishing assistant, produces creative marketing elements from websites to bookmarks.

Thank you, everyone.

—Ron Loveless

FOREWORD

Walmart Inside Out is a fascinating story detailing how a young man can navigate from poor economic circumstances in rural America to become an effective, highly respected management talent with the world's largest retailer.

Ron Loveless takes us on a candid, inspirational journey that explains how he overcame numerous obstacles to fashion a life's work that provides insight and encouragement to all who read this story.

Additionally, Ron paints us a great picture in the early days of Walmart and the basic principles that provided the foundation, which still exists in the company today. By starting at the bottom and progressing through various levels of management, Ron gained an insight that served him well as he ultimately directed large positions within the company's business.

I am pleased Ron included a section in the book on the LEIR Report. I have used this report as I traveled from Washington to New York and abroad. Though intended as humor, I found it to be universally understood and appreciated by business associates throughout the world.

Ron Loveless was one of Sam Walton's favorite associates. Even though Ron grew up in Bentonville and he had a long relationship with Sam, it was Ron's qualities that caught the admiration of Sam . . . hard working, innovative, great integrity, dedicated and effective. A company's success is measured by the contributions of its associates and you can measure those contributions by asking "did he truly make a difference?" Although Ron retired much too young, he certainly did make a difference and Walmart is a better company today because of his contributions.

This book is a must-read for anyone interested in how the American dream is realized.

— DAVID GLASS, FORMER PRESIDENT/CEO,
WALMART STORES, INC.

PART ONE
HUMBLE BEGINNINGS

CHAPTER 1

The "LEIR" Lands at Walmart

1984

> Many bosses feel there's no place for fun at work.
> Today's employees demand that work be fun.
> The challenge is to reconcile these two conflicting expectations.
> Work is most productive when it's fused with fun. Fun can be an
> essential element to conducting business, retaining customers,
> enhancing external perceptions of the business and brand,
> attracting and retaining talented employees — and
> helping to build competitive advantage.
>
> — LESLIE A. YERKES
> *Creating Fun in the Workplace*

Just before dawn on a crisp Monday morning in early 1984, our Walmart twin-engine Aero Commander lifted off from the Bentonville, Arkansas airport for the short jaunt to Dallas, Texas. Jerry Turney sat at the controls. David Glass, CFO for Walmart, had nestled into his seat to enjoy a cup of coffee while perusing the *Wall Street Journal*. I, the recently appointed head of the new Sam's Wholesale Club division, was seated across from him. I reported directly to David and anticipated having time to talk about a few upcoming projects. However, the purpose of today's trip was a visit to the first prototype Sam's Wholesale Club, which was to open soon on Garland Road in Dallas.

Shortly after takeoff, David looked up from his newspaper and said, "Ronnie, isn't it strange that our Walmart store sales are booming, yet

17

these economists back east are forecasting doom-and-gloom? They use indicators such as the GNP, housing starts, interest rates, and all that. Thank goodness our customers aren't paying heed to that stuff. We'll just choose not to participate in the recession."

Thinking about his statement while soaring over the vast stretch of northwest Arkansas "chicken country," I began to reflect on my childhood days in the nearby town of Hiwasse. In fact, reflections like this would prove to serve as a foundation for my personal life, as well as a guide for my career. Anyway, back to the chickens. You see, northwest Arkansas was then, and is even more so today, one of the largest poultry production areas in the country. I recalled the times my mother would wake my sisters and me early in the morning to go look for chickens along the roadside. During the fifties and sixties, residents caught chickens at night and loaded them into wooden crates for transport to the slaughter houses. Many of the chickens would fly off the trucks through broken slats in the crates. For a poor family like ours, these wayward birds served as some pretty good eating come Sunday dinner. (For those readers who are not from the south, dinner is the noon meal, while supper is served in the evening.)

As I stewed on those days, being known as a sort of company clown and comic, a thought came to mind. In fact, this was the birth of the Loveless Economic Indicator Report (LEIR), although I didn't realize at the time the full-scale dynamics of my off-the-cuff idea.

"Mr. Glass," I said, "those so-called economic experts in New York use the wrong indicators. For our company and our customers, a different set of measurements makes more sense. You don't know this, but I have a group of 'Chicken Patrollers' from our General Office count the number of chickens and other road kill they see on the highways as they come to work in the mornings. We adjust our buyer's open-to-buy and inventory planning accordingly."

David looked confused. Then a wry smile crossed his face. "Now there's an original idea," he said. "How's it work?"

"Well," I said, "as the economy gets worse and people are struggling, they pick up these chickens shortly after they hit the road ... so long as they're not smashed too flat. As the economy improves, they buy their chickens at the grocery store, like everyone else. It makes perfect sense to me."

David laughed and said, "It certainly makes more sense than those indicators back east, which don't have an impact on our customers here in Walmart territory. Thanks for sharing your indicators with me."

Several weeks passed, and then one day "Mr. Sam" (Sam Walton, that is) dropped by my office. Although we all loved and respected Mr. Sam, his unexpected visits had a way of making us feel uneasy. A compliment from him was inspiring, but when he was unhappy about something, he had a subtle way of making you want to crawl under a rug.

After a bit of small talk, Mr. Sam said, "Ronnie, David shared with me your chicken economic indicator program. I think it makes a lot of sense. I'd like you to present your report at the analyst forum during this year's shareholders' meeting."

Thinking he *must* be joking, I was taken aback. The annual Walmart shareholders' meeting is unique; a combination of business, circus, pep rally, and motivational show. There's nothing quite like it in the business world. Thousands attend. After taking Walmart stock public in 1970, in addition to the shareholders' meeting, the executive team conducted a very private "analyst forum" in the General Office during the weekend of the shareholders' event. Many of the large investment banks holding Walmart stock assigned their retail analysts to this meeting. Local and state dignitaries, members of the media, and other VIPs were the norm. This particular year, we expected Arkansas Governor Bill Clinton as well.

Apparently unaware of my astonishment, Mr. Sam plowed ahead. "These guys are always looking to find some secret to our success. You and I know it's as simple as low prices, great people, and taking care of our customers. But let's have some fun with them. I'll introduce you as our 'in-house' economic guru, then give up some of my time for you to deliver your chicken report."

"Mr. Sam, are you serious?" I wondered if I looked as uncertain as I felt.

"Sure," he said. "They'll get a kick out of it."

So that was that.

After visiting with David Glass and the folks putting together the agenda for the analysts' meeting, I found that Sam had indeed made room for me to introduce the LEIR.

All in a day's work, right? Not exactly. But I rose to the challenge. Allowing my jokester side to take over, I decided to go the extra mile to create new material for the report. With the help of Bob McCurry, one of my marketing buddies, we assembled a slew of charts and graphs to help bolster my case. I also recruited Stan Moore and Larry King, the early grocery buyers for Sam's Club. Outfitted in Chicken Patrol (CP) outfits, they accompanied me to a brooder house to collect an assortment of live and dead chickens to be featured on my slides.

My preparations were in order as the meeting date rolled around. That Mr. Sam and David Glass required no prior approval of the content indicates a great deal of trust by those gentlemen. Today, Walmart receives such scrutiny that any public comments or presentations are undoubtedly approved by a bevy of attorneys and executives. In the early days we just "winged it." (No chicken pun intended.)

Our top brass held the analyst forum in a small room at the Walmart General Office. When I entered the room, my heart skipped a beat or two when I spotted Governor Clinton and other local dignitaries standing in the back. At that moment, I realized that our little joke was serious business. Members of the press had already sought out their seats. Then, hosted by our buyers, the retail analysts made their way into the room. Pads and pens poised, they quickly readied themselves to take down the scoop. Two particular analysts had followed the company closely from the day our stock went public.

Maggie Gilliam, of First Boston Corporation, and Joe Ellis, of Goldman-Sachs, believed in Sam Walton and Walmart from the outset. Closely following the operations and merchandising strategies of the company, they became very familiar with the executive team and the talent of each member. We placed great importance on keeping them and the rest of the analysts well-informed and positive about Walmart. Knowing this made me realize I was about to make a complete fool of myself and the company. My mouth felt like the Sahara Desert on a particularly dry afternoon as I pondered the possibility of looking for new employment.

Mr. Sam began with his usual up-beat, positive comments, and then presented an overview of his five-year forecast, which he always had ready — usually scrawled on a yellow legal pad. Then he remarked, "Now folks, this is the time when David Glass usually shares his numbers. But so many of you have repeatedly asked for secrets to Walmart's success that I've decided to reveal one of our most closely-guarded company secrets."

In unison, the entire audience leaned forward. Mr. Sam continued, "I've asked our chief in-house economist, Ron Loveless, to give you a report on the economic indicators from which we make our purchasing and merchandising decisions. This information has been proprietary up until now, but I invite you to take notes. Our company is experiencing great success, while the New York economic indicators reflect a rather serious downturn in the economy. Mr. Loveless' numbers indicate quite the opposite, so we've been aggressive. As a result, our bottom line is outstanding."

Here goes nothing, I thought as I stood to begin my presentation, all eyes riveted on me. After all, Sam Walton himself said this was a key secret. *The* secret. With a straight face and an odd sense of calm, I explained that I had based the LEIR on the number of dead chickens that littered the highways of northwest Arkansas. As I proceeded, I assessed the crowd. Some were restless, some were grinning, and some simply looked confused. But, as Mr. Sam suggested, all were diligently scribbling away on their notepads. The analysts and their escorts exchanged furtive glances. Fully aware of our little joke, the buyer escorts assisted me by playing their roles to the hilt, intently whispering to their assigned analysts how committed we were to this program.

I presented the professional graphs, which indicated a gradual increase in the chicken count through the twelve months reflected in the report. Pointing out an unusually high spike in the count, I explained that two chicken trucks had collided on a sharp curve in western Benton County, dumping an inordinate number of chickens onto the roadside. Our audit team, investigating the unusual spike, had come upon the accident. Therefore, we discounted the accident in our overall numbers review. In summation, with the count showing a steady 6–8 percent overall growth over the past six months, we had actually increased our buyer's open-to-buy budget by 10 percent for the holiday selling season.

By the time I finished the numbers portion of the report, the incredulous looks had increased by a much higher percentage than our open-to-buy budget. I sensed that a few folks were on the verge of laughing out loud, but believing this LEIR was important to Sam Walton and Walmart, no one dared show their disdain during the meeting. As a finale, not wanting anyone to leave this meeting thinking we were serious, I launched into my slide show.

In preparation for this presentation, I had commandeered a few guys from the office to dress in white jumpsuits with armbands that read CP (Chicken Patrol). I then used the live and dead chickens as the stars of my show. Maintaining my poker face, which was getting more difficult all the time, I explained that we took the LEIR so seriously, we assigned an internal audit team to go into the field to authenticate that only edible chickens were being counted. A succession of slides demonstrated our Chicken Patrol in action during training:

▸ First, we trained them to identify all sorts of "road kill" from a distance, so as not to confuse the chicken count with other animals. I'm referring here to critters that appear in abundance in the Ozarks (and undoubtedly in other areas): possums, buzzards, coons, armadillos, rabbits, and squirrels.

▸ Second, we taught them to verify the time of death of each chicken with the aid of a kit supplied by the Arkansas State Police. Chickens that had been dead more than three days would be eliminated from the audited count, since most people would not pick them up (because of the smell).

▸ Third, they received instruction on ascertaining the sex of each chicken. I showed a slide or two of our CP people holding up a dead chicken, examining between its legs. I clarified that only female chickens are desirable for consumption. And since we don't eat roosters, we placed extreme importance on determining the sex of each chicken.

▸ Fourth, we trained them to measure the depth and circumference of each chicken. A slide depicted the CP squad down on their knees, measuring the linear depth of a chicken breast with a ruler. I explained that when a car or truck ran over a chicken, if it smashed the breast flatter than one inch, no one would pick up that chicken anyway. Therefore, determining the edibility of each chicken was paramount.

I concluded my presentation by stating, "So, you see, our LEIR is highly sophisticated and meaningful, in that only edible chickens are counted."

From the onset of the slide presentation, everyone in the room had acquiesced that this was, indeed, a big joke — and a good one, at that. When I finally finished, the crowd roared with laughter. I did, too. Even after Mr. Sam took over the reins and we got back to serious matters, the mood in the room remained upbeat.

Shortly after this meeting, several articles appeared in newspapers around the country. Following is the article that ran in the business section of the *Sacramento Bee* on Tuesday, June 19, 1984, written by Capital Accounts editor, Marguaret Peterson. I'm not sure whether it was good or bad for my reputation, but Walmart's stock performance certainly climbed. Perhaps the old adage from the entertainment industry — "any publicity is good publicity" — might apply here.

The Sacramento Bee Tuesday, June 19, 1984

Walmart's secret of success: Counting chickens on the roads

The retail analysts in the auditorium perked up like so many bloodhounds catching the scent. Walmart Stores' annual meeting suddenly held unexpected promise. The fabulously successful discount chain was about to unveil its secret for forecasting the economy, they were told. Analysts have watched over the years — and tried to explain — as the Arkansas-based firm's sales zoomed from $168 million in 1974 to $4.8 billion last year. Net profits last year were $200 million.

As the audience waited breathlessly, Ron Loveless strode to the podium and set up an impressive series of charts and graphs. Then Loveless began talking about the numbers of edible chickens — dead and alive — found on Arkansas highways.

That's the basis of the Loveless Economic Indicator Report (LEIR), created by the vice president and general manager of Sam's Wholesale Club, a Walmart operation similar to California's Price Club.

Chickens, as it turns out, are big business in Arkansas. More than half the nation's fryers are trucked through northwestern Arkansas to slaughterhouses. They are shipped in crates on flatbed trucks and as the trucks careen down the highways, some crates topple off. That's where LEIR comes in.

According to LEIR, when times are bad and people are out of work, the crates are grabbed as fast as they fall. So the edible chicken count goes down. When times are good, there's no incentive to be out on the highway sifting through birds possibly run over and squashed. So the count goes up.

As Loveless tells it, LEIR gets even better. There are official counters who must meet rigid standards. Counters are trained to distinguish chickens from other common roadside fowl — and must be able to do so in blindfold tests. There are also rigid standards for classifying edible chickens. Chickens dead more than twenty-four hours or mashed flatter than one inch are not considered edible.

Loveless last week recalled the meeting and laughed. "There were all these retail analysts sitting there kinda scratching their heads and saying, 'Is this true?'" He also has a written version of LEIR to pass out to visiting analysts. "People pick up on it (LEIR) and put it in their reports. And, honestly, people feel that maybe this is true and they don't really know," said Loveless. "We write the thing seriously, but it's just a joke."

"However," he said, "It is based on half-truth." As a youngster from a poor rural family, Loveless and his siblings often scoured the Arkansas highways for fallen chickens. "We'd pick those chickens off the road and we'd eat good that day," he said. He recalls personally seeing a fallen fowl perched atop a road sign, surrounded by a clamoring mob of would-be diners trying to shake it loose.

Loveless, who has been with Walmart twenty years, began toying with his index at staff meetings. "People would ask did I have a new update on the chicken count, and I'd get up and make some funny remarks," he said.

Recently, he told a meeting that "we had observed eight Southwestern Bell employees picking up chickens, which would support what we've been hearing that the telephone industry is in a state of confusion."

The annual meeting presentation was the high point for the LEIR — or maybe just the beginning. After one bank's retail analyst who attended gave the LEIR a big write-up, complete with charts and graphs, bankers and analysts from all over the country were calling for quarterly updates. Then Senator David Pryor, D-Ark., included LEIR in a presentation before the Senate Finance Committee on the state of the poultry industry.

And, said Loveless, "I have sent a copy to Ronald Reagan. I'm expecting a response back from him." After all, he said, analysts have told him, "this makes more sense than anything they use in Washington today."

I've now been away from the company for as many years as I worked there, yet when I encounter someone from Walmart, he or she still asks about how the chicken count is doing. Like many others, I worked my way up through the ranks. I progressed from stock boy to vice president of the Hardlines Merchandising Division. I ultimately became the first leader of the Sam's Club Division, yet my legacy seems to remain the "guy who did the Chicken Report." I'm not sure whether I should be proud or embarrassed. Maybe a little of both.

I always said that Sam Walton thought of business 110 percent of the time, but he also possessed a very good sense of humor. He loved the unflappable characters that came up with off-the-wall ideas to promote company initiatives. I would be remiss if I didn't mention two close friends who were both creative and entertaining during my Walmart career: Bob Hart and Russ Robertson. They were not only very capable and successful contributors to Walmart's success, but could just as easily have enjoyed careers as stand-up comedians.

Most of the zany and strange antics were known only internally, but without a doubt the most highly-publicized was when Sam Walton bet that our company could not achieve an 8 percent pre-tax profit on sales. We achieved the number and only after a great deal of pressure from his management team, Mr. Sam paid up by donning a grass skirt and leis, and performed a hula dance on Wall Street in New York City to the strains of ukulele music.

☺

I opened this memoir with the invention of the LEIR, which occurred toward the end of my career with Walmart and Sam's, to provide a glimpse into my background and to illustrate the importance of "having fun" while working in the highly stressful and labor-intensive business of retailing. Most people would agree that all work and no play can lead to a myriad of problems. Whether performing a Blues Brother dance routine with Stan Moore or dressing Bob Hart in a Chinese rice farmer's garb to spoof Sam Walton and his bird hunting, I had fun at Walmart. It was part of our culture and Mr. Sam was right in the middle of it.

> Whether it's Saturday morning meetings or stockholders' meetings or store openings or just normal days, we have always tried to make life as interesting and as unpredictable as we can, and to make Walmart a fun proposition. We're constantly doing crazy things to capture the attention of our folks and lead them to think up surprises of their own. We like to see them do wild things in the stores that are fun for the customers and fun for the associates. If you're committed to the Walmart partnership and its core values, the culture encourages you to think up all sorts of ideas that break the mold and fight monotony. We know that our antics—our company cheers or our songs or my hula—can sometimes be pretty corny, or hokey. We couldn't care less.
> — SAM M. WALTON — SAM WALTON, MADE IN AMERICA,
> BY SAM WALTON AND JOHN HUEY

CHAPTER 2

My House, Chicken House, Outhouse

> ## 1943–1953
>
> ▸ In 1945, Sam Walton leases his first store in Newport, Arkansas.
>
> ▸ In 1950, losing his lease, he relocates to Bentonville, Arkansas and buys the Harrison Variety Store, owned by Luther Harrison, located on the town square. He renames it Walton's 5 & 10.
>
> ▸ My mom, sisters, and I live on the Child Assistance Program and pickled pigs feet in Hiwassee.

Okay, so you picked this book up for some reason. It certainly isn't because I'm famous and you longed to read about my background. But hopefully, by getting to know me on a personal basis, you'll better understand the traits and thoughts which guided my life and my career at Walmart. I'm a simple man, but I know that childhood and life experiences contain valuable lessons that serve to build character. I'll share with you the lessons I've learned along the way, in hope that you may glean some knowledge or insight from my experiences that will aid you in your walk through life.

I didn't just fall off the turnip truck yesterday. I was born in the bedroom of my grandmother's house in Hiwassee, Arkansas on October 6, 1943. The population of Hiwassee at that time was fewer than one hundred people. As I tell everyone, the town was so small the city limits were on opposite sides of the same sign and the city utility was a Die Hard battery.

My grandma, Beulah Allmendinger (one of the all-time memorable names), performed the delivery because the doctor, from nearby Gravette, didn't arrive in time. My father, Clifford Loveless, had talked his way out of a jail in Kansas to attend the birth of his second child. However, he chose instead to steal a sheriff's car in Bentonville, six miles east of Hiwassee. They locked him up, once again, the day before I made my debut.

My mother, Angie Beatrice Allmendinger Loveless Crabtree Ritchie (she married four times), is the greatest woman I have ever known. The esteem I have for her is not because of any public measurements of achievement, but because she struggled as a single mom for so many years during very difficult times, just to make ends meet. Her alcoholic, abusive first husband left her with nothing but three children at the end of their three-year marriage. As a result, Mom worked long, hard hours to provide for us.

My earliest and lasting memories of Mom during my childhood are of watching her slave over an iron, which she kept heated with the aid of our wood-burning stove. Mom brought things into our home to iron for people from our community. I remember she charged five cents per piece. That piece could be a blouse, a pair of pants, or a large frilly curtain. Regardless of the size, she charged a nickel.

When we were old enough, my sisters and I helped supplement Mom's income by tackling whatever odd jobs came our way. These jobs often entailed hours of sweaty, back-breaking labor. Now, please note that this was not uncommon back then. When it came time to harvest the crops, many kids worked in the fields and apple orchards prevalent throughout the area. We were happy for the chance to earn money, and not knowing any better, cheerily marched off with Mom to a green bean field or strawberry patch to pick the ripe yield of the day. On occasion, we also helped sell apples from the back of a pick-up truck owned by Mom's boyfriend, Charlie Duncan.

By any measurement then or today, we would have been considered poor folk. However, we were blessed by blindness to our impoverished situation, which left us blissfully happy. Frankly, as we lived out our young lives, we simply didn't acknowledge our condition. While many people measure their happiness by the amount of material possessions they amass, I recall that a small number of little things served us just fine. We were content with our circumstances and appreciative of any little blessing that came our way.

Weekly rations from the Child Assistance Program (now known as the Welfare Program), helped complete our needs. Trailed by our mother, my sisters and I would march, dusty and barefoot, down the gravel road which served as the main street of Hiwassee. Our weekly treks to the General Store to pick up rations afforded us our allotment of powdered milk, peanut butter, and an assortment of other commodities, which we then toted back the quarter-mile stretch to the three-room clapboard dwelling we called home.

We all had chores to do every day. No exceptions. The chores varied over the years, depending on our ages and capabilities or the needs of any particular day. Patricia, the youngest, was often in charge of straightening our bedroom. (I always had to sleep in the middle, which I hated.) Connie, the oldest, usually helped out in the kitchen, while I, the only boy, had the privilege of "slopping" our baby pig, Pinkie. This amounted to trudging out to the pig pen (which could be a hot, muddy, cold, or rainy experience, depending on the season), to deliver the pail of table scraps which served as Pinkie's dinner.

I'll never forget the day that Mom's boyfriend loaded Pinkie into his truck and drove off. A few days later, while frying up bacon, Mom accidentally let slip that she was cooking Pinkie. When my sister, Connie, explained what happened, I cried. I also refused to eat the bacon, hungry as I was.

We ate as a family while gathered around the kitchen table. A typical lunch (or dinner, for that matter) consisted of beans and cornbread, topped off with a sampling from the ever-present gallon jar of pickled pigs feet. A small jar is rather expensive today, but in the 1940s, a gallon jug of pigs feet was cheap, and thus, a staple in our house. I grew to hate the things as I got older. They reminded me of Pinkie.

Most of my favorite toys growing up were homemade. I loved to nail a bent can to the end of a stick and roll a steel hoop around in the yard or out in the road. In the evenings, my sisters and I played with the neighbor kids. We looked forward to games such as "kick the can" or "Annie over." I spent hours building a fort out of any materials I could find. I also enjoyed sitting in the dirt or mud, pushing around my few toy cars or trucks. My sisters, in the meantime, played "dress up" nearby with their miniscule collection of baby dolls.

My favorite pastime, bar none, was baseball. I got my first baseball, bat, and glove for Christmas when I was seven-years-old. Armed with a can of neat's-foot oil, I religiously rubbed that glove every week. With these prized possessions, I could entertain myself daily. Although our town offered no organized sports and very few neighborhood pals to play with, I managed to come up with ways to amuse myself with my baseball gear. I spent hours on end alone, throwing that ball against the side of the house and fielding it on the rebound. Long after the stitches and rawhide gave out, I kept that ball in working order by wrapping it with black electrical tape. That old black ball served its purpose for quite a few years.

There were good times. I remember trips traveling to Gravette in the back of Charlie Duncan's pick-up truck, en-route to the movie theater. Mom and Grandma rode shotgun with Charlie, which left my sisters and me in the back bed of the truck. (That's illegal today, as well it should be. I'm amazed we grew up in one piece.) While this would normally be an exciting adventure, with the wind whistling around the cab and slapping us in our faces, it could also be unpleasant — like whenever Charlie hauled a load of hogs to market. To avoid those stinky pigs, we were forced to precariously perch ourselves on the sideboards of the truck.

Even so, we loved those trips to the movies. The picture show, which we called it in those days, started with a newsreel relaying current affairs, usually a recap of our progress in the Korean War. Next, we watched a cartoon. And finally, the feature show — our favorites being a Gene Autry, Roy Rogers, Tom Mix, or Lash LaRue western.

I'll never forget when our neighbor, Walter Patchin (whom we thought was rich), bought the first television set in Hiwassee. We'd sneak over after dark and peer through his window to catch a glimpse of whatever show he was watching. A Green Bay Packer game made a lasting impression. The reception was so snowy that we could barely make out the blurry little figures running around on the screen. That didn't matter at all to us, as we had only ever listened to such games on the radio. We thought that television was really something. Several weeks after getting his television set, Walter bought a hot new item — a piece of cellophane with red, blue, and green horizontal stripes. He taped that cellophane over his television screen and — voila — color television. It was of no consequence that people on the screen might sport blue hair, red bodies, and green feet. Color was cool.

One of the greatest inventions in history, as far as I'm concerned, was indoor plumbing — specifically, the toilet. During my childhood, about the only thing we had that might be perceived as "keeping up with the Joneses" was our two-holer outhouse. That was one hole more than most folks. I've never quite understood the need for a two-holer, because I never saw two people use it at the same time.

My visits to the outhouse introduced me to the world of merchandising. We always kept the Sears and Roebuck catalog handy. It made interesting reading material and also worked just fine as a suitable toilet paper substitute. Many years later, it became known as the Wish Book, and I thought that was a great name for it. I often lingered in the outhouse, looking at and wishing for all the wonderful things in that catalog.

The one and only schoolhouse in Hiwasse, which my sisters and I attended, was comprised of grades one through six. Mrs. Beasley taught both second and third grade in one classroom. Having difficulty keeping me occupied with second grade work, she apparently recognized that I had the "smarts" to accelerate a bit faster than others. And so I found my-self promoted to the third grade in the middle of the year. This resulted in me joining coursework with my older sister, who wasn't too thrilled about that. Had our family stayed in Hiwassee, my sisters and I would have attended junior high school and high school in neighboring Gra-vette, about six miles to the west.

One of my earliest life lessons occurred on one particular day in the Hiwassee school. I had forgotten to do the arithmetic homework Mrs. Beasley had assigned us the day before. When she asked about it, I claimed to have done it, but left it at home. (Had Pinkie been living, I could have blamed her.) She saw through my lie, and decided to make an example of me. She called me up to the front of the classroom, turned me upside down on her lap, and gave me three swats with her paddle. Hurt and embarrassed, I ran from the schoolroom all the way home. I couldn't face my classmates. Today, schools don't allow "corporal punishment," but I can attest that a good paddling works. I never lied to Mrs. Beasley or any school teacher again.

What turned out to be a foretelling of my future legacy with Walmart occurred during my Hiwasse days. You're now familiar with my chicken story, but here's the way it all came down:

Arkansas, although disputed by the state of Georgia, is arguably the "poultry capital of America." In the early '50s, rural northwest Arkan-sas undoubtedly boasted more chicken houses than homes. Folks caught chickens at night when it was coolest, so the birds wouldn't smother to death when huddled together. After the "chicken catchers" did their thing, they loaded the victims into wooden crates and stacked them on flatbed trucks headed to the slaughterhouses. The crates were made up of a series of slats with spaces in between to allow for airflow, enabling the chickens to breathe en-route. Frequent use caused a number of slats to break, giving the chickens a convenient escape hatch.

Mom would somehow learn of the exact time and route. Early the next morning, she'd wake us kids early in the hopes of "harvesting" a few chickens from the dirt road adjacent to our house. On occasion we found one or two, at which time we chased them down, grabbed them, and struggled all the way home, our wiggling conquests thrashing in our arms. Once home, we proudly presented what would become a tasty Sunday meal.

Of course, the process of killing, cleaning, and dressing a chicken would not be a particularly appealing one to most people today. Unless you grew up or still live on a chicken farm, you'd probably find it hard to wring a chicken's neck and watch it flop around until it died. You may have heard the term "running around like a chicken with its head cut off." Well, this is why that phrase was coined. To complete our task, we had to plop the chicken into a boiling pot, so we could pluck the feathers more easily. Not pleasant by any means, but the end result made it all worthwhile. Thank goodness PETA wasn't around then. They could have had a field day.

☺

Today, I love Jeff Foxworthy's humor. I get a particular kick out of his "you might be a redneck" series. The more I listen to him, the more I realize that I enjoy his jokes because they hit so close to home. His humor depicts the reality of my childhood.

Jeff says, "You might be a redneck if your family business requires a lookout." Well, my grandfather in Sulphur Springs, about fifteen miles from Hiwassee, reputedly housed a sizable moonshine operation. As a result, he *always* posted a lookout around the still during operating hours.

Jeff says, "If your front porch furniture is nicer than your living room furniture, you might be a redneck." Well, we kept a nice old couch out in front of our house that was every bit as good as the one in our living room.

Foxworthy also says, "If you call your wife 'cuz,' you might be a redneck." As far as I know, no one in my family actually married a cousin. But a town of ninety-eight people obviously didn't offer a plethora of available bachelors and maidens from which to choose. The population of Hiwassee primarily consisted of the Cowgur, Galyean, Sandlin, Dunnaway, and Duncan clans. Thus, over the years, most of these families became related to me in one way or another. My grandmother's maiden name was Galyean, and some of their offspring married Cowgurs, and so on, and so on. Years later, when I attended family reunions, I could rarely keep up with all my relations, so would just ask anyone I met, "Are you my cousin?" More often than not, they were.

During my childhood in Hiwassee, downtown consisted of a general store, Cassavetes' Café (a hamburger joint, which eventually became known as the "Hiwassee Hilton"), the Nazarene Church, and the post office. When we picked up our commodity rations on Saturdays, we occasionally had a spare nickel or dime for candy at the general store. I recall finding it hard to choose among my favorites: Sugar Daddy, horehound or peppermint sticks in jars, Fleer's bubble gum with baseball cards, yummy BB Bats, candy cigarettes, or the ever-popular little wax bottles with flavored syrup inside.

My grandmother walked my sisters and me to the Nazarene Church every Sunday morning so we could attend Sunday school and get our weekly dose of preaching. Afterward, when we could afford it, Grandma treated us to a burger or coke at the café. Sunday was always a special day.

One not-so-special incident occurred when I was eight-years-old while walking to church. Our family dog, Mickey, a mixed breed, always followed us to church. As Grandma, Mom, my sisters, and I walked along the road, a pickup truck came barreling down the highway and struck Mickey full on. The force of the impact threw the poor creature a long ways, killing him instantly. Terrified and devastated, I ran to that dog and cradled him in my arms, the tears streaming down my face. To this day, I can still feel the emotional intensity of losing my best friend and hating the driver of that truck. I learned that day how fleeting life can be. Of course, we kids were so upset Mom took us back home. Church would have to wait another week.

The Cassavetes Café on the corner of the main drag and Highway 72 also doubled as the local Greyhound Bus station. Indicative of the lack of entertainment in Hiwassee, my sisters and I would walk down to the Café most Saturdays just to watch for the bus. We thought this was really something, especially if it actually pulled in to collect or disperse someone. However, most of the time, it just went sailing by, blue smoke trailing behind, without even slowing down.

At the end of my sixth grade year, Mom informed us that she needed to find a higher-paying job for us to get by. She had inquired about possible openings in Bentonville and Rogers, the twin-city area just east of Hiwassee. And so, at ten-years-old, my days in Hiwasse drew to a close and in the summer of 1953 we relocated to Bentonville. A neighbor was kind enough to pack us, along with our few possessions, into her Ford coupe. Connie, Pat, and I shared the rumble seat, while Grandma and Mom rode inside with our neighbor. Looking back, I'm reminded of the television show *Beverly Hillbillies*. I suppose our little entourage looked similar to Jed and his clan piled onto their old truck. Off we went, headed for the "big city" — Bentonville, population 2800, the County Seat of Benton County, Arkansas.

As I reflect, I can't help but note the vast differences between children today and children in the days when I grew up. Kids today largely influence, if not drive, the spending of billions of dollars. Electronic game systems and their individually-acquired games, computers, cell phones, the hottest clothes (including $150 jeans and $100 tennis shoes), lessons, organized sports, private schools, and the like require a lot of money. However, the kids of today also face many ongoing challenges unheard of in my day. The ever-increasing need to excel in school, expectations of classroom discipline without corporal punishment, increasing rates of childhood obesity in a nation addicted to a fast-food diet, prescription and non-prescription drugs, violence in their homes and/or neighborhoods, and the ever- present peer pressure put a tremendous amount of strain on today's kids. I really believe that every family in America would benefit from experiencing life as my family lived it in the '40s and '50s. I am who I am today — a stronger, more appreciative person — as a result of my upbringing.

When I look back on my childhood years and contemplate how they may have prepared me for the career I chose and the rewards I ultimately received in my life, two main principles come to mind. These principles, while simple, made me a better man, a better employee, and a better manager.

Strong work ethic. Before I was nine-years-old, I spent long days in a strawberry patch or a field of green beans, not gathering something to eat, but working as fast and hard as I could to earn a few necessary dollars. We spent eight to ten hours a day picking strawberries or green beans, back-breaking labor indeed. I helped pick, load, and sell apples throughout our area from the back of a pickup truck. When you have to work at hard labor to survive as a young child, many job opportunities later in life seem rather easy by comparison. As a Walmart manager, I always looked for applicants whose backgrounds indicated a challenging work ethic. They made the best associates, because they truly appreciated having a job. These types of individuals responded to recognition and took pride in a job well done, even if it was perceived as the simplest of tasks. Perhaps I saw myself in them.

Compassion for others. My family's struggles in the early days made me empathetic and compassionate toward others in similar circumstances. I displayed that same compassion throughout my career at Walmart; it gave me a sincere appreciation for every associate I worked with. I understood that many struggled to survive or feed their families. I recognized their need to know they were making a difference, that they were justified in striving to overcome their difficulties. I made sure they knew that I felt a kinship with them and their circumstances.

> We never thought of ourselves as poor, although we certainly didn't have much of what you'd call disposable income lying around, and we did what we could to raise a dollar here and there. I learned at a very early age that it was important for us kids to help provide for the home, to be contributors rather than just takers. In the process, of course, we learned how much hard work it took to get your hands on a dollar, and when you did, it was worth something.
>
> — Sam M. Walton

CHAPTER 3

Bentonville, Arkansas and the U.S. Air Force

> **1954–1964**
> - The Waltons are growing their chain of Ben Franklin stores in Missouri and Arkansas.
> - Elvis Presley starts his career.
> - The Civil Rights movement begins with Rosa Park's bus incident in Selma, Alabama.
> - IBM and Bell Telephone start producing computers.
> - Color television and transistor radios come into existence.
> - John F. Kennedy is assassinated.
> - Mom, Connie, Pat and I are trying to survive.

We arrived in Bentonville and Mom borrowed money to rent a small two-bedroom house a couple blocks north of the town square. Mom and Grandma shared a bedroom; my sisters, Connie and Pat, bunked together, and I slept on the living room couch. Mom got a job at the Munsingwear factory in Rogers, sewing nylon hosiery. Grandma went to work as a housekeeper for the prominent local physician, Dr. Neil Compton.

Because we moved during the summer, my sisters and I had a difficult time adjusting. Not knowing anyone left us feeling isolated in the "big town." As luck would have it, the boy across the street told me about little league tryouts. I had never played organized baseball, but had thrown that worn-out baseball against my house for the past three years. I felt I had become adept at throwing and catching, and hoped my hours of dedication might win me a spot on the team. Regularly tuning in to the St. Louis Cardinals on the radio (hearing Harry Caray's famous, "It might be outta here . . . it could be . . . IT IS!"), I dreamed of becoming a major league baseball player.

I attended the tryout with a skip in my heart and a gleam in my eye. All that catching and throwing paid off by earning me a place on the farm team for the Little League Cardinals, coached by County Sheriff John Black. As a result of my baseball activities, I made a lot of friends throughout the summer. Although Sam Walton's boys — John, Rob, and Jim — played on one team or another, I hardly knew who they were in 1954, my first year in little league (Jim Walton did play on my Cardinal team in my second year). A few months later, however, I would become very aware of the Walton kids.

The Waltons' Housekeeper

The Munsingwear factory laid Mom off after a few months and she became, once again, desperate for work. Grandma relayed Mom's predicament to Dr. Compton and asked if he knew anyone who could use some help. It just so happened that his friends, Sam and Helen Walton, had expressed an interest in hiring someone to clean their house and watch their kids when they were busy. That's how Mom went to work for Sam and Helen in 1955. Mom worked as the Waltons' housekeeper for only about a year, because of an incident with the kids.

Each day at the Waltons' house, Mom mopped the kitchen floor so it would be pristine when Helen came home. On numerous occasions, when the kids got home from school, they tracked dirt and mud across the floor, requiring Mom to clean the floor all over again. After repeatedly asking the kids to take off or clean their shoes, she had reached her wit's end. One day, Rob, the eldest, burst through the door with mud-caked shoes, creating more work for Mom. She pulled him aside, got right in his face and said, "Rob, I warned you about tracking dirt across the floor. If you do it again, I'll have to spank you!" She "swatted" a towel at him to emphasize her point. Of course, Mom would never spank someone else's kid, but that was the only way she knew to make an impression on Rob.

The next morning, when Mom showed up for work, Helen called her aside and said, "Angie, we love you and appreciate what you do for us, but I just can't have you threatening to spank my children. I'm going to have to let you go." Rob had ratted out Mom. Mom told me this story much later in life and said she realized Helen was right; she had no regrets. After losing that job, Mom went to work for Emerson Electric, an electric motor manufacturer in Rogers, for a couple of years. Following that job, she worked at the original Walmart warehouse in Bentonville, where she packed and shipped health and beauty aids until she reached retirement age.

Now back to my life in Bentonville. Following the tradition established in Hiwassee, my grandmother walked my sisters and me to church every Sunday morning. The Nazarene Church was just across the street from our house, making it easy for us to regularly attend. Religion and ethics were ingrained in us from an early age and played an important role in our everyday lives. I became a member of the "Trailblazers," the Nazarene church's youth group.

While the church taught us right from wrong, and instilled the proper moral values, something altogether different was taking place outside of church. A neighbor boy across the street introduced me to smoking "grapevines" in the woods. We thought it was cool, but those vines really burnt our lips. We graduated from that to sneaking smokes from cigars he sometimes provided. On one occasion, Mom smelled the cigar odor on me, made me confess, and taught me a lesson I've never forgotten. She brought home a cigar, sat me in a chair, and made me smoke the entire thing, inhaling all the way. I got so ill I vomited for about an hour; to this day I can't stand the thought of smoking a cigar. Too bad she didn't have the same effect on me with cigarettes.

According to the tenets of the time, Mom was a strict disciplinarian. She ruled the old-fashioned way. When we did something wrong, she instructed us to "cut our own switch" from any nearby tree. She then applied said switch to the seat of our pants . . . or any body part within reach. We quickly learned not to choose from the willow trees, because those branches were strong and the whipping action created bigger welts than other types of flora. If she considered our transgressions especially dire, the dreaded belt made its appearance. Let me tell you, the threat of the belt versus the switch really ratcheted up the old fear quotient. Regardless of the opinion of Dr. Spock and other so-called child-rearing experts, I can attest that this old-fashioned discipline is far more effective than taking a "time out."

Shoplifting at Walton's

One of the most embarrassing and harsh incidents of my life occurred in the summer of 1955. My cousin from Joplin, Missouri, came down to spend a week with us that summer. Bobby Lee Allmendinger was a year older than me, and unbeknownst to me, had a "bad" streak in him — the tendency to steal things. In those days we called a young guy like that a "juvenile delinquent."

One Saturday afternoon, as Bobby Lee and I strolled around the Bentonville town square, he said to me, "Ronnie, why don't we go look around in the Walton's store?"

"Sure, let's do it," I said. I loved going to Walton's and since I had about twenty cents burning a hole in my pocket, I could even afford to buy something. As we headed toward the store, I decided to purchase some Fleer's bubble gum with baseball cards inside to add to my collection.

I pondered over the candy shelves while Bobby Lee looked at some other stuff. Suddenly, he brushed right past me and said, "Let's go, Ronnie." Once we left the store and rounded the corner, he held out a gleaming new pocket knife and said, "Look what I got from the store."

I asked, "Where'd you get the money to buy that?"

"I didn't have the money, man. I stole it," he said with an air of cocky pride.

"Man, you could go to jail for doing that if they caught you," I said, flabbergasted.

"Don't be a baby. It's easy to steal things. Try it; I dare you."

I held out as long as I could, but his third "double-dare" wore me down. I didn't want to seem like a wimp, and besides, I really wanted a knife like that.

We went back into the store, and shaking like a leaf, I picked up a new pocket knife and simply slipped it into my pocket. When a bolt of lightning didn't strike me dead on the spot, I let out a long sigh of relief.

The next morning, I was lounging around the living room with Bobby Lee when Mom burst in with *that* look on her face and said, "Ronnie Leroy, get yourself into the kitchen right now!" It didn't take a genius to know I was in some kind of real trouble, because Mom never used my middle name unless I was in deep doo-doo. Man, I felt sick to my stomach. Whatever was up, I knew it wasn't good. A moment later, my worst fears were realized when she held out her hand and produced the pocket knife.

Mom didn't have to be Sherlock Holmes to get to the bottom of this case. You see, I never owned more than two pairs of jeans, so Mom washed daily to keep a pair clean. The night before, she had washed my jeans and discovered the knife in my pocket.

"Ronnie, I know you didn't have the money to buy this knife, so you have one chance to tell me where you got it." The look on her face told me she meant business.

Thinking fast (maybe a little too fast), I blurted out, "Mom, I found it . . . honest." Big mistake. After retrieving her belt, she gave me the old "you've got one more chance to tell me the truth" routine. She also let me know she was going to whip me anyway. Plus, she grounded me for a week. That was the worst of all, because it meant missing my little league game.

In full "damage control" mode, I decided to fess up. I knew it was too late to avoid the belt. But maybe Mom would feel sorry for me and let me go to my game. Before meting out my punishment, she said, "This is going to hurt me worse than you." I never understood what she meant by that, since she was the one holding the belt.

While that whipping is rooted in my memory as one of the most painful I ever received, the situation soon got worse. Mom made Bobby Lee and me walk down to the Walton's store with her. No death row prisoner ever feared a walk more. She promptly asked for Mr. Sam Walton. Thankfully, Mr. Sam wasn't in. Neither was Bob Bogle, the store manager. But their right-hand gal and cashier, a nice lady named Inez Threet, filled in admirably. Mom made us hand the contraband items to Inez and confess that we had stolen them from the store. Inez must have felt sorry for us because she just gave us a good "talking to" and made us promise never to do it again. I honestly swore that I wouldn't. That's one promise I had no trouble keeping.

About a week later, Sam Walton stopped by our house carrying a little white puppy. Since losing my only dog, Micky, in Hiwasse, I had always wanted a dog, but Mom wouldn't let us have one (too much of a hassle). I didn't know why Sam Walton came to the house that day with this dog, because he and Mom were outside having a private conversation. Mom shared the story with me after he left.

Mom said, "Ronnie, Mr. Walton brought this puppy over. He told me, 'Angie, every boy needs a dog. It's a special kind of relationship and I think it helps keep them both out of trouble.'" When Mom told me these details of the conversation, I had no doubt that Mr. Sam had learned of the shoplifting incident. This was his way of trying to help a young boy go down the right path.

During my twenty-three-year career with Walmart and Sam Walton, he never once mentioned the shoplifting. I like to pretend he never knew about it, but then I think about the dog.

School and Friends

Being accustomed to our grade school in Hiwasse, which had consisted of as many as three grades per classroom and no more than fifteen kids total, my sisters and I were intimidated and insecure our first year of school in Bentonville. My seventh grade class had a whopping ninety-three students. Worse yet, I knew only a couple of kids from little league.

We walked four city blocks to school, taking the same route as the Walton brood. Throughout my years at Bentonville High School, I came to know Rob, Jim, John, and Alice on a casual basis. We weren't particularly close friends, but from my position, I garnered a lot of respect for the family. Gaining insight from Mom's association with them and my own observations of how they lived, I grew to hold the Walton family in high esteem.

As with any high school, we had kids whose families earned enough money for them to dress well, drive new cars, and the like. Even though the Walton kids could undoubtedly have been at the top of that category, they were obviously taught the value of a dollar early on. They walked or rode bicycles to school, just like the rest of us. And, I must say, their bikes were not the best. I would often see them trying to fix something on their older bikes or airing up a flat tire.

Sam Walton's frugal philosophy has been well-documented in both his autobiography, *Sam Walton — Made in America*, and in Vance Trimble's book, *Sam Walton: The Inside Story of America's Richest Man*. That he passed his beliefs on to his children was evident to all of us who attended school with them. They were simply regular kids who certainly did not consider themselves any better than the rest of us.

School lunches in those days cost ten cents. Mom gave each of us a dime per day to pay for lunch at school. I usually chose to skip the school lunch in favor of my favorite treats: a Nehi orange soda and a Zero candy bar. Eventually, a friend introduced me to the Bentonville pool hall, just a block from our high school. At lunchtime, we'd walk from the school down to the pool hall, and I would quickly blow my lunch money on a couple of games. I'd then go back and tell my sisters I had "lost my dime." On numerous occasions, Pat or Connie felt sorry for me and forked over their lunch money. When I think back on it, I feel bad. I was wrong to "con" my sisters, and it showed how much they loved me. They went without lunch, while I wasted my money on pool. We laugh about it today, but it's one of those things from my past that I would do differently if I had the opportunity to re-live my life.

Throughout my high school years, we all hung out at the businesses typical of small-town America in the 1950s and '60s. There was Gus' Newsstand, the Tinnin Drugstore/Soda Shop, the Cozy Theater (which ultimately closed as we favored the new Plaza Theater), Mayhall's Barber Shop, Otasco, Western Auto, Overstreet Jewelry, and of course, the Bank of Bentonville. Oftentimes, we just sat around the Confederate Statue in the middle of the town square. When we were lucky enough to ride with someone who had a car, we'd go "parking" and do a little "petting." (For you youngsters, that was our term for "making out." All very mild stuff by today's standards.)

This was the era of the true rock-'n-roll explosion, and we all listened to Elvis Presley and the Motown artists. We'd hurry home from school to catch Dick Clark's *American Bandstand* on TV, and a few of my fortunate classmates got to go up to Joplin, Missouri, one Saturday to appear on a local area television dance show. I wasn't part of the "in group," so they didn't include me in that excursion. It didn't matter much, since I hadn't yet honed my dancing skills.

My best friends were Larry Joe Rogers, Roger Lee Harrison, and Max McGaugh. Much later in life, like a lot of people in Bentonville, Larry Joe worked for Walmart in one capacity or another. During our school days, Larry was a darn good baseball player and his mother, Nellie, staunchly kept all the statistics for the Bentonville Little League organization. As I write this, Larry is still working in the Rogers Walmart store – store #1.

I'll never forget the time when Larry and I, while sleeping out in the yard in a tent, decided to sneak off and climb the Bentonville water tower. It was the tallest structure in town and provided a view of the entire "metropolis." I don't know exactly how high it was, but it might as well have been the Empire State Building in our minds. This was illegal, of course, based on the signs attached that said so, but we were young and foolish. After viewing the square from the top of the tower, I made it safely to the ground. Larry wasn't so fortunate. He lost his grip about twenty feet from the bottom, plunged the rest of the way, and broke his arm. A ragged bone literally stuck out of his arm, but I wouldn't let him go to the hospital. I knew Mom would kill us and we were more afraid of her. I half-carried him back to our house, ignoring his pleas to go to the hospital and trying to keep him from passing out. I laid him down in the yard as gently as I could, and then screamed for Mom.

"Mom, Larry tripped over a chair!" It was the best I could do on short notice. Years later, I finally told Mom what had really happened, and of course, she said, "I knew all along you were lying." Mom's instincts were better than any FBI agent's. She was really angry, even after all those years. Even though I was twenty-years-old and almost out of the Air Force, she still threatened to spank me.

Max McGaugh was one of those young geniuses who was always building and creating unique things. He took an old motor scooter and stuck an aluminum box on the front end. I don't know what purpose the box was supposed to serve, but he'd stuff me in the box and ride the thing all over town. It had to be a weird sight as we tore around the Bentonville square on Saturdays.

Max was also into building rockets. These weren't just kits. Like a mad scientist, he played around with the amount of chemicals to see how high and how big of a blast he could make for takeoff. A couple of times, the rocket misfired and set fire to the back lawn. It's a miracle we didn't blow ourselves to kingdom come. Who knows, Max might have had something to do with the early space program. Some of his rockets flew so high, they just disappeared.

Roger Lee Harrison was an out-going popular classmate and an entertainer by nature. He taught me to play the baritone ukulele and we performed duets at class assemblies. I was shy at the time and I must credit Roger Lee with making a "ham" out of me. Learning to love the stage and an audience served me well for the rest of my life.

After a stint as a stock broker in New Orleans, Roger Lee chased his dream of making movies and dealing in the topsy-turvy world of entertainment. His first involvement with films enjoyed a measure of success. He served as executive producer of *The Chosen*, starring Maximillian Schell, Rod Steiger, and Robby Benson. A later project, the documentary,

Bullets Over Hollywood, continues to do well. Similar to my path later in life, Roger Lee experienced the ups and downs and financial disappointments of his industry, but remains one of the most positive-thinking guys I've ever known.

When Sam Walton arrived in Bentonville seeking a store to buy, he acquired the Harrisons' variety store on the square from Roger Lee's grandfather, Luther Harrison. Roger Lee's father, Tom, owned a dairy supply company just off the square and became a close friend of Sam's early on. While talking to Tom Harrison, Sam learned that Tom's son was involved with investment banking people. He sought out Roger Lee when he decided to take Walmart public. Roger Lee told me that Sam came to his office with three legal pads full of hand-written notes and figures, a typical Sam Walton "business plan." Roger guided him toward people he knew with Merrill-Lynch, though they were never involved with the public offering. The story of the company going public has been told in detail. No need to repeat them here. But in essence, Jimmy Jones (whom Sam first met when he worked with Republic Bank in Dallas) with First Commerce Bank in New Orleans, Buck Remmell with White, Weld & Co. in New York City, and Mike Smith and J. D. Simpson with the Stephens family in Little Rock were very involved in the initial public offering of the Walmart Company's stock.

My First True Love

Like most of us at that age, I had my share of crushes on the girls. As a matter of fact, I think I had a crush on almost every girl in my class at one time or another. Unfortunately, I had no car and was two years younger than everyone in my class, which put me at a severe disadvantage. Most of the girls in my class liked me, but referred to me as "Little Ronnie," not exactly the image I hoped to project. I acted in the senior class play, *Our Town*, by Thornton Wilder, playing the role of George Gibbs. That's where I developed a real crush on Maybelle Osborne, who played Emily. She proved not to be "the one." Soon after, I did experience my first real "puppy love." Her name was Nancy Covey, a junior, and we were the same age.

Work and Play

Because of our circumstances, my sisters and I needed to work to help supplement the family income. My first official job (I don't count picking up soda pop bottles, which were redeemable for two cents each) was mowing lawns for Gary Black, who had a sizeable operation up and running at the time.

Gary, the son of County Sheriff John Black, my baseball coach, had a trailer, several mowers, and a steady network of regular customers all over town. A few of his patrons lived on West Central Street, known to the locals as "Silk Stocking Row." The folks who lived on this street were considered the upper crust of Bentonville. Believing that Sheriff Black had influenced my hiring, I set out to show everyone I could do a good job. However, one unfortunate incident cut my mowing career short (so to speak).

The Knotts owned an impressive home on West Central, known far and wide for its immaculate landscaping. On my first trip with Gary, he assigned me the job of mowing the front lawn while he trimmed the shrubs. As I cranked up the mower, I noticed unusual outcroppings of what I thought were taller weeds here and there on the lawn. I thought it odd that these weeds had been allowed to pop up, but eager to prove myself, I made sure to mow over them to create a nice, even lawn.

Much to my consternation and disappointment, Gary was appalled when he checked my work. It turns out that those tall weeds had been some of the Knotts most prized flowers, which were not yet in bloom. I recall Gary saying, "Ronnie, you just don't have the experience to mow lawns. Maybe you should look for something else to do." That might have been the shortest landscaping career on record.

Gary himself went on to a long and successful career with Walmart, after which he was elected Benton County Judge (the CEO of Benton County). The Blacks were a noted family in Bentonville through the years, and played a significant role in my life. As I've mentioned, John Black, Gary's father, served as the County Sheriff, my little league baseball coach and a father-figure in my young life. His wife, Maxine, worked at the Walton's store for years.

Following my failed bid at lawn-mowing, I sought other employment. A big, gruff local businessman named Wiley Wolfe managed an opposing little league team, the despised Yankees. I realize his name sounds like something from a Disney movie or newspaper cartoon, but that was his actual name. Wiley owned the Western Auto store on the town square. With a bit of trepidation, but desperate for a regular summer job, I asked Wiley if he needed any help at the store. Surprisingly, he said he could use some part-time help, so I went to work for him. That was my introduction to retail. For two summers, I helped stock the store, dusted shelves, and performed a number of other assorted tasks, such as assembling bicycles. When this job started interfering with my baseball practices, though, I again sought other opportunities. I learned a few things about merchandising at the Western Auto store, but by the time I returned to Bentonville following a stint in the Air Force, the store had gone out of business.

I became something of a local baseball star as I moved up through the ranks of little league, Babe Ruth, and one season of American Legion ball. It turns out Sam Walton loved baseball and followed the local teams and their constituents closely. In the summer of 1959, I went undefeated as a pitcher in the Babe Ruth League. At the conclusion of one memorable game, a man named Fred Hawn stuck out his hand and introduced himself. He turned out to be the St. Louis Cardinal scout for the southwest region. He said he was in town to look at me and another fellow, Melvin Coffelt. I knew Melvin. He was a far better player than I and one heck of a hitter. The scout went on to say that his friend, Sam Walton, had suggested he take a look at the talent in Bentonville, that he thought "there were some kids with real potential." Talk about flattering. I had no idea that Sam Walton followed our local baseball leagues as closely as he did. Mr. Sam kept touching my life in unexpected ways.

Because I was entering my senior year of high school at only fifteen-years-old, nothing came of this visit by the Cardinal scout. I was simply too young to be considered for the big leagues, but it surely gave me continued hope for a career in baseball. Life, however, takes some odd turns and we can't always predict the outcome.

Family Ties

My mom had four brothers; Jack, Leroy, Dick, and Bill Allmendinger and one sister, Esther Hufford. They all influenced my early life in one way or another. Uncle Jack moved off to California and established a career as an auctioneer. Uncle Leroy, from whom my middle name was taken, was an Army career enlisted man, retiring from Fort Benning, Georgia. Uncle Bill and his wife, Betty, were long-time residents of Bentonville. Betty worked for years at the Walton-owned Bank of Bentonville and Uncle Bill retired from the local Kraft Foods plant.

I owe a great deal to my Uncle Georald Hufford. With two sons of his own, Gary and Jerry, and daughters Karen and Brenda, he included me in most of the family's outdoor activities. He taught me to shoot a .22 rifle and .410 shotgun, taking me hunting for rabbits and squirrels. We went frog-gigging on Osage Creek, and fishing on the White River (before it was dammed up to form Beaver Lake). In those days, we hunted and fished for meat . . . not just pleasure. Uncle Georald was the only guy I've known who could make a good edible dish out of just about any wild critter he could catch or kill. His specialties were turtle stew, and turtle and dumplings. I imagine that turtles tried to scamper (which isn't all that fast) when they saw Uncle Georald heading their way.

My Sisters

My siblings and I were somewhat typical, I suppose. We stair-stepped down from Connie, the oldest, to me, to Pat, the youngest. They always accused Mom of favoring "Little Ronnie" — the only boy. Maybe they were right, but if so, how come I got the most spankings? We had some sibling spats, but also some downright "knock-down, drag-outs." I recall one incident when Pat threw a pair of scissors at me, which stuck in the door beside my head as I tore out of the room. We'd been fighting and she became irate just because I had her down in a chokehold. She was turning kinda blue (a good color for her, actually), but of course I quit before causing any serious injury. She could have killed me, though, if those scissors had been on target. I don't even remember what we were fighting about, but I remember the spanking, as usual.

Perhaps because Mom married so many times, and we saw what bad choices can do, or perhaps because of our poor circumstances, we depended on one another. We were not prone to acknowledge how much we cared, but I recall my sisters defending me to the end when necessary. We'd fight, argue, and criticize each other, but let someone else threaten one of us and they had us all to contend with. We weren't quick to express love and affection, but those emotions always lurked just beneath the surface. And we all knew it.

At this writing, Connie and I are closer than we seemingly were as children. She lives in Joplin, Missouri, with her husband, Frank Hollis. Our sister Pat died of a massive heart attack at the far too early age of forty-seven. She was married to Dale Musteen and resided in Rogers. Her twin sons, David and Doug, currently work for Walmart, as did Pat. Pat was the assistant to Dick Mahan at Walmart in the Sporting Goods category.

The creator of the Peanuts comic strip, Charles Schultz, is credited with this philosophical statement; "The people who make a difference in your life are not the ones with the most money, or the most awards. They simply are the ones who care the most." My sisters, Connie and Pat, fit this description to a tee.

My Last Job in Bentonville

During my senior year, 1960, I went to work at Earl Bright's Texaco station on the corner of 8th Street and SW A Street in Bentonville. Mom had married a much younger man and we moved to the southwest side of town, three blocks from our high school. Our house was walking distance to the service station, which was across the street from the baseball fields; a good location for me. Back then, a gas station was truly a "service" station. We pumped the customers' gas and asked if they wanted us to check the oil. We cleaned the windshield and checked the air in the tires. When folks sometimes talk about "the good old days," that's one reason why.

My primary job at the station was to steam-clean engines. This had to be one of the foulest, dirtiest, most miserable jobs in existence. With a hose spewing high-pressured scalding water, I blasted the accumulated scum, oil, and grease off the engine, with much of it accumulating on my uniform (and on me). I went home most days with burns on my face and arms from that scalding hot water. It didn't matter. They paid me the princely sum of $1.50 an hour and I was happy to get it.

The United States Air Force

Following high school graduation, I continued to work at the gas station while playing on a local independent team, keeping my hopes for a baseball career alive. One Saturday, three of my old high school classmates dropped by the station sporting their spiffy Air Force uniforms, complemented by some pretty cool "shades." They had just gotten out of basic training and were on the way to their base assignments. I thought they looked really cool. They turned out to be excellent recruiters for the Air Force, as they explained why it would be a great match for me. They told me that each of the Air Force bases had baseball teams which were made up of pros and semi-pros, so while getting a paycheck and three square meals per day, I could continue my dream of baseball, while learning some skills for a career after the service.

Because I didn't have the money to attend college, I decided the Air Force was the answer for me. After making this decision, with my mom and sisters realizing that "little Ronnie" would be leaving soon, Mom took the family on our first real traveling vacation. Nancy Covey, my girlfriend, was invited along. I had always dreamed of seeing the ocean. We went to the Panama City area of Florida. One evening, while Nancy and I stood under a palm tree gazing out at a magnificent sunset, I gave her a small engagement ring and we made plans to be married at some point in the future. I was in love. The ending of this story deeply impacted my life, as you will learn.

On October 6, 1960, the day I turned seventeen, I enlisted in the United States Air Force together with two friends, Gary Bates and Billy Wilkerson. For a seventeen-year-old young man who had traveled outside of northwest Arkansas only once in his life, the thought of leaving the comforts of home, family, and a new fiancée traumatized me. After tearful goodbyes, I left on the Greyhound bus for basic training, my heart heavy and my mind running away with possibilities.

While in basic training at Lackland Air Force Base (AFB) in San Antonio, Texas, recruits were subjected to a series of tests to determine the best career path for each of us. In high school, I had taken a course in typing my senior year. I signed up for this course because it was considered easy, with no homework, and therefore, wouldn't interfere with my baseball time. My buddies ridiculed me for it because typing was for "sissies." (No one at that time could realize the benefit this held for computer skills in the unknown future.)

During the Air Force exams, my typing skills helped me ace one test in particular. It was the Morse Intercept test, which involved copying Morse code on a typewriter. For me, it seemed like the most natural thing in the world. That's when the brass transferred me to the Morse Intercept Training School at Keesler AFB in Biloxi, Mississippi, on a career path in a branch called U.S. Air Force Intelligence Service. I didn't know it at the time, but it required "remote" duty service, which I'll explain in a moment.

It was in Biloxi that my so-called friends introduced me to alcohol. It became one of those "do-overs" we wish life would hand us from time to time. On my eighteenth birthday, my Air Force buddies took me down to the beach, bought me a pint of Seagram's 7 whiskey, and watched as I guzzled the entire bottle. This would be a good time to explain that throughout my young life in Bentonville, I had never even tasted alcohol. Mom was dead set against drinking because of her first two alcoholic husbands. When other high school classmates would occasionally "sneak" a beer or two, I passed. So that first pint hit me hard and fast. I don't recall how I got back to the base and into my barracks. But I woke up in a bed full of vomit (I assume it was mine), my head pounding from my first (and worst) hangover. I was sick all day Sunday and swore to never drink alcohol again. Of course, I didn't live up to that promise. But I never liked the taste of Seagram's 7 after that.

After graduating from the Morse Intercept School with a Top Secret security clearance, I was sent to a remote island in Alaska — St. Lawrence Island. Needless to say, there was no baseball team. So, I had to put my dreams on the back burner for a couple of years. Although I didn't like the remote duty, I enjoyed my work in the Air Force and found it easy in comparison to jobs I had performed in the past.

While on the Alaskan island for my one-year tour, they allowed us two phone calls home via radio. On one of these calls in 1962, Mom mentioned something that didn't mean much to me at the time, but became prophetic two years later. She said, "Ronnie, Sam Walton opened this big store in Rogers. It's called Walmart. The prices are so good. It's the talk of the town." I found that comment interesting, but didn't think much more about it. I had no idea at that time the impact Walmart would have on my life.

The second phone call with Mom resulted in my receiving some very bad news. My tour of duty on an island in the middle of the Bering Sea was tough. Approximately 200 men lived isolated in a solitary concrete building without benefit of girls for a year. I don't know about the others, but every night I would fall asleep thinking about a warm homecoming with my fiancée, Nancy, running into my arms as I got off the plane. From the time I arrived on the island until this phone call, I had been writing her every single day, and receiving an equal number of letters in return. All at once, after three months, the letters stopped. I had no idea why. When I talked to Mom, she informed me that Nancy had married my third cousin, Kendall Galyean. This news hit me like a punch in the gut. To say I was devastated would be an understatement. Now I under-

stood what it meant to have a broken heart. I look back on this episode
and realize the toll it took. I found it difficult to trust women in my life
for years to come, even when I had no cause.

Entertainment options on our island were, shall we say, lacking. We
spent most of our off-time in the airmen's dayroom, where I became
highly skilled at pool and snooker. As soon as we got our hands on our
paychecks, we'd head for the dayroom, where we could lose our wages or
win someone else's in a matter of days. There was also a small gymnasium
and a basketball league. I became proficient at shooting the long ball (before it was worth three points). Unfortunately, my baseball fielding skills
didn't prepare me for handling a basketball. I was more likely to dribble
one off my foot than off the floor.

There's one story from St. Lawrence Island I like to tell. During my
stay, an enormous herd of reindeer migrated from one end of the island
to the other a couple of times. Before I arrived, the airmen made a pet
of one of them they had found injured. They named him "Buck." They
kept that reindeer on a tether outside our building. Unbeknownst to
us newcomers, when the herd got within sniffing distance of Buck, his
sexual instincts took over. He'd go crazy and would try to mount any
human within striking distance. So the fellows who'd been there awhile
would always try to get the new guys to carry the feed to Buck as soon as
the herd came around. It's a miracle Buck didn't seriously hurt someone.
Usually, they managed to dart out of range when Buck reached the end of
his tether. Just before I left the island, a new lieutenant got too close and
Buck pinned him up against the building with his antlers. He escaped
injury, but the incident scared the dickens out of him. So he had old Buck
shot. A sad story. We liked the reindeer much more than the lieutenant.

Following my stint with the Intelligence Service in Alaska, I chose the
option of a second military career path and went on to serve two years in
Air Traffic Control. After a month of leave in Bentonville, I was to report
to a fighter base squadron in Duluth, Minnesota.

Between the two assignments, a significant event occurred in my life
while I was home on leave. My sister Pat and I went to the local bowling

alley for a soda pop and to roll a few frames. While on the lanes, Pat came up to me and said, "Ronnie, Nancy Covey is over there having a Coke and would like for you to talk to her." I glanced over, and there sat Nancy with an infant. Her marriage to my cousin hadn't lasted very long, just long enough to produce a baby. I suppose it wasn't right, but still suffering from a broken heart, I let my bitterness get the best of me. I told my sister I had absolutely no interest in talking to her, and didn't. I still had feelings for Nancy, but I was a stubborn guy.

That same night, still at the bowling alley, I met a pretty girl working behind the counter. Her brother-in-law, Bob Miller, owned the lanes. I asked Bob what her name was and he told me "Cindy." It turns out that wasn't her name at all, but funny-guy Bob set me up. I strolled up to the counter where she was busy taking care of other customers and said, "Hey, Cindy." No response. I said more loudly, "Hi there, Cindy."

She spun around this time and said, "Are you talking to me? My name is Murlene." That's how I met my future wife, Murlene Stearns, from Mt. Vernon, Missouri. Over the next two years, we stayed in touch and saw each other as often as we could. Much later, I thought about the significance of that night in the bowling alley, and how strange life can be. I ran into the girl who broke my heart, and thirty minutes later met the girl I married. A few days later, I left once again, for my new duties in Minnesota.

Duluth, Minnesota — the Air Force Base

Duluth Air Force Base was located on property at the Duluth Municipal Airport. I enjoyed my job as flight scheduling supervisor. Although I was an enlisted man, I supervised the scheduling of flight time for all the fighter pilots and brass at the base. They flew F-106s at the time. The officers would "kiss up" to me to get the easiest flights and maintain their "flight status." I had both good and bad experiences while there.

It was during my stint in Duluth that the Cuban Missile Crisis arose. The Soviets were moving ballistic nuclear missiles into Cuba, and the general public was not aware, at the time, how close we came to World

War III. Our fighters were all deployed to Pensacola, Florida. B-52s from Offutt AFB in Omaha, headquarters for SAC (Strategic Air Command) were sent to our little fighter base, which in the event of war, would give them a chance to take off after the first wave of missiles hit Offutt. (Part of a brilliant master strategy.)

But the best-laid plans can look much different in actual practice than on paper. When these heavily-loaded B-52s landed at Duluth, they caused the aprons to collapse and broke up the parking areas from sheer weight. Had we actually gone to hostilities, these planes could not have taken off. We eventually stripped them down to the bare bones and they still struggled to get off the ground when the crisis ended. I recall all of this because on take-off for Pensacola, one of our F-106 fighters "flamed-out" and crashed near Superior, Wisconsin (neighbor of Duluth). Our pilot, one of the most popular on our small base, died when he ejected from the plane. One of my responsibilities, while on duty, was to implement the "crash plan." It was the first and only time, other than drills, this had to be put into effect. I'll never forget how tragic and difficult it was for this close-knit family of pilots.

While in Duluth, I played for the base fast-pitch softball team. We won the Minnesota State Championship and traveled all over to play softball. What a wonderful experience. As taxpayers, readers may not appreciate their tax money going to subsidize a C-123 cargo plane full of softball players. The pilots had to fly anyway to keep their hours current, so we weren't truly wasting taxpayers' dollars.

My entertainment and stage experiences continued while in Duluth when I joined the Duluth Amateur Theater troupe and acted in a couple of stage dramas, one of which I particularly enjoyed — "Desperate Hours" — because I got to kiss the leading lady (a gorgeous blonde).

I'll also never forget when our base hosted a visit by President John F. Kennedy. He arrived one evening while I was on duty at Base Operations. I watched him exit the aircraft and climb into a limousine just a few hundred feet from me. Being a serviceman, seeing your Commander-in-Chief in the flesh is a gripping experience. A few months later, he was assassinated in Dallas and our entire base was absolutely mortified. Consisting of a relatively small group of officers flying F-106 fighter jets, we took the news especially hard. The pilots in Base Operations at the time all shed a tear while watching the news on television.

Another incident which meant little to me at the time occurred when I headed into town with a couple of my airmen buddies. We spotted signs for the "Grand Opening" of a huge new retail store close to the base. We decided to stop and check it out. I was extremely impressed with the size of the store, the excitement of the shoppers, and the vast array of merchandise. I had never seen anything quite like it. I thought the name "Target" was sort of strange, but I'll never forget that first exposure to big box retail.

In October 1964, the Air Force handed me my discharge papers (honorable), and in my 1954 Ford, I headed home to Bentonville, Arkansas, and an unknown future.

Sam Walton Job Offer

Still without money for college and clinging to the remote possibility of a baseball career, I went back to Earl Bright's Texaco station and resumed my position (usually prone) steam-cleaning engines. One Saturday morning in late October, I was lying on a dolly underneath a car with hot grease and grime raining down on my already filthy station uniform, when I heard a horn honk over at the gas pumps.

Rolling out from under the car, I got up and walked over to the pumps to find Sam Walton standing there. "Fill 'er up, Ronnie," he said. I was always nervous around Mr. Walton, partly because my mother had worked for him and partly because I had gained a deep respect for the man. Although he had never acted as if he was better than anyone else, in my mind the Walton family was "above my status in life." As I started the pump and began washing his windshield, he said to me, "Ronnie, I heard you just got out of the Air Force. What are your plans?"

I took a deep breath. "Well, Mr. Walton, I still hope to play baseball, but I gotta work and I'm just not sure what I'm gonna do yet."

Sam Walton had piercing eyes that could look right through you. Now he fixed those eyes on me and said, "Ronnie, I've always admired your work ethic. If you're thinking about going back to school, maybe I could help you out. But if not, how'd you like to come work for me?" For reasons unknown to me, I had never seriously considered college and I was still not inclined to do so. Looking back on this moment, I surely wish I had taken him up on that school offer. Although I enjoyed a successful career with Walmart (which is what this book is all about), there comes a time and a "level" of management responsibility that require a deeper knowledge that can only be acquired through a formal education. An MBA serves a person well when dealing with the financial and strategic decisions so much a part of "big business." This is not to say a person can't achieve anything he or she desires in life without going to college. But it certainly helps.

With this job offer coming out of the blue, I just stood there, a million thoughts running through my brain. But one particular thought seemed more important than the rest: buying a car and getting away from the gas station. So I said, "Mr. Walton, what would I be doing?"

"I'm opening a new store in St. Robert, Missouri, and you could go to work up there and learn the retail business. What do you think?"

This notion was awfully sudden and might normally have required careful consideration. But respecting Sam Walton as I did, thinking about my dirty uniform, and reflecting on my current options (which were none) I replied, "Well, Mr. Walton, it sounds good to me. When would I start?"

"I just hired a manager for the St. Robert store. His name is Gary Reinboth. My brother Bud is in charge of those Missouri stores and that store is already under construction. I'll just call Bud and Gary and tell them I hired you. Could you be up there on Monday?"

My immediate thought was *Oh, crap*. My current situation flashed through my mind; it's Saturday, I have no idea where St. Robert, Missouri is, I don't own a car, I have to tell Earl Bright I'm quitting, and Sam hasn't even mentioned pay. None of this made any sense, but I did my best to sound confident. "Sure, Mr. Walton, I'll be there on Monday." That was the end of the interview and the beginning of my life in retail.

☺

I believe the teen years of one's life provide lasting memories, but are wrought with many challenges. These years are made difficult by peer pressure, the struggle to find one's inner self, leaving the comfort of home, and the challenge of choosing a direction in life. I would be the first to tell any young person, no matter what it takes, to go get that college education ... and take education seriously. Looking backward, I would also tell them to have fun — but, good clean fun.

There will always be ups and down in life, but the compilation of the hard times and rewarding times shape the future, both personally and professionally. Interaction with classmates and teachers, the feeling of achievement when good grades are earned, being active in the community and/or playing sports all contribute to lifelong memories and help form lasting values and ethics. You don't truly think about or even know how great those teen years are until they are long past. When you eventually face the challenges of work, raising a family, and adulthood, you only then begin to realize what those years meant to you and the ultimate impact of each event.

Lastly, though I now know I should have gone to college first, I realize that my time in the U.S. military was a godsend for me in many ways. I honestly believe that every young man in this country should be required to serve a minimum of two years in a branch of our military service. When entrenched in the military, you grow up very quickly — you simply have no choice. You can't just get angry and quit or sass your superiors. In the military, our young folks learn discipline, respect, and an appreciation for the defenders of our freedom that cannot be fully understood without experiencing it.

Later in my career at Walmart, when I was responsible for hiring and supervising a large number of people, I found that some of our best associates were military veterans, school teachers, and individuals who had worked their way through life from an early age. A college education was always a big plus, but working hard, appreciating others, and learning the retail business from the ground up reigned paramount in my mind.

Trahey's Simple Rule: Would you hire you?

— JANE TRAHEY

Never let formal education get in the way of your learning.

— MARK TWAIN

PART TWO
MY CAREER

CHAPTER 4

Learning the Ropes — Stock Boy

1964–1965

▸ Sam Walton has a chain of fifteen Ben Franklin stores and is getting ready to open his second Walmart store in Harrison, Arkansas.

▸ The Beatles take the music scene by storm.

▸ The Vietnam War heats up.

▸ Congress passes the Civil Rights Act.

▸ Cassius Clay (known today as Muhammad Ali) wins the heavyweight boxing championship.

▸ I am beginning to find out that retailing is a lot of hard work and life is not easy.

'd been driving a 1954 Ford when I got out of the Air Force, but blew the engine soon after. So I was on foot when I accepted Mr. Sam's job offer. My stepfather loaned me his '58 Oldsmobile to use until I could get a car of my own, which I promised to do as soon as possible. He and Mom loaned me $60 and I headed for Missouri.

I drove into the brand new Bobby's Shopping Center just off I-44 in St. Robert and located the Ben Franklin Family Center. Crews were hard at work installing the windows. Not knowing what my new career held in store, I gathered my courage, walked inside, and asked for the manager.

In those days management folks always wore ties, but because I didn't own one and didn't consider myself management, I never thought to worry about my appearance. My entire wardrobe fit into an overnight bag. Apparently, my inattention to appropriate attire resulted in a not-so-great first impression on my new boss, Gary Reinboth. I guess you might say I fit the stereotype of the early '60s; beltless, low-slung jeans with the cuffs rolled up and white tee-shirt with a pack of Winston's lodged in the sleeve. Picture "The Fonz" on *Happy Days*, my hair long, combed back in a duck-tail and held in place with an ample supply of Brylcreem (a little dab'll do ya) hair dressing.

Gary's recollection of our first meeting reflected his skepticism. He recalls that I walked in the front door and said, "Mr. Walton sent me up here to help you." He remembers taking one look at me and thinking, "Oh my, what do I have here?" He says he then called Bud Walton (Sam's brother who supervised the Missouri stores) to ask if he knew anything about Mr. Sam hiring me. He wanted to know exactly what Mr. Sam had gotten him into. Bud told Gary that Sam had mentioned hiring me; my salary was to be $50 per week and to just use me to do whatever he needed.

Why the Waynesville/St. Robert Store was Unique

Here's a puzzler for you. A 1964 map of Missouri shows two tiny dots representing the sister towns of Waynesville and St. Robert. The index indicates populations of 1,200 and 500, respectively. So, why did Sam Walton choose to build his largest store to date in the town with only 500 people?

I found out the answer when Bud Walton explained to me the unique methods they established early-on for store site selection. The plan was simple, but had far-reaching potential. Noting that most discount chain stores were being opened in large population centers, the Walton's simply chose the alternative — small town America. Mr. Sam had a vision of bringing large store discounting to small towns, but drawing customers from the entire "trade territory."

Mr. Sam and Bud looked at three key factors when determining site selection:

1. Retail sales for the county (not just the town). This gave them an idea of how much business activity existed or could exist in the area.

2. Bank deposits. These numbers gave an indication of the wealth and spendable income in the market.

3. Population. This was always a county-wide number. The Waltons believed a large store in a community would draw customers from many miles around.

After determining an interest in a particular location, Mr. Sam would jump in his plane and fly over the area to check out the competitors and traffic patterns, and to scout potential locations. During this process, he discovered the key to St. Robert's potential.

The population number was deceiving, because he noticed something that didn't show up on a map. St. Robert was, and still is, the home of Fort Leonardwood, one of the largest Army training bases in the United States. It was difficult to determine just how many military personnel were stationed there, but the base was huge. After a bit of research, they heard numbers that exceeded 100,000 men and women. Sam Walton discovered this base had only one shopping outlet, the Post Exchange. He decided a large store just outside the entrance to the base would produce a lot of volume. He was so right.

The Ben Franklin Family Center

Sam Walton's early retail expansion and success has been well documented and won't be repeated here. However, this particular store in St. Robert merits a bit of explanation. Even before this store became a Walmart, it generated the company's largest sales volume and highest profitability and continued to for many years to come. To fully understand the success of Walmart, I'd like to discuss how and why this store was so successful. The St. Robert store, under the leadership and guidance of Gary Reinboth, became the organization's benchmark for managing a high volume store. Two key strategies in particular proved to make the biggest difference.

Merchandise

At this period in time, Mr. Sam owned fifteen Ben Franklin Family Centers. He ran these franchise stores, but had to follow the guidelines mandated in his contract with the mother company, City Products Corporation. City Products owned a warehousing distribution center in Chicago called Butler Brothers. Owners of Ben Franklin franchises were required to purchase a minimum percentage of their inventory from the Butler Brothers' warehouse. Mr. Sam knew that he was paying a premium for his goods through Ben Franklin, but didn't have the structure or buying power to buy direct from the manufacturers. As a result, he stocked his Ben Franklin Family Centers with a basic assortment of merchandise from Butler Brothers, but bolstered his inventory with promotional merchandise from other sources. Sam Walton's early Ben Franklin Family Centers carried many more promotional products, and considerably more sporting goods and automotive and outdoor items than typically found in other Ben Franklin stores. (This "outside" buying proved to be the better business decision and eventually led to a parting of ways with City Products/Butler Brothers and to the development of Walmart.) From the beginning, Mr. Sam and his team stocked Walmart stores with merchandise purchased directly from manufacturers or various distributors.

The expanded variety of products offered by Ben Franklin Family Centers made it necessary to establish a clear definition of product departments. Walmart kept these department distinctions in place for many years. In fact, most still exist today.

Store Operational Structure

These early large stores were operated by a store manager with, usually, two assistant managers, but high volume stores largely depended on a cadre of department managers — hourly associates — responsible for each or a combination of several of these departments within each store. The store manager position was an important one, to be sure. But a well-

Hardlines

01-Candy
02-Health & Beauty Aids
03-Stationery
04-Paper Goods
05-Electronics
06-Photo
07-Toys
08-Pet Supplies
09-Sporting Goods
10-Automotive
11-Hardware
12-Paint
13-Household Chemicals
14-Housewares
15-Appliances
16-Horticulture
18-Seasonal

Softlines

17-Home Furnishings
19-Fabrics
20-Domestics
21-Curtains/Drapes
22-Bedding
23-Men's Wear
24-Boy's Wear
25-Shoes
26-Infants/Toddlers
27-Socks
28-Nylon Hosiery
29-Sleepwear
30-Lingerie
31-Accessories/Handbags
32-Jewelry
33-Girl's Wear
34-Ladies' Wear
35-Maternity
36-Outer Wear/Coats

trained, motivated department manager group was paramount to achieving excellent operating results. Openly sharing the sales, markdown, and inventory numbers with these hourly associates empowered and motivated them. They were literally running their own small business operation. The best department managers managed their areas so well they often trained the ever-changing management folks.

In my opinion, Gary Reinboth's store set the standard for the department manager program at Walmart. Many of them managed their departments until they retired with generous retirement accounts — thanks to the company's profit-sharing program. I'll never forget the key folks from this group — Loreen Gordon, Fabrics and Pansy Dye, Ladies' Wear. Other department managers at the opening of this store included: Vera Cotton, Men's Wear; Violet Collins. Lingerie; Ann Stewart, Girl's Wear; Ann Sands and Catherine Ogle, who worked in a number of Wearables departments; Bea Shipley, Plants; Jackie Morrison, Cashier; and Nita Gann, Health & Beauty Aids. Thelma York manned the service desk. Associates in the stores represent the company in the eyes of the consumer. The selection, training, and appearance of store-level associates were important elements of a Walmart store's success in the early years (and are just as important today).

Gary Reinboth, Store Manager — St. Robert, Missouri

Gary Reinboth represented an enigma in my mind. On the one hand, he was a tough, demanding taskmaster when I worked under him. On the other hand, he showed compassion, cared about my family, and helped prepare me for a successful career in retailing (not to mention that he chose not to fire me on a number of occasions when he might have been justified in doing so). One thing is clear; Gary was a talented store manager who served as an excellent role model and mentor.

Sam Walton personally hired a number of store managers in those early Ben Franklin growth years. I came to know a number of them. Willard Walker, Claude Harris, Charlie Baum, Larry Woods, Ray Stephens, Merle Gilbraith, Charlie Cate, and Bob Bogle stand out. At the time, Mr. Sam couldn't have known they would work out as well as they did. Or did he? He certainly had an uncanny knack for choosing the right people at the right time (maybe even me). These are the qualities and capabilities he looked for in his management team:

1. They had variety store backgrounds that gave them knowledge of basic merchandise demanded by customers. They also possessed a unique skill-set for selecting items that could be sold in large quantities at a good gross margin. In other words, they were good merchants.

2. Like Sam Walton, these early managers understood the very fine line between making a profit and losing money; as a result, they were very "tight with a dollar." Expense control was part of each manager's basic make-up.

3. They were honest, ethical, and good businessmen.

4. They had a passion for the retail business, their chosen career, and weren't afraid of hard work.

5. Like many people today, most of these early managers were also committed to their families, which required a consideration and dedication to work-life balances on the part of both spouses.

Gary worked for the Hested's chain in Nebraska before moving over to Walmart. Because big box retailing was a relatively new industry, these early managers came primarily from the variety store chains. You can imagine how difficult it was to entice the manager of a large discount store in a major city to relocate to Bentonville, Arkansas, and take a chance on a start-up outfit that might fold at any time.

When I reported to work at St. Robert, Gary and his wife, Lois, were driving a beat-up Chevrolet Corvair. As my store manager, I assumed he must have been financially well-off. The truth is that he had taken a big risk by leaving Hested's and was gambling with his future by joining the Waltons in this early stage of their growth. However, it didn't take long for that risk to pay off. From the day we opened the doors in this store, Gary earned some of the highest store manager bonuses in the company.

Learning the Ropes

I rented a two-room cabin in Waynesville and Gary put me to work right away. Although I was never given an official job description, I quickly realized I was a stock boy. My first assignment: a towering stack of "wheel goods" in the stockroom. Bicycles, tricycles, grills, and anything else that featured the instructions, "Assembly required." Lucky for me, this happened to be my forté, because of the two months I had spent at Western Auto in Bentonville performing exactly the same tasks.

As one of the lowest men on the totem pole, I learned that a stock boy is expected to do anything and everything asked of him. Because the store was being stocked for a Grand Opening, a steady stream of merchandise arrived on the loading docks at all hours. In those days (prior to bar-coding and scanning), workers had to manually unload every single item from the truck, match it to a purchase order, label it with a price ticket, and take it to the floor to be stocked on the shelves for sale. Each step was time-consuming and costly, but unavoidable in any retail environment of that time. After all, this was 1964.

The store's Grand Opening was truly grand. In addition to Sam and Bud Walton meeting and greeting the customers, their father Tom helped out by actually shagging shopping carts from the parking lot. Everybody pitched in as "one of the team" when things needed to be done. We never

heard anyone say, "That's not my job." Most communities in our country today have a "big box" retailer in or near their town. But in the early
'60s, stores of this size were truly a novel attraction. A Grand Opening of
this kind was a big deal. Mr. Sam, Gary and Claude Harris negotiated
special pricing for the items most in demand and offered customers the
lowest prices they'd ever seen. We stacked merchandise on the sidewalk,
gave away free popcorn and balloons for the kids, and brought in radio
announcers for live remote broadcasts. All of this activity really did the
trick. People flocked to the store from many miles away. The mayor and
available beauty queens (state and city) helped cut the opening ribbon.
For me, never having experienced something like this, it was like attending the largest circus in the world. I felt I had contributed to a very important happening and was very proud of myself and our team.

A typical day for me that first year of my retail education included
an abundance of different tasks. I was responsible for unloading trucks
arriving with new merchandise, checking that merchandise in, and two-
wheeling it out to the department managers. I also helped apply price la-
bels to the merchandise and place it on the counters. I answered requests
over the in-store paging system to carry out goods for customers, clean up
spills on the floor, put together display items, re-lay merchandise counters,
sweep the sidewalk (several times per day), pick up carts and trash from
the parking lot, clean the bathrooms, and a variety of other jobs. Each
evening, after closing at 9:00 p.m., I would scrub and strip old floor wax,
apply new wax, and buff-shine a few aisles of the store. A typical work
shift would begin at 7:00 in the morning and end at 10:30 in the evening.
Because I was on salary rather than hourly pay, the math computes to approximately 50¢ per hour. After figuring this out, I decided my old job at
the gas station wasn't so bad after all.

At that time, I wasn't exactly what you'd call an early riser, and such
long, physical hours at work led to my tendency to oversleep. On a few
too many occasions, a loud banging on my door would jolt me out of a
sound sleep. It was Gary telling me to "get my butt to work." Years later, I
asked him why he was willing to put up with my behavior rather than just

fire me. He said, "The truth is, you were more productive than anybody else. I didn't want to lose you." (Years later, I discovered a good excuse for over-sleeping or even dozing on the job. I wish I'd known of it back then. Just tell the boss you're using the "Stress Level Energy Exercise Plan," or SLEEP, they taught you at the last management seminar.)

Although I was just a stock boy, Gary took the time to teach me about retail and the store's operation. He was *very* patient. In addition to the day-to-day requirements of cash register operation, handling of money and deposits, cash reports and opening/closing procedures, he explained retailing terms, profit and loss statements, and the intricacies of making a profit in the retail business. He also told me about the store manager's bonus program and helped me see that a future in this business could be rewarding.

As the months went by, I became very proficient at checking in freight. We received a weekly warehouse truck from Butler Brothers. Because of our store's high volume, I could count on this being a very large shipment. It frequently included a big supply of "inner-packs" — smaller basic items combined in one huge box. When I first started, I had to carefully look at the stock numbers on each item, check those numbers against the shipping invoice, and identify the price to put on each item. One truckload could take as many as three days to process. I became so proficient at this that I could tell at a glance what most boxes contained. Ultimately, I could have a truckload of merchandise checked in, marked, and out on the floor in one afternoon. At the same time, I learned which items were selling the best according to the volume of basic merchandise going through the store. I rapidly came to identify the best-selling basic items in the store: the optimum sizes and colors of zippers, thread, underwear, health-and-beauty supplies, and so on. Later, that knowledge would become invaluable.

My Personal Life

Shortly after arriving in St. Robert, I married Murlene (Cindy) Stearns, the pretty girl I had met in Bentonville at the bowling alley. Looking back on it, we probably should have waited until I was making a decent salary. But with her living in Kansas City with airline stewardess roommates, and me being rather jealous, I was afraid I might lose her. And now, with a real job and all, I thought it made sense.

We were married in Mt. Vernon, Missouri, at her family's church, the First Baptist. Roger Lee Harrison, my best friend, served as my best man. Unfortunately, we overslept on the morning of the wedding and arrived forty-five minutes late. The family, pastor, and guests were none too happy with us. To add to the mayhem, I had purchased a new pair of black socks to wear with my rented black suit. (I had always worn only white socks). Cindy shared with me that a friend of hers had once remarked that if she was marrying a boy from Arkansas, he would probably be the "redneck" type who would wear white socks to a wedding. Well, when I got dressed that morning, I couldn't find my black socks and had to put on my white ones instead. Later, in the wedding pictures, kneeling at the altar with Cindy, those white socks shined like a hillbilly beacon. After the wedding, I found my new black socks in the inside breast pocket of the suit; I must have put them there for safe-keeping, but couldn't for the life of me remember doing it. (Perhaps because Roger Lee and I tilted back a few drinks the previous evening.) I'm sure Cindy's friend reminded her of the "redneck in white socks" comment.

We had our first child, Kimberly Murlene Loveless, in 1965, and rented a very small trailer house close to the store. The baby crib took up almost all the space in our living room. At my salary level, we quickly realized just how tough it was to make ends meet. Just about every week, after paying bills, our money ran out a few days before the next paycheck arrived. To supplement my income, Cindy would babysit Lois and Gary's kids, Scott and Stephanie, as often as possible. Many times we didn't know how we would buy milk or formula for the baby.

Loreen Gordon and Pansy Dye, two of the department managers I mentioned previously, were like angels to us. They knew Cindy and I were struggling and often brought us food, left us a few dollars, or helped in a number of other ways. Mom and a few other folks helped us out, too, as did Cindy's parents, Leonard and DoraLee Stearns. Somehow we got by. I had grown up poor, but this was different. As a husband and father, other people depended on me, people I loved. I had no choice but to succeed. I also developed a new understanding and compassion for others. Living and working through really hard times honed my insight and empathy for future employees in similar circumstances.

With the advantage of age and wisdom, I look back on this early marriage and realize that I really wasn't ready to marry and start a family at that stage of my maturity or finances. My advice to young people would be to become financially stable and be sure you're ready for a lifelong commitment before taking the giant leap into marriage. Although our marriage lasted for eighteen years, the first seven years were tough indeed.

Mr. "Bud" Walton

Because of my background in Bentonville and my connection with Mr. Sam, most of this book relates to those personal experiences. But during my stint in St. Robert, I came to know Mr. Bud almost as well. He was in charge of the Missouri stores. Mr. Bud was the type of person who put you immediately at ease. He had the same piercing gaze as Mr. Sam, the gaze that activated the butterflies in your stomach, but you knew he genuinely cared about you as a person. His wife, Audie, was one of the nicest people I've ever met. Bud and I had one thing in common — we liked to fish. Bud introduced me to his long-time friend, Harold Ensley from Kansas City, and we embarked on many wonderful fishing trips years later. Harold was a pioneer in the televised fishing show industry with his program, *The Sportsman's Friend*. I later accompanied Harold and Mr. Bud on fishing adventures to the Northwest Territories and Costa Rica. When Bud Walton passed away in 1995, I was honored to be one of the individuals asked to speak at his memorial service in the home office. Bud was the quiet, behind-the-scenes partner of Mr. Sam and played an integral role in the development and growth of Walmart. I was proud to call him my friend.

My First Promotion

After a year of long hours and low pay in the stockroom, I began to seek a new challenge and started bugging Gary to give me a department to manage. Gary delayed as long as he could while trying not to discourage me. I'm sure he thought I wasn't ready. Eventually he conceded. In late 1965, he rewarded me with a small raise and a promotion to Pet Department Manager in St. Robert.

> We seriously undervalue the passion . . . a person brings to an enterprise. You can rent a brain but you can't rent a heart.
>
> — MARK MCCORMACK

When I reflect on my experience as a stock boy checking in all that freight, I realize how much it increased my knowledge of basic merchandising. Throughout the early years of rapid growth with Sam Walton's stores, one of the keys to success was the merchandising ability of individual store managers. Starting at the very bottom of the supply chain exposed me to the "basic assortment" needed to attract a solid customer base in small communities. This essential store-level merchandising knowledge is not taught in college.

As a stock boy in St. Robert, I was treated with respect by Bud Walton, Gary Reinboth, and all the supervisors with whom I had contact. I was made to feel "one of a team," not just a stock boy. This management attribute is one which I adopted and practiced throughout my career, and one which I believe comes from the heart. I have observed many management executives who give "lip service" to respecting and appreciating lower-level associates, but those who believe in and practice these principles become true "servant leaders."

> A good manager is a man who isn't worried about his own career but rather the careers of those who work for him.
>
> — H.S.M. BURNS

> You can't treat people like an expense item.
>
> — ANDREW S. GROVE

CHAPTER 5

Ocelots, Monkeys & Mynahs (Oh My!) — Confessions of a Pet Department Manager

> ## 1966
>
> ▸ Two Walmart Discount City stores are now open in Rogers and Harrison, and Sam Walton is committed to growing the chain with openings in Springdale and Siloam Springs, Arkansas. Plans are underway for stores in Conway, Fayetteville, North Little Rock, and Morrilton, Arkansas.
>
> ▸ The Beatles, Rolling Stones, and Beach Boys are the hottest groups in music.
>
> ▸ *Doctor Zhivago* is a box office hit.
>
> ▸ Both the U.S. and Russia land unmanned vehicles on the moon in a space race.
>
> ▸ 500,000 troops are now fighting in Vietnam.
>
> ▸ I've set a goal to become the number one Pet Department manager in the company.

From the beginning of the Walton's store operations, company policy required managers and department managers to carry a 'Beat Yesterday' book at all times. This was our management bible. On any surprise visit by Mr. Sam, he fully expected you to recite the numbers in that book — your comparative sales year-to-year, inventory comparisons, markdown, and gross profit figures. Upper level management believed in the importance of openly sharing all numbers with the folks working in the stores. They insisted we keep our own department's numbers, while the store managers tracked the store's overall numbers.

With my promotion to manager of the Pet Department in the St. Robert store, I now carried my own record of daily, weekly, monthly, and annual sales. Merely looking at that book motivated me to excel. That competitive streak has always been part of my makeup. Plus, I was determined to show Gary that I could not only increase sales in the pet department, but that I could be the number one department manager in the whole company. I needed to prove to him that he'd made the right decision.

Gators of Miami, a pet supply wholesaler located in Miami, Florida, shipped us the live pets sold in our store. A big wall of aquariums stocked every sort of tropical fish and literally thousands of gold fish. We also carried common pets like hamsters, mice, tiny turtles, and guinea pigs. To boost sales and create the best pet department in the chain, I wanted to offer a larger variety of pets and began researching the entire inventory of Gators of Miami.

Understandably, Gary was a little wary of giving me free rein, but allowed me to start "testing" some things. So I ordered two squirrel monkeys. We sold them as soon as they hit the cages. I ordered two more with the same outcome. Ultimately, we sold 192 squirrel monkeys in the first twelve months. These monkeys had a high profit margin and retail price, which pleased Gary (and me).

We did experience one minor setback when I opened a cage door and was promptly bitten by a monkey that escaped into the rafters of our store. (Mind you, in those days, we had no wild animal control centers, protective organizations, or activist groups to reckon with.) After exhausting all hope of *ever* catching that monkey, and because he was now loose in a large store that catered to the public, Gary assigned me the task of shooting the critter. Now these little squirrel monkeys had cute faces, and I had grown attached somewhat, so it wasn't a pleasant task. But armed with a

Daisy pellet gun, I thought of my teen years in Bentonville when Uncle Georald took me rabbit and squirrel huntin'. Imagining this was no different, I managed to do the dastardly deed. This subsequent depletion of the monkey inventory resulted in a costly markdown that Gary certainly didn't appreciate.

My next venture into exotic creatures involved iguana lizards. These proved to be another hit, so I started stocking them regularly, followed by baby alligators, which customers also gobbled up (as opposed to the natural order of things). Easter time, the sales of baby yellow chicks and fluffy white rabbits made me look good. I was on a roll, leading the company in pet sales. Gary was happy with his decision to make me the Pet Department manager.

The Ocelot

But it wasn't all peaches and pet food. First, a guy came into the store and asked if I could order him an ocelot. One might wonder why. A lion or tiger or cheetah would seem feasible, but an ocelot? Not wanting to offend the customer and still striving to be an outstanding department manager, I called Gators of Miami and found that they could, indeed, supply a baby ocelot. We required a 50 percent down-payment on any special orders and we had to pay freight costs. What a fair freight charge would be, we could only guess. This was, after all, our first ocelot sale. The animal itself would cost us about $100. To play safe, we charged the customer $500. We figured he would never go for that, but to our surprise he said, "Fine, I'll take it." He ponied up half the money on the spot and we placed the order.

When the ocelot arrived we kept it in a cage in the stockroom. Now this little kitty was the cutest thing any of us had ever seen. We went crazy over it. When our customer showed up all excited about his new exotic acquisition and reached into the cage to pet it, the darned thing started snarling and hissing just before it bit him. Despite the flesh wound, the new ocelot owner asked if we could keep it in the stockroom for a few days to allow it to acclimate to its surroundings. We agreed. He came in every day to pet it before finally paying the remaining balance and leaving with the cat.

That $500 alone boosted me to number one in sales for the week. My happiness didn't last long, however. Soon after, Gary came to my department and said, "Ronnie, I got a call from a motel here in town. The manager's really upset. It seems the guy who bought the ocelot had been living there. They're gone now, but the cat ripped the hotel room to shreds. The furniture, draperies, everything. He wants *us* to pay for it." Of course, we refused to be held responsible, but it got hairy when the motel owner threatened to come down and beat Gary's butt. That was my first and last order for exotic cats.

The Mynah Bird

I did, however, order a mynah bird. My sales rep at Gators of Miami told me they had one that could already talk "real plain." Man, I thought, a real talking bird could be a hit and draw a lot of attention to my department — besides, this mynah bird was a high-ticket item. If I actually sold it, my sales would look better than ever. The mynah bird arrived, and talked to just right, could say "I love you" as clearly as a human being. I began whistling at the bird — the old "wolf-whistle" we used when flirting with a pretty woman. Soon that bird was wolf-whistling, then saying, "I love you."

Apparently our customers weren't all that impressed. While folks found it intriguing and interesting, it didn't sell. To attract more attention to our talking bird, I hung up a cage high in the aisle in front of the pet department. I got a kick out of watching the ladies walk down the aisle, hear a wolf-whistle and "I love you," then spin around trying to identify the offending party. More often than not, they thought it was me. I'd waste no time blaming the bird, and we'd share a chuckle. All well and good, until a *little* problem arose.

We held department manager meetings with Gary every morning before opening. In a meeting about this time, Loreen Gordon in fabrics and Pansy Dye in lingerie said they had been noticing a lot of bird poop on their merchandise. Now, occasionally sparrows flew into the store or stockroom through the open doors, warranting that I grab a BB gun to "take care of them" after hours. Gary and I decided that was probably the cause of the problem. But after looking high and low, we couldn't find one bird. This complaint continued to surface for the next two weeks. Finally, I just happened to glance at the mynah bird in time to see him lift his tail and "shoot" his poop like a shotgun shell toward the fabric department. Just like that, the "case of the mysterious bird poop" had been solved.

But not yet fixed. I took care of the problem by covering the cage half-way-up with clear plastic. Learning through experience is invaluable. I asked Gators of Miami about this issue and they said they didn't know anything about projectile mynah bird poop. Mynah birds didn't produce a huge sales volume (not nearly as large as their waste volume), but they did create a lot of interest and buzz. I sold that bird about three weeks after I hung it up in the department, and then moved a few more along with a number of cockatoos and a couple of parrots for Christmas that year. The biggest sellers, of course, were parakeets and canaries.

The Elephant

I won't get into all the gory details, but I started "pulling in my horns" on the exotic animals after the "big one." I ordered a baby elephant for a sergeant on the base. When it arrived, we all gathered excitedly around the truck, watching the workers off-load the crate. I slowly pried the wood slats back, trying to get a peek at my prized purchase. Once I caught a glimpse of the gray hulk inside, I thought it must be asleep. Probing further, I came to realize that the baby elephant was, in fact, "deader than a doornail." It was a sad affair, made sadder when I learned that I was liable once that elephant set foot on that truck. That was the day I learned what F.O.B. (Free on Board) stood for. I also discovered that, after this markdown, Gary was becoming a little more than peeved at my aggressiveness.

PETA did not exist at that time and no one camped out in front of the store with picket signs. Laws today prohibit importing most exotic animals and after our experience with the elephant, I believe that is the way it should be.

The Tornado

I was working one late Friday afternoon when a line of severe thunderstorms slammed into the St. Robert area. As I stared at a massive dark cloud out the front window, I saw the giant shopping center sign beside the highway just bend over to the ground. I'll never forget the loud roar and horrific ripping noise it made. In mere seconds, rain gushed into the store. Half of our roof literally disappeared, exposing the store to the torrential downpour and gale force winds. I looked out toward Bobby's Grocery store, which was adjacent to our space, and saw that the front of the building had caved in. The whole area looked like a battle zone.

I learned a lot about our company that night. Bud Walton arrived within three hours. Gary, Bud, a few other folks from the Bentonville office, and our store team worked all night long with squeegees and mops to get the water out of the store. We threw tarps over the gaps in the roof, marked down damaged merchandise, and by Monday morning drew a huge crowd to shop the "Big Tornado Sale." We turned a disaster into a record sales day. I only got two hours of sleep during that three-day period, but I was young, full of vinegar, and loved the challenge. Many of my colleagues were cut from the same cloth. We worked hard, played hard, and felt we were truly part of a family who cared about us.

Later in 1966, Gary began to trust me with the keys to the store, allowing me to occasionally open and close. I started to feel more like a member of the management team, though the salary certainly hadn't increased accordingly. I think both Gary and I realized that I could now take on added responsibilities. So in 1966, he promoted me to the position of assistant store manager.

Working as Pet Department manager was my first exposure to the responsibility of decision-making and the empowerment of controlling sales, inventory, and profits. This made me feel included, important, and productive. I also learned the terminology and methodology involved in the process of buying and selling for a profit. I discovered the meaning of the old adage, "retail is detail." Lastly, I learned to always keep plastic around a mynah bird's cage.

> There are no secrets to success: don't waste time looking for them. Success is the result of perfection, hard work, learning from failure, loyalty to those for whom you work, and persistence.
>
> — COLIN POWELL

CHAPTER 6

Movin' and Shakin' — Assistant Store Manager

1967–1969

▸ "One Small Step for Man" — Neil Armstrong and Buzz Aldrin land on the moon in Apollo 11.

▸ The Vietnam War sparks protests nationwide.

▸ Dr. Martin Luther King and Robert F. Kennedy are assassinated.

▸ The Woodstock music festival is staged in New York.

▸ Green Bay Packers and Kansas City Chiefs play in the first Super Bowl.

▸ Gas is 33¢ per gallon and the average house costs $15,000.

▸ Walmart incorporates as Walmart Stores, Inc. in October, 1969.

▸ Me, I'm an assistant manager, moving from store-to-store with dreams of becoming a manager.

I was officially promoted to assistant store manager, received a raise, and was transferred to the Walton Family Center in Berryville, Arkansas. With the slightly higher salary, Cindy and I were able to rent a small house in town. At last, we could get into our living room without maneuvering around the baby crib. It felt good to be moving up in the world. The store manager at the Family Center was Jack Carmichael, a great guy and family man who was well-liked in the community. Along with his beautiful wife, Elizabeth, and two sweet children, he gave us a warm welcome and made us feel like part of the family from the beginning.

Nothing of consequence happened in the few months I worked in Berryville. (Perhaps I was too devoted to performing my new job and presenting myself as a worthy contender for a store manager position to even think about pulling off any of the antics for which I had already become known. There were no spider monkeys, iguanas, baby ocelots, or talking, squirting mynah birds.)

Most stores at that time had one assistant manager for the "Hard-lines" side of the store and one for the "Softlines" (wearables and home furnishings) side. I went back and forth between both sides during my time at Berryville, absorbing the merchandising details in all categories. As an assistant manager, I became more involved in hiring practices. I conducted employment interviews and associate evaluations for the first time. Every step in a career furthers one's education and increases one's responsibilities. After a few short months, in 1967, I received a transfer to the Bentonville Walton Family Center — company headquarters and my old hometown.

Two changes had already taken place before I arrived at the Bentonville store. The name of the store had been changed from Walton's 5 & 10 to the Walton Family Center. And the store itself had been relocated from its original spot on the square to a small strip center just off the square. The Walton store shared a wall with Phillips' Grocery, owned and operated by a close friend of Sam's, Harlan Phillips, one of the truly nicest people I have ever met.

The Walton store featured the typical assortment of goods carried by variety stores at the time, but with a larger sporting goods/automotive department. This department had a separate entrance to the street, but was also accessible from inside the main store. Bob Bogle, Mr. Sam's first store manager for his Walton's 5 & 10, hired in 1955, was my manager. Bob was your typical detail-oriented, profit-driven merchant, the model executive favored by Mr. Sam. He treated me with respect, and as with

Gary Reinboth and Jack Carmichael, taught me a lot about merchandising the store. Over the years, I heard stories about how tough it was to work for some managers. I guess I was fortunate, because all my managers, while demanding, were polite and respectful to me. Perhaps it was that I expected them to be tough or that I just didn't know any better, but I always returned their respect and held them in high regard.

Bob's son, David Bogle, was a fellow assistant manager during my time there. David didn't work for Walmart very long. He preferred to make his own way, and went into business for himself in Bentonville. He remains a friend to this day. Bob's wife, Marilyn, was also a very nice lady. Bob and Marilyn continue to reside in Bentonville at the time of this writing. Over the years, the Bogle family contributed greatly to the community in many different ways. They are also big supporters of the University of Arkansas in Fayetteville and their Razorback Athletic programs. "Wooooooooo Pig, Soooie!"

On my first day of work at this store, I noticed a bespectacled young lady working behind the customer service desk at the front of the store. I asked Bob her name and he informed me that the girl was Alice Walton. I couldn't believe it. I hadn't seen Alice since high school and she looked much different than the girl I remembered. Like David Bogle, Alice didn't stay at the store long. She went on to become an accessories and girl's wear buyer for the company for a brief period of time, before realizing retailing just wasn't for her.

The General Office

At this time in the late '60s, Mr. Sam's vision of building a chain of Walmart Discount City stores was becoming a reality. The initial stores proved successful and he was hiring experienced management people from outside the company whom he felt could manage the growth and help plan the future. He leased office space for the General Office on the southeast corner of the Bentonville square. The space was on the second floor of the building, with access only by a narrow, curving stairwell. It wouldn't necessarily impress anyone, but it was much fancier than the old office Mr. Sam occupied when I was growing up in Bentonville — an ex-tire shop in a back alley.

You'd think that, being only a city block from the General Office, we would see the Walmart management folks on a regular basis. Perhaps Bob did, but as a young assistant manager, our paths rarely crossed. No doubt Mr. Sam kept them busy planning and managing this young but rapidly growing company. I'd occasionally be asked to deliver something to the General Office. In doing so, I came to know most of the early management team.

Considering the company now consisted of several Walmart stores and fifteen or so Ben Franklin and Walton 5 & 10 stores, Mr. Sam had an awfully small General Office (G.O.) team when I got to Bentonville. With two women, Wanda Nichols and Loretta Boss working in the G.O., big Don Whitaker overseeing the stores, and Claude Harris serving as the merchandising guy, Mr. Sam added some accomplished management talent for his fast-growth plan. Along with a handful of others, key roles were filled by Ferold Arend, Bob Thornton, Jim Dismore, and Ray Gash. The reference to the headquarters as the "General Office" was later changed to the "Home Office," as it sounded more store-supportive. It continues to be referred to as both, depending on who is discussing the company. Also, as the organization grew through the years, the Walmart logo and signage continued to evolve. The original "Wal-Mart Discount City" contained the hyphen. The next incarnation was "Wal*Mart" with a star in the middle, then "Wal-Mart" without the Discount City, and lastly "Walmart," followed by a "spark" symbol. That's the same logo in use today.

During my years as an Assistant Manager, the number of company stores and the volume of sales grew at a fast clip: 1967 — 24 stores, $12.6 million; 1968 — 27 stores, $21.4 million; 1969 — 32 stores, $30.9 million.

On The Personal Side

Another key event in my life occurred while I served as assistant manager in Bentonville. Cindy and I welcomed the birth of our second child, Ronald L. Loveless II. (I'm kind of partial to that name.) He was born at Bates Hospital on April 26, 1968. We still struggled financially, but with Kim and now little Ronnie, our family was complete. We hung in there, with the hope that better things awaited us just around the bend.

Moved Again

In late 1968, I was transferred once again, to Walmart store # 4 in Siloam Springs, Arkansas. The manager was a slightly-built officious little man named Rex Chase. Rex had a tendency to micromanage. He often stood a few feet away from me while I performed whatever task he had assigned, just to ensure I was doing the job properly. I quietly referred to Rex as "The Professor." While our management styles differed significantly, I suppose Rex taught me, more than anyone, that "retail is detail."

This was my first job in an actual Walmart store. Being larger, there was far more space in the store devoted to feature tables and stack bases for greater quantities of promotional merchandise. I had to adjust to a number of differences in the Walmart format versus that of the Walton Family Center concept. Ben Franklin no longer supplied the basic assortment. I had to learn everything all over again.

Paul Dunnaway and the Blackhawk Lounge

I'll never forget one of my fellow assistant managers in this Siloam Springs store — Paul Dunnaway. Paul's relatives single-handedly made up a considerable percentage of the population in my hometown of Hiwassee. For all I knew, he might have been my cousin. Paul was a tall, rambunctious guy, and he and I would occasionally head over to the local watering hole, the Blackhawk Lounge. The lounge was actually located in Oklahoma. Siloam Springs lies on the Oklahoma/Arkansas border. Let's just say that the Blackhawk was one of those bars that might have spawned the legendary reference, "It was so rough, if you didn't have a gun when you entered, they'd *give* you one."

On one visit, Paul and I won some money from a couple of guys in a pool game, but they had no intention of paying up. Being assistant managers at the local Walmart store, I didn't want to make a big deal of it. Trouble was the last thing I needed. But Paul was having none of that. Trying to avoid an inevitable confrontation, I left to go wait in the car. Paul stayed behind, but not for long. Soon he came flying through the door, tossed out bodily by three or four hefty patrons, his face bleeding. He looked even worse when he arrived for work the next morning, not exactly what you'd expect in an assistant manager. (For the record, we never set foot in the Blackhawk again. This little incident added to my education. Along with management responsibility comes a heightened awareness of your public image, and of course, my role as husband and father was ever-present on my mind.)

Store Set-Up Crews

One of my tasks as assistant manager involved helping with the opening of other stores as a member of a "store set-up" crew. While in Siloam Springs, I participated in a number of these set-ups, which provided valuable experience for opening my own store (if and when I was promoted to store manager). The store opening process in those days was a sight to behold. From the time the contractor turned the vacant building over to us, we would whip the entire store into 'Grand Opening' shape in less than thirty days. I know of some stores that came online even more quickly than that.

I met some real characters during these set-ups, some of the hardest working folks I've ever seen. Guys like Jackie Brewer, Larry English, Al Miles, Dale Walkup, Charley Cate, Gary Smith, Bill Smith, and many, many others. We worked *very* hard, generally arriving around 6:00 a.m. and finishing up around 10:00 p.m. We had to set the fixtures, lay out the merchandise on the counters, train the associates, and attend to hundreds of tasks required for the opening of a new 40,000 square-foot Walmart store in less than a month. It was truly a challenge. None of us were "specialists." We did it all. How smoothly the process took place was largely dependent upon the knowledge of the crew. The men I mentioned here were the best of the best.

A key individual in those early days deserves a tremendous amount of credit for his contributions. Mr. Sam hired a fellow named Gene Lauer, a carpenter by trade, to build our store fixtures. Gene became a "master" at constructing, delivering, and setting up the fixtures in new Walmart stores for years to come. From a small shop in Bentonville, he amazed us with the sheer volume of fixtures he could mass-produce, ship, and install. I would describe Gene as the "Henry Ford" of store fixtures.

At Last, My Own Store, But . . .

In September, 1969, at twenty-six years of age, I got *the call*. Don Whitaker, Director of Operations at the General Office, informed me that I had been selected as store manager for the new Walmart store #18, to be opened in Newport, Arkansas. I was elated; all my hard work had turned the dream of running my own store into a reality. My time had arrived. I was confident and intent on showing the company what I could do. I knew merchandising, how to motivate people, and the company policies and procedures. How could I fail?

A few doubts crept into my mind as the conversation call continued. Don said, "Ronnie, there are a lot of us in the G.O. who don't think you're ready yet, but the 'old man' wants you to have the store. We gotta talk, boy."

This was Don Whitaker's way. He was an imposing figure, a big burly man who was a bit "cock-eyed." (Later, I learned he actually had one artificial eye.) He looked at you with a perpetual scowl on his face and spoke with a very deep, gruff voice that put the fear in you. All of us in the stores nicknamed him "the Bear," though we never dared call him that to his face. He referred to us as "boy," but it wasn't meant to be degrading. He referred to Mr. Sam as the "old man," though Mr. Sam was only a few years older. The truth was, as most of us eventually found out, Don "the Bear" Whitaker was actually a "teddy bear." He had a big heart and would defend his people to the end, so long as you were doing your best.

Don went on to say, "I need to go down to Newport next week, and I want you to ride along with me. I need to tell you some things. After this trip, you can give me your final answer about taking the store. It's not too late to back out. Come over to Bentonville on Monday and we'll drive down together." This conversation dampened my enthusiasm. I thought I was capable and ready to handle the job. Just as important, Mr. Sam thought I was ready and had mandated the assignment. So what was the problem?

On Monday, I met the Bear in Bentonville and we took off for Newport. Everyone in the company was aware of the Walton's history regarding Newport, the location of Mr. Sam's first retail venture in 1945. In a nutshell, he had built a successful business in his variety store there, but lost his lease because he hadn't bothered to note the lack of a renewal clause. The landlord wanted the business for himself. This resulted in Sam Walton ultimately relocating to Bentonville. The opening of a big, new Walmart store there in Newport, in our collective opinion, must have had special significance and a degree of redemption for Mr. Sam, though he would never express it openly. This all added up to extra pressure on the manager who opened this new store. (In other words, me.)

As we drove down to Newport, the Bear filled me in on a number of things I didn't know. He informed me that he felt the store was too large for the community at that time. This was going to be our largest prototype to date, 40,000 square feet, about one-fifth the size of a current Supercenter, and would be located "quite a ways" from downtown. He said that the largest employer in town, the Brown Shoe Factory, had just closed its doors. The town's economy was in bad shape. Newport was nestled in the delta farming area of Arkansas and this was a hard time for farmers — they were "hurting." He didn't think the store would do well under the current economic conditions. All things considered, he questioned my willingness to take that risk.

As I had learned in St. Robert, one of Mr. Sam's measurements of the potential business in a town was city and county sales tax revenue, which indicated sales potential. As the Bear and I entered the Newport city limits, he pointed out something I'll never forget. Passing a number of large farm equipment dealerships, he said, "Ronnie, Mr. Sam talks about the high sales tax numbers for Newport, but you see all that farm machinery over there? It doesn't take many $25,000 to $50,000 pieces of equipment to show some high numbers. That's why this county looks good to Mr. Sam, but it doesn't mean people are buying that much toothpaste and panties . . . got it?" Bottom line, he was letting me know that he and others felt sales would be tough for any new store, much less a huge new Walmart.

My personal bottom line was different. The lure of getting my own big, new store to manage, coupled with my near-cocky "I'll show them" determination, led me to dismiss the Bear's misgivings. I squared my jaw, looked him dead in the eyes, and said, "I still want the job."

In October, 1969, I moved my family to Newport and reported for work as a new store manager.

I look back on this period of my career and see how tough it was on my family to move from town to town. I now realize how fortunate I was to have a supportive wife. There were many assistant managers then, as there are today, who relocated more than I did. It was just the way things were done. That was the downside. But the upside was the opportunity to work for a number of store managers, each with different strengths and weaknesses. Astute assistant managers could learn from the weaknesses, as well as the strengths, to determine how best to manage their own stores when given the chance. The advantage of exposure to a variety of management skills and philosophies provided an invaluable education that can't be learned in business schools.

Webster's New World Dictionary defines experience as: 1: the act of living through an event; 2: anything or everything observed or lived through; 3: a) training and personal participation b) knowledge, skill, etc., resulting from this.

CHAPTER 7

Store Manager, Newport, Arkansas — A Perilous Experience

1969–1970

▶ 100,000 demonstrate in Washington, D.C. against the Vietnam War.

▶ Nixon is president.

▶ The EPA is established.

▶ The National Guard kills four students at a Kent State University protest.

▶ Gas prices rise to 36¢ per gallon.

▶ Walmart builds its first warehouse/General Office (60,000 square feet).

▶ The Walmart Company goes public at $16.50 per share.

▶ Thirty-eight Walmart stores produce $44.2 million in sales with 1,500 associates.

▶ I am the proud new manager of Walmart store #18, Newport, Arkansas.

Just before Christmas of 1969, we opened store #18 in Newport, Arkansas. It was a beautiful store and initial sales were good, thanks primarily to Christmas. Unfortunately, January followed. (I hate it when that happens.) Even though I was adhering to company guidelines and standards to the nth degree, sales continued to drop precipitously.

Mr. Sam himself called me once a week, usually on Saturday after the General Office tallied the week's sales, payroll costs, and inventory numbers. As January, February, and March progressed (and I use that term loosely), sales continued to plummet. I could tell Mr. Sam was very concerned. He felt I had to be doing something wrong. After all, he had increased his initial variety store's business multi-fold when he operated here in the late '40s; it should be a good town for this new store. Or so he thought.

On his March visit, he found everything satisfactory. The store was clean, neat, and well-merchandised, but was running a very high payroll cost in relation to the low volume of sales. He asked me what I was doing about expenses, and I told him I had slashed costs as low as I possibly could. We just needed more sales volume.

A couple of months later, I cut my store staff to the bone, with department managers overseeing multiple departments. I released my cash report clerk and handled the weekly cash reports myself after closing each day. I was working long, long hours, yet my payroll costs were running 15 to18 percent, almost twice the acceptable level. Despite my growing frustration and disappointment, I remained confident in my efforts, refusing to believe that the problems were directly my fault. Recalling Don Whitaker's warning about this store, I realized he'd been correct in his assessment of the area's current economic challenges. Even now, I can think of nothing more I might have done to improve the store's performance at that time. In later years, Newport became a typically-good Walmart location (but that's not pertinent to my situation in 1970.)

As I sat preparing the weekly cash report after the close of a very long, very exhausting Saturday in May, the phone rang. When I answered, an all-too-familiar voice said, "Ronnie, what in the world is going on down there? You ran an 18 percent payroll this week and your sales are terrible. I've had enough of this. Am I going to have to change managers? Did I make a mistake on you?"

Between Mr. Sam's foul mood and me at my wit's end, we had a recipe for trouble. This is probably the appropriate time to mention that my competitive spirit and determination to win could, at any time, reveal itself in an explosion of temper. The pressure that had been building finally burst at this, the most inopportune, time.

"Mr. Walton," I replied, my voice rising, "I have done everything I can to make this store successful. Everyone says the store looks great, so I just don't know what else to do. I guess if you think I'm not good enough, maybe you should come down here and run it yourself!" And with that said, I hung up the phone. After a brief moment to reflect on what I just done, I thought to myself, *Oh, my God, what have I just done?*

After closing the store, I dragged myself home and told Cindy, "Well, are you ready to go back to Bentonville? I just hung up on Sam Walton and I know I'm out of a job." I fully expected the phone to ring any minute, confirming my worst fears. I collapsed into bed that night with my mind swirling, finally drifting into a fitful sleep around 2:00 a.m. Two hours later, my doorbell rang. I got up, staggered groggily to the door, and found Don "the Bear" Whitaker on my doorstep.

"What in the world did you say to the old man, boy?" he asked. "He sent me down here to fire you. You got any coffee? We really need to talk."

I put on a pot, told him the whole story, and we chewed over the particulars for some time. Finally, Don leaned forward in his chair and said, "I think I can talk him into giving you another chance, but boy, I'll really be sticking my neck out. You know I don't think the situation here is your fault. I have a store in mind that I could move you to, but I'm telling you, if you screw up again, you're finished. You understand?"

"Yes, sir, I do understand and I'd really appreciate another chance. I know I can run a store, and I'll prove it to Mr. Sam." And to myself.

So in 1970 they shipped me to Walmart store #11 in Mountain Home, Arkansas. Little did I know at the time that I was going from my own personal "hell" to "a little bit of heaven."

This first experience as a store manager was a serious blow to my ego. It left me with questions about myself and doubts about my ability. Most importantly, though, I knew I had disappointed Sam Walton. He had become a sort of "father figure" to me. I felt like I had failed him and wondered if I could ever turn that around. Yet, deep down, I still knew I was capable and ready to take on this job.

When things go wrong as they sometimes will

When the road you're trudging seems all uphill,

When the funds are low and the debts are high,

And you want to smile, but you have to sigh.

☺

When care is pressing you down a bit,

Rest if you must, but don't you quit.

Life is strange with its twists and turns,

As every one of us sometimes learns.

And many a failure turns about,

When he might have won, had he stuck it out.

Don't give up though the pace seems slow,

You may succeed with another blow.

Success is failure – turned inside out

The silver flint of the clouds of doubt.

And you never can tell how close you are,

It may be near when it seems so far.

☺

So stick to the fight when you're hardest hit,

It's when things seem worst that you must not quit.

— AUTHOR UNKNOWN

CHAPTER 8:

Managing in Paradise — Mountain Home, Arkansas

1970–1975

- Walt Disney World opens.

- FedEx, HBO, and Atari's PONG debut.

- Intel introduces the first microprocessor.

- First known act of international terrorism: Palestinian militants massacre Israeli athletes at Munich Olympics.

- The Watergate scandal results in President Nixon's forced resignation.

- Vietnam War ends.

- World Trade Center and Sear's Tower completed.

- Secretariat wins horse racing's Triple Crown.

- First UPC scanners installed in Marsh's Market — Troy, Ohio.

- Future billionaires Bill Gates and Paul Allen create Microsoft Company.

- Walmart grows from 52 stores ($78 million in revenue) to 125 stores ($340 million in revenue). Stock splits for the third time and now trades on the NYSE.

- My new store is making money. We buy our first new car and a house.

Mountain Home is situated in extreme north central Arkansas,
nestled in the hills of the Ozark Mountain range. Surrounded
by two huge, beautiful lakes (Lake Norfork and Bull Shoals Lake) and
three bountiful rivers (the Northfork, White, and Buffalo National Rivers), the city is truly a sportsman's paradise. At some point in the '60s, the
word must have gotten out in the northern part of the country that this
was an idyllic retirement spot, because by the time we arrived in 1970, a
large population of older folks had taken up residence. The natives referred to the area as "Little Chicago." We southerners kiddingly referred
to them as "Yankees." With its abundant lakes and rivers, Mountain
Home's robust economy was largely driven by tourism.

Coming out of my less-than-stellar experience in Newport, I was dis-
illusioned by the Walmart store to which I had been assigned. I figured
it was upper management's way of making it clear that I had been "demoted." Located in a very old strip center, Walmart store #11 was *small;*
on the scale of an oversized convenience store. The sporting goods and
automotive departments had to be operated out of an annex adjacent to
the main store. The main building was 12,000 square feet, as opposed to
40,000 square feet for the Newport store. Yet our volume was considerably higher.

By the end of my first week, I found that we had more customer traffic
in a week than the Newport store had in a month. Everything seemed
wonderful. My family and I immediately fell in love with the town and
the area. There was just one snag, a problem exactly the opposite of the
one I experienced in Newport. Sales were *too* good. Let me explain.

In those days, we received a weekly delivery from the Walmart warehouse, two-and-a-half hours west in Bentonville. In this small Mountain Home store, we were moving so much merchandise so quickly that
when we ordered what we needed, we couldn't fit it all in the stockroom.
Weather permitting, we unloaded the truck in the alley behind the store,
checked in the merchandise outdoors, took all we could fit on the shelves
to the sales floor, and tried to squeeze the rest into the *extremely* small
stockroom long after the truck had gone. On rainy or snowy days, we

WALMART INSIDE OUT — CHAPTER 8

were forced to do all this receiving in the middle of the store aisles, a major inconvenience for our customers (and for us).

Walmart published and ran weekly sales circulars. Featuring sixty to one hundred items for a three-day sale, stores were required to fill out "return sheets," indicating how much of each item they needed for the event. I quickly discovered there was no way to buy enough of this merchandise to last three days. As a stopgap, I finally rented a small storage space about a block from the store to house some of the merchandise. After noting the rent charge on my profit & loss statement, my district manager (DM), Jim Dismore, reminded me that outside storage units were a violation of company policy. So, back to my original problem — running out of sale merchandise.

The warehouse truck arrived on Tuesday or Wednesday. For the next few days the store looked great — full end caps, counters, and promotional tables. Sales soared. But by late Saturday, the counters and displays looked barren and uninviting, much like the store itself. We couldn't wait for the next truckload.

Another Close Call with Mr. Sam

One Saturday afternoon, as I sat in my office at the front of the store, Sam Walton paid a surprise visit. This was our first face-to-face encounter since the "Newport hang-up" incident. I broke out in a sweat. I just knew the store wouldn't meet with his approval. He said, "Ronnie, just do what you're doing. I'm gonna walk around a bit."

Do what I was doing? Yeah, right. About thirty minutes later, Mr. Sam called me out to the parking lot (his version of taking me to the woodshed) and said, "Ronnie, your store looks horrible. You're badly out-of-stock. What are we going to do with you?"

"Mr. Walton," I pleaded, "you know the sales of this store are way up. The problem is I can't get enough merchandise into the store to keep up with demand. One warehouse truck per week isn't enough. I either need more than one truck per week or a bigger store . . . or both."

He frowned, looked me in the eye, and said, "I don't want to hear excuses. A good manager would figure out a way to get the job done, no matter what it takes. We've got to take care of these customers. I'm gonna give this some thought on the way home."

The next Monday morning, I received a call at the store. Jim Dismore, never one to mince words, got right to the point. "Ronnie, Mr. Sam was not happy with your store last Saturday. He's wondering if he should fire you." Déjà vu all over again, as Yogi Berra once said. I immediately thought of the similar call from "the Bear." Of course, Jim already knew the situation; I had discussed the problem with him often. Don Whitaker, who directed all Walmart store operations, also understood what I was up against. I begged Mr. Dismore to ask Mr. Sam to commit to another visit, but try to make it on a Thursday. I knew my store would look a thousand percent better after receiving my weekly shipment.

Two weeks later, on a Thursday, Jim Dismore pulled into my parking lot with Sam Walton. The night before, we had finished restocking the store and it was as near perfect as I could get that old building. Once again, Mr. Sam instructed me to do what I needed to do and proceeded to walk the store with Mr. Dismore. Just before leaving, Mr. Sam stuck out his hand to shake mine and simply said, "Thank you, Ronnie." End of conversation. (Thank you, Jim Dismore.)

A Newer, Bigger Store

A few months after my second "near miss" with Mr. Sam, Jim Dismore told me that the company had approved a new store to be built in Mountain Home. It would be the biggest, most modern prototype to date — 45,000 square feet, slightly larger than the Newport store. This proved to me that Sam Walton listened. He knew we needed the space and took action.

Our Grand Opening took place in 1973. Business surpassed everyone's expectations. We won a number of awards over the next two years, including "Store of the Region" and "Store of the Year." We were always highly-ranked in sales and profits. Most important to my family, the store managers received a generous bonus on annual store profits. I recall the excitement of that first big check, around $18,000 (back when that was real money). I felt like I had won the lottery. All the hard work and scrimping to eke out a living had finally begun to pay off. But instead of buying Walmart stock, which I should have done, I spent it on things I'd always dreamed of owning: our first house and a brand new car.

I joined the Chamber of Commerce and became acquainted with the important folks around town. We made a lot of new friends. I ensured our store became a "community" gathering place and a good corporate citizen by participating in local fund-raising activities, helping the schools, and advertising with the local print and broadcast media. I also taught Sunday school at the First Baptist Church. Ah, life was good. And I was only thirty-years-old.

The Maverick Sales Promoter

I would have to say that my time in Mountain Home served as the catalyst for my eventual reputation as a "maverick" (well before John McCain and Sarah Palin made it a household word). Frankly, this served me well with Sam Walton over the years. He liked mavericks. He liked to see us try new things and take risks, so long as sales and profits kept heading in the right direction.

That was me, alright. A maverick. I never knew Mr. Sam to fire someone over a single mistake, but he wouldn't hesitate to get rid of "non-performers." I also learned to navigate my way through the tough choices. For example, a manager could get in trouble and "chewed out" for payroll costs that were too high in relation to percentage of sales, but could get *fired* for running a poor store operation. A no-brainer, actually: take the payroll heat, but keep the store in good shape. But back to the "maverick" story...

One of my sales promotions went a little too far. In 1974, the nation was riveted by the famed Evel Knievel's up-coming motorcycle jump over the Snake River Canyon in Idaho. Evel was at the top of his fame, if not his game, at this time. Concurrently, I had been informed by the G.O. merchandising staff that they were putting the "Big Wheel" toy on the fast track. Introduced in 1969, the Big Wheel was a three-wheeled plastic tricycle-type riding toy for little kids. It was a consistently good seller. In the middle of a conversation with my assistant managers I said, "Let's see how many of these things we can sell." Walmart gave us managers a lot of leeway in those days, not even requiring approval for local ads and sale events. So without the knowledge of my bosses, I came up with an idea.

I dreamed up this big Saturday event, complete with a couple of "Truckload Sales" and a "Sidewalk Sale," which we held on a regular basis. Plus, we would order a huge quantity of the Big Wheels, "stack 'em high and sell 'em cheap." We would draw traffic to the store by advertising that "Evel K-Roger (my assistant, Roger Shipley) would be jumping his Big Wheel cycle over a swimming pool on the Walmart parking lot on Saturday at 10:00 a.m. I ran two teaser ads a week prior to this big event, declaring: "IT'S COMING ... THE BIG JUMP ... EVEL K-ROGER WILL ATTEMPT TO JUMP THE SWIMMING POOL AT WALMART NEXT SATURDAY, 10:00 a.m ... DON'T MISS IT!!" Included with this verbiage, of course, were the sale items with hot prices and a "heckuva" price on the Big Wheels.

On the big day, cars began pouring into the parking lot well before we opened our doors. We drew one of the best crowds ever — perhaps as large as our Grand Opening. The night before, we had constructed a wooden ramp with a rather steep incline. Directly below the end of the ramp, we had placed one of those inflatable kids' swimming pools. We thought the plan was simple and foolproof: Evel K-Roger would pedal the Big Wheel to the top of the ramp and just fall into the swimming pool (ha-ha-ha). Everybody would get a good laugh and buy bunches of stuff.

At 9:45 a.m. I climbed to the top of a tall ladder right next to the "event site" and clicked on a PA system to emcee the event. Right on cue, Evel K-Roger pedaled the Big Wheel out of the store, stopping at the base of the ramp. Having donned the helmet we had painted with stars, not to mention the handmade red, white, and blue jumpsuit, he gave a hesitant wave to the crowd. With my store associates having a good laugh, about

half of the crowd seemed to be joining them while many other customers seemed confused and not necessarily enthused about the goings-on.
Unfortunately, we had not pre-tested this "jump." The thinking was: if
Roger got hurt, he would only get hurt once. It seemed like a good idea
at the time.

I called out "GO!" and K-Roger started pedaling that Big Wheel as
furiously as his legs would let him. He made it about half-way up the
ramp when the plastic wheels lost traction and started spinning — back
down the ramp. I could detect a few boos and negative comments around
the crowd — others were laughing — and the associates were absolutely
cracking up. After three tries, we had no choice. My other assistants positioned themselves behind Evel K-Roger and pushed the Big Wheel up
and over the end of the ramp. Of course, gravity took it from there. He
dropped like a rock straight into the pool, hurting himself slightly (since
we hadn't bothered to figure out how deep the water should be for a fif-
teen-foot fall).

Many in the crowd cheered, but just as many booed. I overheard a
few comments like "false advertising" and "rip-off." Several customers informed me of their intent to complain to the home office in Bentonville.
I learned that while the retirees in that area were good people and great
customers, they felt cheated out of witnessing a spectacular motorcycle
jump. Evel K-Roger and his Big Wheel did not come close to qualifying.

Jim Dismore called first thing Monday to inform me of the complaints
he'd already received. "What in the world did you do?" he asked. "You
had the best Saturday sales of anyone in the company."

I explained it all, and thanks to the sales results, he let me off with a
slap on the wrist. (By the way, we led the company in Big Wheel sales that
Christmas.)

The Maverick Merchant

During this time, Walmart gave its store managers a great deal of leeway
in sourcing and stocking merchandise. With Mountain Home situated
smack dab in the middle of the best fresh-water fishing in the country,

we led the company in sporting goods sales. This area became the home of three of the leading bass boat manufacturers: Ranger, Champion, and Bass Cat. I joined my first Bass Club and learned the ins and outs of the sport from some well-known current (and future) BASS professional anglers. I was fortunate to fish in a couple of tournaments with Max Atkinson, as well as a few others. As a result, I came to know which lures and baits were in high demand.

Another big name in the fishing world, Bill Newland, made his own line of jigs and spinner baits right there in Mountain Home. They were "hot" and "everyone" was using them. Our buyers in the G.O. shipped us the nationally-known products, but would approve the sale of local brands if you could convince them they would do well. I got approval to purchase some Newland lures and displayed an end cap of them in our sporting goods department. We sold more of those lures than all the other jigs and spinners combined. That store generated a tremendous amount of sales volume from a vast assortment of unique, locally-produced products.

The company buyers determined and purchased the basic assortment of merchandise, plus items to be featured in the monthly sales circulars, keeping the warehouse stocked with these items. Each store replenished basic items by ordering from these warehouse goods on a weekly basis. "Assembly orders," which were basic items not regularly stocked in the warehouse, shipped to the warehouse every two weeks. There, they were broken out for each store and loaded onto the same trucks with our basic warehouse goods. Store managers determined the quantities of sale items needed and ordered via "return sheets," based on recommended quantities by size and volume of stores. The largest stores in size and/or volume bought "A" quantities, while the smallest volume stores bought "D" quantities. Beyond these established company replenishment programs, managers could enhance their stores' sales with merchandise bought directly from suppliers based on their local community needs. Having been trained by people I deemed to be great "merchants," I had learned to be a good merchant myself; therefore, I bought directly from some of the big suppliers, which resulted in impressive sales volume on promotions in feature aisles.

During my tenure in Mountain Home, the lawn and garden (horticulture) department led the company in sales. In the spring, we purchased literally truckloads of plants, peat moss, fertilizer, and a host of other products that were not necessarily offered by the G.O. buying staff. The retirees in the Mountain Home area loved their flowers and gardens. This attention to the needs of specific geographic and demographic populations was a key to Walmart's success during this peak growth period. Stores leading the company in sales were doing so because they were managed by the best "merchants" in the company; managers who were directly involved with the department managers in buying ample basic merchandise while selecting items to buy in larger quantities for end cap and feature aisle promotions.

As I've said, the Mountain Home store was a top performer. When a store generated exceptional sales and profits, it wasn't unusual for Sam Walton to drop by to see first-hand what was driving such results. My store was no exception. On his occasional visits, Mr. Sam showed a genuine interest in learning about the hottest-selling items — quite a change from previous visits I had experienced. Yep, life was good.

The Maverick Manager

I like to consider myself a "people person" and a good manager. During my store manager days, I treated my team of assistant and department managers like members of my extended family. I truly cared about them. I was eager and willing to do unusual things to motivate them. Even in this new and larger store, we couldn't cram all the goods into the stockroom on our Tuesday receiving days. Walmart designed its new stores with only 5 percent of the total space devoted to storage. So even after taking full cases of merchandise straight to the floor for marking, we always had a stockroom full of inner-pack cartons. Each had to be individually checked in and price-marked with the "ticket guns" in use at that time. If the items were "advertised sale items," we had to mark them with the regular price, and then mark them again with the "sale price tags." This usually took all day, a source of frustration because we needed to move the goods on the floor immediately to maximize sales.

My team of assistants was really into sports. Rick Russell, whom I had hired from the Sears Catalogue store downtown, was an exceptional athlete. We even fielded a store softball team and basketball team. This all led to my "brilliant" idea — a basketball goal hung from the stockroom rafters. We rigged it so we could pull it up out of sight when necessary, and lower it when we wanted to play. The "court" was tiny, but we managed to dribble around a bit, play a little "horse," and have a good time. As an incentive, I made a deal with the guys. On freight truck day, if they had the merchandise checked-in, marked and on the sales floor by noon, they could play basketball the remainder of the day. Those guys moved more freight more quickly than I ever thought possible. Unorthodox? Sure, but it worked. I call it an employee motivational technique.

I got a little nervous, though, when my new district manager, M.I. Dillard, paid an unannounced visit one freight day. My previous D.M., Jim Dismore, had recently been promoted. As was customary, Mr. Dillard and I toured the store discussing merchandise, sales, and the like. When we neared the stockroom door, I could hear the usual freight-day dribbling. I quickly excused myself from the boss and tracked down a clerk, telling him "Go to the stockroom and tell the guys to stop right now and pull the goal up into the rafters. The boss is here!" The whole scene must have looked like time-lapse photography. By the time we walked into the stockroom, there was no evidence in sight. I had no idea if my motivational techniques would sit well with the bosses. Fortunately, it never became an issue. The way I looked at it, our sales and profits compensated for any potential criticism of my maverick methods.

At our annual store Christmas party, I wanted to come up with something unusual to entertain the store associates. I decided to hold a "Miss Walmart Beauty Pageant," with one slight wrinkle: the contestants would be my assistant managers dressed as women. They included: "Miss Kozy Korner, Kansas," played by Arvin Clemans; "Miss Chapped

Cheeks, Minnesota," played by Roger Shipley; "Miss Farkle's Flat, Vermont," played by Joe Coonrod; and "Miss Hooker Hill, Hawaii," played by Rick Russell. We went all out, with evening gown, talent, swimsuit, and interview competitions. It turned out to be one of the most successful parties we ever threw. The associates absolutely cracked up seeing their management team make fools of themselves. Doing things like this brought the team together and made for an enjoyable work atmosphere.

When I talk with people today about these sorts of antics, they tell me it's "demeaning" to women; that "you can't do that, it is politically incorrect." I say, "Get over it." The only people "demeaned" by this event were the assistant managers. Our female associates hooted and hollered louder than anyone; they thought it was the best thing they'd ever seen. By the way, Rick Russell won the event. (He aced the swimsuit competition.)

A Little Too Comfortable

During my last year in Mountain Home, perhaps I had become a little too complacent. My store was one of the tops in the company. My team could practically run it without me. Our Walmart-sponsored softball team played a full slate of weekend tournaments, which meant Rick and I missed quite a few Saturdays during the season. In addition, I loved fishing and had purchased my first bass boat, which I kept docked at the Quarry Marina on Lake Norfork. Softball and fishing conflicted with my Saturday work schedule (which happens to be the busiest day in retailing). The company fully expected all managers to be in their stores on that day. On two occasions, I took off early to go fishing. The first incident quickly became a problem, when "the Bear" Whitaker called for me shortly after I left the store. Rick took the call, and thinking fast, made up some cock-and-bull story regarding my whereabouts. In those days, the closest things to cell phones were the imaginary two-way wrist radios in Dick Tracy comics. Rick had no choice but to call the dock to try to intercept me before I went out on the lake. Fortunately, he caught me and tipped me off that Whitaker was looking for me. I was able to return to the store and return the call (a *close* call, at that).

On the second occasion, my luck ran out. Once again, I'd left the store mid-day on Saturday, telling the assistants that I was heading to a Chamber of Commerce meeting. (You'd think I'd learn.) As I stepped onto the dock at the marina, the owner informed me that I had a phone call waiting. Uh-oh. I answered the phone to find Jack Shewmaker on the other end of the line. You'll learn more about Jack later, but at this point he was one of the top executives in the company. Frankly, I was more scared of Jack than I ever was of "the Bear."

Meekly, I said, "Hello?"

"Hello, Ronnie, how's the Chamber meeting going?"

I think my heart stopped for a second. Stunned, I simply stammered, "Hello, Mr. Shewmaker . . . uh, ya caught me, didn't ya?"

Jack had called the store to check on sales and to discuss another matter of no particular significance. Being a very astute and intuitive person, when the boys told him I was at a Chamber meeting, he didn't buy it for a moment. Over the years, I've asked him many times how he figured it out. In addition to knowing there were no Chamber meetings on Saturday, all he'll ever say is, "Ronnie, I knew more than you thought I knew about you." Now that's a scary thought . . . which you'll learn more about by the time you finish this book. Neither Jack nor anyone else ever mentioned this particular incident again. I think my bosses knew the embarrassment of being caught was enough to teach me a good lesson.

The Store Team

Typical of the '70s-era Walmart stores, we had two assistant managers — one responsible for hardlines and one for softlines. While I don't recall exactly when each assistant came or went during my more-than-four-year stint at this store, I have fond memories of each assistant who worked there during my tenure. Gordon Hodges and Steve Thornton were assistants during the same period of time. (Steve was the son of Bob Thornton. Bob, an executive in the G.O., was initially hired by Sam Walton to design and build the first distribution center.) Arvin Clemens and Roger Shipley were long-timers. David Seay ran our sporting goods department.

Joe Coonrod, who came to us from K-Mart, brought his years of experience to Walmart, as did Ken Morrow and David Dust.

The assistant manager in Mountain Home I am most proud of, largely because I found and hired him myself, is Rick Russell. Rick went on to a long, successful career with Walmart, eventually managing a store in my district, and ultimately retiring from a position as head of loss prevention in 2005. My greatest satisfaction came from seeing people succeed and knowing that I helped them in some way.

As in St. Robert, we had some great department managers in Mountain Home. Actually, any good Walmart store in those days was dependent on good hourly associates and department managers. These folks were a vital ingredient in our success. My "cash clerk" and confidante in this store, Pat Trivett, often served as my right hand. Dorothy McGuire, a key associate, was a reporter for the company's internal newspaper, *The Wal-Mart World*. Every associate and manager looked forward to reading the latest monthly edition, which devoted most of its space to recognizing top performing stores, assistant managers, and department managers. We all took pride in being recognized in this publication. It was a true morale-builder.

Key Merchandising Change and the RC Factor

While I was managing the Mountain Home store, Walmart introduced a program that turned out to be one of the most important elements of the company's success for years to come. It was called the Modular Program. It is also known in the industry today as a "Plan-o-Gram." Keith Binkelman, in the Home Office, developed and managed this new initiative.

Although we used basic merchandise listings, up to this date in Walmart history, managers simply filled each counter (gondola) with whatever merchandise was available on any given day. Their individual assessments determined what went into creating "full" or "nice-looking" counters of merchandise. The Modular Program was designed to give a "permanent home" for all basic items in each department, in every store, companywide.

When the top brass rolled out this program and told us to implement it, we didn't handle it well. In fact, we were outraged! How in the world could the buyers in Bentonville possibly know how we should set up the stores in all the different communities? What about judgment, experience, and individuality? Didn't that count for something? The onset of the modular program represented my introduction to the Resistance to Change Factor (RC Factor), a term now commonly recognized in the business world. Business gurus espouse the merits of a "low" RC Factor. This program put it to the test.

After much negative store-level feedback and pleading to the Home Office, we found we had no choice. They ordered us to execute this program immediately. (Some of us, I believe, would have rather executed the folks at the Home Office.) As we started re-laying each department with shelf tags, indentifying the designated spot for each of the everyday basics in the program, we were in for quite a shock. In any given department, 20 to 40 percent of the items were actually out-of-stock at any point in time. Prior to this program, when we noticed an empty space on a counter, we simply spread out other merchandise to keep the shelves from looking thin. To keep the counters fully-stocked at all times, this program forced us to order enough weekly merchandise. After setting up the Modular Program, company sales began to climb sharply. This sort of program, now standard practice in the entire retail industry, marked a radical change for us in the '70s. I learned two important things: maybe I wasn't as good a merchant as I thought, and to be careful about prejudging corporate programs. In other words, keep your mind open and your RC Factor low.

Meeting Thomas Jefferson

Because of his role in the next chapter, I must tell the story of meeting Thomas Jefferson. (No, not *that* Thomas Jefferson. He'd already been dead for years.) In Mountain Home, there was a Sterling store downtown. Sterling was one of Mr. Sam's early variety store competitors. The company was based in Little Rock, Arkansas, and ran a good operation. Mr.

Jefferson, their executive over operations, was a unique individual. He had a deep, rumbling voice and some definite opinions on the way I ran my store.

I was out on the floor one day when Tom approached. He said, "Boy, aren't you the store manager?"

"Yes, I am."

"Well, I'm Tom Jefferson and I just want you to know you've got a lot to learn about running a store. See those holes in the merchandise layout? And those pieces of tape all over the windows where you took down some signs? A good manager doesn't let little things go."

My blood pressure shot up a couple of points. Who the heck was this guy, anyway? And why was he telling me how to run my operation?

"Who are you?" I asked.

"I run the Sterling store, son, and I've been at this business thirty years. I've forgotten more than you'll ever know about running a store, boy."

I have to admit, I was already tired of him calling me "boy." I wondered if he could see the steam rising from under my collar.

Rather than embarrass myself, I just said, "Well, we'll see about that." I was well aware that our big Walmart store was kicking Sterling's butt. I didn't like this Tom Jefferson and it became an issue about a year later, which you'll read about in the ensuing chapter.

Company Functions and Alcohol Don't Mix

During my twenty-plus years at Walmart, I attended countless annual meetings. We all understood that the company frowned upon drinking at these types of functions. This position stems from one specific event, which I'll share here for the first time.

From early on, Mr. Sam would gather the G.O. and store management folks for an annual business retreat/fishing trip. While at Mountain Home, I attended these events, which were held at the Lost Bridge Resort on Beaver Lake. One particular annual retreat changed our corporate culture for good.

More than one hundred of us gathered at the Lost Bridge Resort,

which crowns a tall hill about twelve miles north of Rogers. This site offered the most picturesque view of sprawling Beaver Lake in the area. The
Lost Bridge Marina provided everything a person needed for enjoying
the lake — boat rentals, guides, snacks, soft drinks, etc., and made an
ideal location for the Walmart annual business meeting/fishing contest.
Our three-day agenda consisted of half-day business and half-day fishing
sessions each day.

Not unlike most groups of men out to have a good time while conducting business, many of the guys in our group enjoyed a few drinks at night
and/or while fishing. A large contingent also liked a good poker game.
Two of the upper-echelon men in operation management occupied one
of the largest rooms, which became the staging area for the first night's
festivities. Having fished all afternoon, consuming a fair amount of alcohol in the process, a number of us sat down for a friendly game of poker.

Well, as the night wore on, the party got rowdier and the die-hards were
still playing when it came time to shower up for the 7:00 a.m. business
meeting. I happened to be one of them. I'll never forget it. The meeting
room was so small that many of us, despite our inebriated and half-asleep
conditions, had to stand or lean against the wall. At one point, Mr. Sam
finished his talk and asked Ferold Arend, our president, to address the
group. To reach the front of the room, Ferold had to negotiate the narrow
aisle between the chairs and the "leaners." That's the very moment one of
our party participants chose to pass out. (Luckily, it wasn't me.) As his
lifeless body oozed down the wall, Ferold had to make a tricky maneuver
to avoid doing a header and joining him on the floor. Dumbfounded, we
watched as a couple of guys hurriedly escorted our buddy from the room.
Later, we explained that he had not been feeling well (not a lie, exactly).

That scene was embarrassing enough. But nothing compared to what
followed. The manager of the resort personally presented Sam Walton
with a bill to repair the damage to the poker room. I've only heard rumors
about that bill, but it must have been significant. It reportedly claimed
the room had been littered with broken whiskey bottles, carpet damage
from cigars and cigarettes, spilled beer, and burn holes in the linens. I

can only imagine the look on Mr. Sam's face as he reviewed the itemized destruction.

We were all a lot more reserved and prudent on the second afternoon of fishing. Perhaps the hangovers had something to do with it. No poker game took place that night. At the closing meeting, Mr. Sam announced in his own smooth, inimitable manner that the expense of bringing us together each year should result in more time to discuss and plan our business. Therefore, fishing would be eliminated at future retreats. Secondly, although he couldn't tell us how we should conduct ourselves, drinking at company functions should be banned.

From that time forward, the annual Walmart corporate meetings have grown dramatically larger, as has the company. They are now conducted in huge convention centers and fill several large hotels. I understand the restrictions have changed a great deal now, but for years following the infamous Lost Bridge incident, hotel bars and clubs were closed or declared "off-limits" to Walmart associates. It didn't exactly please the resorts, but it had the desired effect. During the rest of my days with Walmart, I don't recall seeing anyone pass out at another meeting.

Good Friends

I made many good friends in Mountain Home — most of them through business and some from activities with the church. I know I'll leave some out, but among those who stayed in touch through the years is the advertising salesman for the local *Baxter Bulletin* newspaper, Charles Howard. He and his wife, Shirley, were wonderful people, and we got to know them very well. Many years later, Charlie would invite me back over to Mountain Home to hunt on property he owned. That's where I shot my first deer. Shirley always cooked up homemade bread and donuts. I liked to tell Charlie that was the primary reason I stayed friends with him all those years. Bill and Joyce Fletcher, along with Larry and Brenda Nelson, the banker at Peoples Bank & Trust, were also great local people and good friends.

Perhaps my family's best friends while in Mountain Home were Fred and Virginia Young, some of the nicest folks I've ever known. Fred was a manager of the Norfork Dam for the Corps of Engineers. He was eventually transferred to Dardanelle, Arkansas, where he and Virginia still reside.

We advertised some on the local radio station KTLO. I became friends with Monte Manchester and Bobby Knight, who both worked for the station. They also played on the softball team I put together. We had a good team, won the city championship, and played in a couple of state tournaments. We also had an outstanding shortstop, Danny Keeter. Others on that team included Rocky Fratesi and Dick House. To be honest, that team was more like an adult version of *The Bad News Bears*, but with more talent. One of the best baseball players to come out of Mountain Home was Galen Pitts, who played for the Oakland Athletics organization for many years. I always admired guys with that kind of ability, no doubt because of my love of baseball when growing up. Galen would have made it to "the Show," but he played third base, a position mightily filled by Sal Bando at the time. The last I heard, Galen was still managing in baseball.

A Big Decision

I was happy and had no desire to leave Mountain Home, but the company was applying pressure for me to take a district manager's position. I resisted this promotion for about six months, but in a private conversation with Don Whitaker, he explained that there comes a time when you must decide whether or not you want a "career" with the company. If so, you should be willing to progress and take on increased responsibilities. "Otherwise," he said, "management might consider you to be 'too comfortable,' at which point you might just come under added scrutiny."

I thought about his comments, and let it be known that I did want to move up in the company. In 1975, I was promoted to manager over district #8 in northern Missouri and Kansas.

Being a store manager in retailing, and particularly at Walmart in the 1970s, required a set of skills so diversified that rarely did someone possess them all. A manager needed a broad knowledge of merchandising and operations, the ability to hire, train, motivate, and discipline associates, and the people skills necessary in dealing with customers and the local community leaders. Creativity and innovation played essential roles, as did learning how to cope with the constant pressure of new programs emanating from the General Office. Managers had to figure out how to tackle these challenges while maintaining some sort of stable home life. Today this is known as "work-life balance." Store management was, and remains, a tough but potentially rewarding experience and career.

The primary lesson I learned during my experience as store manager was that the General Office existed to develop merchandising programs and operating guidelines which could enable even the weakest store managers to operate a store satisfactorily, simply by following company guidelines. However, managers could excel if they studied their markets and their customers' needs. The corporate structure empowered them to feature and maximize sales by ordering the right items at the right time. In turn, the good managers empowered their assistant managers and department managers to aid them in this quest.

I believe that top store managers understand the value of building a "team" in their stores. A manager must be a "coach." A poor "people manager" can quickly turn a "good" store into a "bad" one if they are unappreciative of or act disparagingly toward their associates. On an everyday basis, store managers must train, communicate, manage by walking around (MBWA), and when warranted, dole out praise and recognition. Not every associate is going to work out for the best, and while not a pleasant task, one of the most important functions of a top store manager is to recognize when someone is not an asset to the team and to make changes accordingly and without hesitation.

Lastly, I found that one of my most gratifying responsibilities was the opportunity to teach, train, counsel, and generally prepare the assistant store managers for their own future successes with the company. Much later in my career, I had the privilege of observing some of my young assistants from the Mountain Home store as they continued to develop and prosper with the company. It is satisfying and rewarding to believe that I had something to do with that.

> If you look after the customers and look after the people who look after the customers, you should be successful.
>
> — CHARLES DUNSTONE

> Progress is mostly the product of rogues.
>
> — TOM PETERS

CHAPTER 9

Bigger Bucks and Bigger Problems — District Manager

1975–1978

▸ Apple Computer is founded.

▸ Elvis Presley dies at age forty-two.

▸ Star Wars arrives from a galaxy far, far away.

▸ First cellular phone is introduced by Illinois Bell.

▸ Space Invaders video game invades arcades.

▸ Walmart grows from 125 stores ($340 million) to 229 stores (just under $1.0 billion). First acquisition, Mohr-Value Stores. VPI (Volume Producing Item) program is launched. "Walmart Cheer" is initiated.

▸ The Loveless family experiences "living without a dad" because of constant travel. I receive my first "stock option."

After my promotion to district manager (DM), I was ready to find a place to live in the Kansas City area. Just before leaving, I was ordered to the Home Office for "orientation." It turned out my orientation was a conversation with Jim Dismore, my supervisor. Jim told me I would never succeed as a district manager, and that I was making a mistake. I thought: *why is it every time I take a promotion, someone tells me I'm not ready?* I like to think it was Jim's way of challenging and motivating me.

By saying he didn't believe I could make it, he had just ensured that I would, because I was determined to prove him wrong.

Cindy and I found a home in Harrisonville, Missouri, a nice, small bedroom community about fifteen miles south of the Kansas City metro area. The Harrisonville Walmart store, managed by Phil Clifton, would serve as "base store" for my district. I was eager to face the new challenges in store for me (pardon the pun).

District #8 consisted of the following stores:

#20 – Clinton, MO

#26 – Leavenworth, KS

#34 – Nevada, MO

#35 – Manhattan, KS

#39 – Ft. Scott, KS

#43 – Junction City, KS

#61 – Warrensburg, MO

#109 – Cameron, MO

#96 – Harrisonville, MO

#135 – Chillicothe, MO

This district, in 1975, was in bad shape. The DM I was promoted to replace had been demoted back to a store manager's position. The district performed at below average levels for sales and profits, while its "shrinkage" was one of the highest. (Shrinkage represents unaccounted-for losses of inventory or dollars within the operation from year-to-year.) Although only one element of the total operating statement, this item alone can spell the difference between profit and loss for an entire year. The average rate of shrinkage in the retail industry at that time was from 3.5 to 4.5 percent. Walmart stores generally ran from 1.8 to 3.5 percent. This district, when I arrived, was running shrinkage numbers approaching 4.0 percent. While this figure fell within the average range in the industry, it was unacceptable by Walmart standards.

The store managers' morale was suffering, and the stores were, in many cases, dirty and poorly merchandised. I recognized the challenge, but also believed it would not be too difficult to correct the problems and turn things around. All I had to do was insist the managers adhere to the company's merchandising programs and operating guidelines, pass on what I had learned, and give them support, as needed.

The Company, circa 1976

As I took over this district, the entire Walmart company consisted of only three operating regions. The alignment was as follows:

Northern Region

Regional vice-president — Tom Jefferson (the same guy; keep reading)

District managers — Bob Hart, Gary Reinboth, A.R. (Mac) McDonald, Ron Loveless, Bill Adams

Central Region

Regional vice-president — John Hawks

District managers — Al Miles, Jack Mackey, Mel Acree, Clarence Leis, Phil Green

Southern Region

Regional vice-president — M. I. Dillard

District managers — Richard Cudd, Ray Thomas, Rex Chase, Gary Smith, John Jacobs

Also during this period, the Home Office had promoted or reassigned many of the management team, while hiring new management people from "outside." They announced promotions and changes every week. I mention the following folks in particular, because I had direct involvement with each during this period of my career.

The Walmart Home Office management team had evolved into a talented group that ignited the company's explosive growth over the next decade. Ferold Arend left his chief operating officer (COO) position due to health reasons, but remained as vice-chairman and a board member. David Glass joined the company as head of finance. Jack Shewmaker, as president/COO, handled operations and merchandising. Other key folks included: Bob Thornton, distribution and warehousing; Glenn Habern, data processing; Al Johnson, advertising/sales promotion; David Washburn, personnel; Keith Binkelman, modular planning; Joe White, store planning; Theo Ashcraft, loss prevention; Ray Gash, controller.

Tom Jefferson

Within a week after making the first tour around my new district and meeting all my store managers, I received a call that immediately dampened my enthusiasm. The news in a nutshell: Jim Dismore had left the company and the new regional vice-president, my boss, was to be none other than Thomas Jefferson, the gruff, critical Sterling store man I met in Mountain Home; the guy who told me I had a lot to learn about running a store.

That night, I told my wife I couldn't work for this guy. No way. I came *this* close to quitting. After discussing the situation at length, we realized it boiled down to two alternatives. I could either throw away what I had worked for over the past eleven years because of someone I hardly knew. Or I could try to make it work. That is, if he even gave me a chance. Based on my earlier contact with him, I knew he didn't think much of me. Still, I decided to hang in there and give it my best shot. If I was going down, I was going down swinging.

A couple of days later, Tom Jefferson called and scheduled a tour of the district with me. He drove up from Bentonville, picked me up in Harrisonville, and we spent the next three days visiting many of my stores. As soon as I got into the car, T.J. (which he would come to be called throughout his career at Walmart) said, "Boy, I remember you from Mountain Home. I'm going to teach you how to run stores."

I held my tongue and replied, "Okay, Mr. Jefferson, I'm ready to learn."

Punching me on the arm, he said, "Just call me T.J., boy." With that little exchange behind us, we headed for the first store.

T.J. had spent thirty plus years with Sterling stores, so I figured he had to know a lot about running retail operations. However, I found him to be very "old school," always noticing what I considered minor details: pieces of cellophane tape on the windows, a string hanging from the ceiling with nothing on it, some dust around a display, or shopping baskets scattered around the parking lot. Although I was interested in what I felt were more important issues on my store visits, I indulged him, always responding with the appropriate, "Yes, sir" and "No, sir."

Over time, I came to respect T.J. and recognize the significance of the "little things." If a manager left the small details undone, it signaled larger problems behind the scenes. We ultimately got along very well, and T.J. gave me license to run my district my way. I heard from him only in the event of a problem with the numbers. He never tried to impose his will on me. This is a textbook illustration of how wrong we might be when we prejudge people based on first impressions. Had my wife and I not mapped out a conscientious game plan, my career with Walmart might have ended then and there.

People Management

I had a talented group of managers in the district. They included: Dan Fuller, Frank Gatschet, Phil Clifton, Les Gerhardt, G.W. Metz, Rick Russell, Dale Shinault, and my first female manager, a good one, Jane Marshall, in Clinton, Missouri.

As I made the rounds and came to know the strengths and weaknesses of each store manager, I learned some key components of successful management. First, I realized the mistake in trying to manage everyone the same way. Second, I learned to recognize and praise people for the things they did well before suggesting improvements they needed to make; then they were much more open to constructive criticism and eager to correct problems.

The company introduced the "self-evaluation" process in the late '70s. It became a business buzzword later on, referred to as the "360-degree evaluation." Here's the basis of the process: First, prior to undergoing an evaluation from management, associates were required to evaluate themselves on the same management form. Second, two levels of management conducted the evaluation. This prevented an immediate supervisor from stifling a career or promoting an undeserving person based on bias, impartiality, or politics. The self-evaluation process opened a lot of eyes, revealing the difference in how people viewed themselves versus how they were viewed by the manager or even fellow associates.

Although it wasn't yet time for the company's annual evaluations, I asked the managers to evaluate themselves on the standard form. I felt it was the best way for me to get quickly up-to-speed. This valuable process resulted in my being able to work with the managers in the areas we agreed needed improvement.

Communication is a key to successful management in the field. We conducted weekly conference calls with our managers, thoroughly covering all important company programs. The regional vice-presidents and merchandising team in the Home Office conducted operations meetings every Friday, which resulted in "weekly priority notes." These notes designated the most important merchandising and operational problems to be addressed and corrected each week. Instructions went out on Friday afternoon, and stores were to execute and complete them no later than the following Monday. This program served Walmart well, in that many dollars were saved and/or sales achieved by simultaneously addressing major problems practically overnight in every store in the company.

A typical week for me included visiting approximately three stores. On each visit, I'd walk the store with the manager and his assistants. To ensure compliance, I came armed with a checklist of the current programs and instructions from the Home Office. But primarily the visit was to evaluate the store's cleanliness, merchandise presentation, and "in-stock" situation. Of no less importance, however, was the enthusiasm generated by simply saying "hello" or thanking the hourly associates for jobs well done. I made a point to learn first names, so after a few trips around the district, I could greet many associates personally. They were quick to return my empathy and trust by revealing problems often not apparent to the store manager.

When Sam Walton visited my stores, more often than not, he preferred to walk around the store without the manager or assistants. He would form an opinion based on comments from the hourly associates. If they were enthusiastic, motivated, and happy, it usually showed in the appearance of the store. He knew that a store's ultimate success was determined by how the manager treated his associates, which in turn, determined how they treated the customers.

The Frank Gatschet Story

I had many good managers in district #8 who helped accomplish a remarkable turnaround in the district in one short year. The story of Frank Gatschet, though, best exemplifies our efforts. When I first took the district, T.J. told me that the company wanted to make a "manager change" in Pittsburgh, Kansas. He supplied no other details, other than one of the "bosses" had visited the store and felt the manager should be fired.

I went down to Pittsburgh, met the manager, Frank Gatschet, and walked the store with him. The store was very well-merchandised. The people liked Frank. His office detail, claims area, stockroom, and sales floor were as good as any I had seen. The main problems cited by upper management were shrinkage in the store and failure to report monthly "markdowns," a company requirement. These were problematic issues throughout the entire district, not just Frank's store. (I found out a while later that the managers had actually turned in the markdowns to the previous district manager, but he had hidden them or simply thrown them away, a short-sighted "fix" ultimately resulting in higher shrinkage numbers.)

After our store walk-through, I was impressed with Frank's operation. Over lunch that day, I learned that Frank and his wife, Amy, were a devout Catholic family. They had ten children and Frank needed this job badly. I saw something in Frank, felt he could be a good manager, and determined that I would go to bat for him with the company. He deserved a chance to prove himself. After a conversation with T.J., we agreed I could move him to store #35 in Manhattan, Kansas. The manager there was being transferred to another area. So in late 1975, Frank became manager at the Manhattan store, home of the Kansas State University (KSU) Wildcats.

The Manhattan Walmart was one of the few stores in a town of that size in direct competition with our formidable competitor, K-Mart. Although K-mart was in close proximity to us, we nevertheless were "holding our own," despite problems with associates and low profits from the ever-present "shrinkage."

A few weeks after Frank moved to Manhattan, I went down for a visit and took him out for a cup of coffee. He told me that the store's biggest problem was that a couple of long-term associates thought they "ran the place" and had free rein to impose their will on the other associates. When the previous managers tried to correct the situation, these long-term associates threatened to report their mistreatment to the Home Office and/or Mr. Sam, who "knew them personally." The managers had backed down, which implied to the other associates that they condoned this behavior, allowing these miscreants to remain at the top of the pecking order. The result? Terrible morale and rampant internal merchandise theft.

I told Frank that I trusted his judgment and would support him in his decisions. I suggested he start compiling a dossier on the troublemakers to substantiate and document his findings. "Sit them down and tell them what they're doing wrong. Explain that if they don't correct their behavior, they will be terminated. It's that simple. We have to do what's right for the store."

Within three months, Frank had eliminated three people who had created problems in the store. These folks had been there since day one, and they followed through on their threats by complaining to the Home Office. I supported Frank's moves and stood my ground. Eventually the complaints stopped, Frank managed the store properly, and morale improved immediately. To this day, Frank gives credit to several store associates who were instrumental in turning the store around: Delmer Peters, Vesta Sargent, Nancy Westgate, and Joyce McGinnis, to name a few. A succession of assistant managers who contributed a great deal in the improvement of the store included: Joe Chapelle, Dennis Ankrum, Don Arrick, and David Page.

While Frank ran the store, his daughter became a "flag girl" with the KSU band. Frank and his wife, Amy, became well acquainted with members of the band and the band director, Phil Hewlett. It turned out that the band was in dire need of new uniforms, but had no money to purchase new ones. Frank's daughter designed a clock to be sold to raise funds for new uniforms. Frank, other store folks, and the band members sold these clocks to local businesses and supporters for $500 each, quickly raising enough money to completely outfit the team.

As this was going on, Frank realized that KSU employees, teachers, and students accounted for a large portion of the business in town. He was determined to make Walmart the "students' store." He began by hiring student applicants who needed part-time jobs. Our company, at that time, kept track of the average age of associates. The older the average age, the better (or so the conventional thinking went). In Frank's case, his college hires made his average the youngest of any store.

Within six months of Frank's tenure at the Manhattan store, sales were booming. Associates were reporting other associates known to have been stealing merchandise. The students were "bad-mouthing" the K-Mart store. This Walmart was "their" store. On one particular trip to the store, I pulled into the parking lot and noticed these two *huge* young men moving fifty-pound bags of peat moss from one side of the front entrance to the other side. When I asked Frank about it, he replied, "Well, Doctor" (he called me *Dr. Loveless*, possibly a reference to the bad guy on the *Wild, Wild West*?), "those are two K-State football players and they needed a part-time job. They only come in six hours per week. I have to keep them busy, you know." I just shook my head. It's hard to question success.

On another visit, I experienced first-hand how well-known Frank had become with the university crowd. Every college town has an area where students, faculty, and others might gather for a drink or two. In Manhattan, it was Aggieville. As we walked into one of the clubs, a number of students recognized Frank and greeted him by name. Very impressive. One table in particular seemed to be drawing extraordinary attention. I asked Frank what was going on. He said, "That's Jack Hartman, the Kansas State basketball coach. There's a game tonight. He's a nice guy. Want to meet him?"

Being a sports fan, I had heard about Coach Hartman. He was well known in NCAA basketball circles and enjoyed celebrity status in Manhattan. Without missing a beat, I said, "I sure would."

Frank walked me over to the table, and Coach Hartman said, "Hi, Frank, how's it going?" This episode caused me to instantly connect the success of Frank's store with his involvement in the community. I could see that the benefits were mutually beneficial.

A short time later, the KSU band received an invitation to play during half-time at a Dallas Cowboys football game. Frank and Amy made the trip with the band, more confirmation (as if I needed any) that Frank's Walmart had truly become a "store-of-the-community." And not coincidentally, we kicked K-Mart's butt in that town.

While I was district manager, store #35 became one of the highest profit stores in the region. Frank Gatschet eventually received the Store Manager of the Year Award for the entire company — despite the fact that I had been sent to fire him in 1975. He was ultimately promoted to district manager. I like to tell this story because I learned that hasty judgments can ruin a good associate's career. And it can cost the company a valuable employee.

Union Difficulties

About a year after I took over the district, I learned that my base store in Harrisonville was experiencing some union organizing activity. I knew the company had faced this elsewhere, but I had no knowledge or training in how to deal with it.

The unions had a strong presence in the KC area and always kept an eye on Walmart as a potentially lucrative target. Unfortunately, they zeroed in on the Harrisonville store because one of our associates was "upset about the way she was being treated." This woman had caused problems in the store from the time she was hired. Phil Clifton, the store manager, had "counseled" her and she resented it. Her husband, who happened to be a union member, goaded her into promoting a union effort with her fellow associates. The ensuing "battle" became a real education for me.

As Phil and I discussed the situation, I learned that a number of associates had signed cards expressing an interest in unionizing the store. The General Office provided me with the guidance I needed, quickly dispatching a team of labor relations specialists who taught me what management could "legally" say and do (which was very limited). On the other hand, union representatives could say or do anything they wished, which gave them a real advantage in visiting with our people.

We ultimately put a stop to this effort, with our people choosing to keep the union out. The deciding factor came when we obtained a copy of a Retail Clerk's Union Contract from another operation in Missouri. This contract proved that employees had fewer benefits and opportunities with the union than with our company. The truth is Walmart has historically: (1) paid as well as the industry in general, (2) offered a profit-sharing program second to none in retailing, (3) provided many other incentive programs for the financial benefit of hourly associates (4) offered one of the best health care insurance programs in retailing (contrary to anti-Walmart propaganda), and (5) last, but certainly not least, gave any capable associate the opportunity to advance in management and build a career with the company.

It's important to note that through the early years of Walmart's growth, the bulk of our store management teams consisted of people who had been promoted from within the stores. I'm just one example. In unions, "seniority" is the primary criteria for salary increases and there is no opportunity to achieve personal advancement in management. Personally, I simply cannot fathom why anyone with a choice would subject himself or herself to that environment. I have relatives who are, or have been, union members and they seem to be okay with it. However, they are also working at the same jobs today as they were ten or fifteen years ago . . . that is, those who still have a union job at all.

My stepfather was a Walmart truck driver, and on several occasions the Teamster's Union made attempts to organize our company's drivers.

He told me about many incidents that conjured up scenes from *The God-father.* Reportedly, thugs and ruffians threatened physical harm, actually threw objects at our trucks, and pressured our drivers in many other ways. The Walmart drivers were loyal to the company, and the unions have never been successful in organizing them. I believe unions are their own worst enemies. As long as management is treating people right, paying fair wages while still making a profit, communicating and sharing information, truly caring about associates, and most importantly, *listening* to them, Walmart will continue to beat the unions.

In my opinion, unions have driven many of the U.S. jobs offshore ... not Walmart, as the company's "haters" would have you believe. When they first started, unions were a good thing. They became necessary because of company or industry abuse of employees. The mining industry (and its deplorable conditions) comes to mind. Over the years, however, as the unions became entrenched in certain industries, they became too demanding. In industries such as steel, textile, and automotive, as union contracts came up for renewal, the threat of strikes and unreasonable demands forced management to accept deals that eventually made them uncompetitive in the marketplace. While union bosses lined their pockets, the very people they were supposedly "looking out for" were losing their jobs. Union organizations would be better off if they hired business leaders to run them — people who understand the economy and the free enterprise system. But this is just my opinion.

One of my Harrisonville neighbors was David Kinney. Our sons were friends and spent a lot of time together during our three years there. Dave owned and operated a manufacturing facility in the KC area. His company produced wooden-cased audio speakers, which were the rage of that era for many noted brands, including JVC. The company did a lot of business with Walmart and other major retailers. After I retired from Walmart and was living in Rogers, David called me, saying he was tired of "fighting the battles" with the union, and wanted to relocate his plant. Arkansas made sense to him because of its "right-to-work" laws (meaning employees have the right to work whether they are union members or not). The city of Rogers embraced the possibility of adding a new manufacturer and the jobs that came with it. Today, Wood Specialty Products, operated by David Kinney, Jr., continues to do business in Rogers.

Much like Wood Specialty Products, the steel and textile industries, the U.S. automobile industry, the airlines, and the U.S. Postal Service, it doesn't take a "rocket scientist" to realize that unions and government over-regulation are driving our U.S. industrial base offshore. Companies simply must remain competitive or they disappear.

Today, an organization called "Walmart Watch" exists for the sole purpose of finding and publicizing mistakes made by the company. Funded by union organizations such as UFCW (United Food and Commercial Workers), FAST (Fast Food and Allied Services Trade), and UNITE (Union of Needles Trades, Industrial & Textile Workers), they do everything they can to harm Walmart's image. Obviously, their goal is to eventually unionize Walmart, given that it is the largest, juiciest target to reverse their declining membership roles in the U.S. As I write this memoir, the politicians in Washington, under pressure from organized labor, are considering legislation called "The Free Choice Act." This legislation, if passed, would be one of the most harmful laws to American business and the free enterprise system upon which America was built.

Leaving Harrisonville

Following is an excerpt from Sam Walton's column in the company newspaper in 1977:

> On Wednesday, I visited a group of stores in district #8 where Ron Loveless is district manager — Leavenworth, Cameron, Chillicothe, Excelsior Springs, and Harrisonville. I was accompanied by a staff writer from Forbes magazine, Mr. Harry Seneker, who was doing an article on Walmart. I must admit that most of those stores knew we were coming, but regardless, they were in terrific shape — well-merchandised, standards good throughout, and best of all, I've never seen the enthusiasm and morale of our associates any better. I can't tell you what Mr. Seneker will write about, but I do know he was tremendously impressed with the people he met in these stores and the job that they are doing for Walmart. But regardless of the topic, I'm

convinced that our company is a story of people — working together, listening to one another, having fun, improvising new techniques and directions daily — and with it all, creating a very effective and competitive retail machine called Walmart. Let's keep it going... Thanks.

I received my first "stock option" while district manager, a perk of unrealized importance at the time. It would become highly significant to me (and my family) later on. By 1978, district #8 was a top-performer and I had received a wealth of experience as district manager. As a result, the powers that be approached me about a promotion to regional vice-president over a newly-formed region based in Bentonville — lah-di-dah, home again. I didn't hesitate for a moment. The thought of moving back to my hometown with my family really appealed to me. My only reservation involved operating so close to the General Office and the attendant scrutiny of executive management.

The district manager position in Walmart was then, and remains today, one of the most important positions in the company. DMs are close to the action. Their primary task is to make sure that each store under their supervision lives up to company standards. They are responsible for retaining the corporate culture, maintaining and enacting the merchandising programs of the company, ensuring that procedures are followed, and selecting, supervising, promoting, and demoting management folks within their district.

In essence, they are the CEOs of their own smaller companies. As Walmart has grown in scope to become such a huge global entity, it is impossible to manage the stores solely from the Home Office. It is more important than ever to select the right field management people at every level, empower them with the authority to make decisions, and give them the support they need. When someone experiences a bad-looking or poorly-merchandised Walmart store, the DM is as much to blame as the store manager.

As a stock boy, department manager, and assistant manager, I remember watching these "bosses" come into the store in their coats and ties, walk around, give instructions, and leave. I thought, *Man, they've got it made. They don't really have to do any work — they just get paid a lot of money.* Once I actually performed the DM duties, I knew the truth. District managers carried the responsibility and were literally "at risk" for every mistake made in any of their ten stores. The district manager received every customer or associate complaint. We earned every penny of our salaries. The stress, travel, and workload were tremendous. Tom Jefferson and Jack Shewmaker gave me the support I needed as a young DM, and we turned a poor district into a very good one.

> *There are two important factors in building a self-motivated team of people — the opportunity to learn through increased effort and trust in management to give the utmost support.*
> — TOM FARMER

> *The difference between a leader and a boss is the difference between good and bad management.*
> — HENRY KISSINGER

CHAPTER 10

Regional VP — Assistant to the President/Special Projects

> ## 1978–1979
>
> - ▸ Sony Walkman is introduced at a cost of $200.
> - ▸ The snowboard is invented.
> - ▸ Three Mile Island nuclear accident narrowly averts meltdown.
> - ▸ Millions of people start playing the hot new game, Trivial Pursuit.
> - ▸ Walmart has 276 stores and celebrates its first BILLION DOLLAR YEAR, with sales of $1.248 billion.
> - ▸ We're back at home now. Ronnie and Kim attend school in Rogers. I'm traveling more than ever.

moved back to northwest Arkansas with my family and bought a home in Rogers, the site of the first Walmart store, which had opened in 1962. The store had been relocated and was one of our largest at this time. My region included area stores, as well as Missouri and Oklahoma. But yet another turn of events curtailed my chance to serve in the regional manager capacity. Before even visiting the stores in my new territory, I re-

133

ceived a call from Jack Shewmaker, President and COO, telling me to drop everything and get my butt over to the Home Office for a meeting.

Project 79

During the meeting, Jack filled me in on the company's plans to build a couple of pilot stores that would serve as "tests" for upgrading Walmart facilities. Rapid expansion into new states and the expectation of encountering more challenging competitors had spurred the need to offer a better shopping environment for our customers. We retained the Ohio-based Doody Company and their consultant, John Geisse, to work with us on the project. John, with an enviable industry track record, had been instrumental in the design and opening of the early Target and Venture stores. These stores represented the best-looking of the current big box retailers. To top it off, John and Sam Walton had been friends for quite some time. It never hurts being buddy-buddy with the big boss.

I was shocked when Jack Shewmaker said I had been selected to supervise the project, and would be working with the merchandising & store planning teams, as well as John and the Doody Company. He informed me that I would carry the temporary title of "Assistant to the President, Special Projects." This would bestow the authority to get what I needed, when I needed it, during this challenging effort. As with just about everything at Walmart, the project would be "fast-tracked." The name of the initiative would be "Project 79" (I suppose because it was a project and it was 1979.) For no other reason than the two properties had already been purchased and were the next available, the "test" stores would be built in Pine Bluff, Arkansas, and Moore, Oklahoma.

By this time, Al Johnson was running the merchandise division and this project would require a close working relationship with the buyers who worked under him. To help you understand what I was up against, I'll need to explain the open communication culture the company had always cultivated. Typically, the whole gamut of store management folks (operations) was critical of the merchandising division (buyers). The operations team was mainly concerned with achieving their budgeted numbers for inventory, markdowns, and store profitability. Merchandising, on the other hand, was primarily interested in reaching their budgeted sales numbers and wanted their merchandising programs implemented without question. In their minds, if something didn't sell well, poor execution at the store level was to blame. The back-and-forth fireworks between the two divisions took place at our weekly "Friday Merchandise Meetings." They were interesting, to say the least.

Having worked only in operations to this point, I had been just as critical as anyone of the buyers, although I think they knew I respected the job they did. We had a competent group of buyers at the time. Now, with Project 79, I would need to solicit and coordinate the help of the entire merchandise division. Two factors assured things would go smoothly during all stages of this project: my job title, which clarified I worked directly for Jack Shewmaker, and the unqualified support of Al Johnson. Although nobody ever confirmed who initiated this project, I suspect Al was as much behind the push as anyone in the company. Later, when I came to understand just how much this project and its implementation in the stores would cost, I'm convinced that Mr. Sam had been pressured into giving it the green light.

My instructions were simple. There were no barriers. Nothing was sacred. Create a store that would be visually pleasing, well-merchandised, and customer-friendly. Utilize the latest lighting, fixtures, and merchandising techniques recommended by the Doody folks.

The scope of my knowledge grew exponentially during that six-month project. I learned new terminology: race-track aisles, wing walls, visual focal points, front-facing, floor-to-ceiling merchandising, traffic flow, and myriad other references encompassing every aspect of store design. Though some of our store planners were probably familiar with at least some of the terms, it was all new to me. As the company coordinator for the project, I found myself "in the middle" of many disagreements. The design team insisted on certain layout features which contrasted, if not directly conflicted, with our current merchandising strategies.

The upgraded fixtures to be installed were often not conducive to our product packaging. We had to work out literally thousands of details. Within six short months, we were speeding toward the Grand Opening of the first test store in Pine Bluff.

The week before opening, Sam Walton came down to get his first look at the new store. I met Mr. Sam at the airport and will never forget the visit. I had a bad case of nerves, because I knew we had made two major changes that would not sit well with him.

First, we had eliminated the feature tables and promotional stack bases in the aisles. The hot button for Target and Venture was a spacious, empty "race-track" aisle around the store to facilitate easy traffic flow. The feature displays in what we called 'ACTION ALLEY' had always given our stores the promotional and volume/price image for which we were noted. The in-aisle feature displays were Mr. Sam's idea, starting with the first Walmart store. I knew he wouldn't give them up without a fight.

Second, we had spent far more money than I knew would be acceptable to Mr. Sam. We installed glass shelving and carpeting in the wearables areas; we eliminated the cold fluorescent strips in favor of recessed halide lighting, giving a soft customer-friendly glow throughout the store. It made all our merchandise look "richer." To "front-face" our wearables, we purchased expensive chrome hooks, waterfall display racks and "T-racks," as opposed to the drab circle racks in typical stores of the time. Up until this test store, we used wooden ledges around the perimeter walls to hold cartons of excess merchandise. The weight of the cartons caused sagging and in a few cases led to the collapse of the ledges. At best, this technique of overhead storage was a visual disaster. In this store we removed the ledges, took all merchandise out of the cartons, and built displays from floor to ceiling with attractive "ribbons" of merchandise. We considered anything above seventy-two inches in height to be beyond a customer's reach, and therefore excess stock or idle inventory. Our primary reason for this approach was that customers walking around the race-track aisle could look in any direction and identify the merchandise category with "focal points" of merchandise on the walls.

We overhauled the store front and sign as well. Up to this time, we were still installing the original highway signs, "Wal-Mart Discount City — We Sell For Less, Satisfaction Guaranteed," and the signs on the building fronts still sported the original western lettering, painted on and lit by external floodlights. With this test store, we constructed a bulky, tiered façade with soft brown, orange and blue stripes, and designed the new, clean, interior-lit sign that simply read: "WALMART."

Getting back to the visit . . . when Mr. Sam and I got out of the car, he just stood out front staring up at the new sign and store front. It seemed like he stood there for a very long time. Eventually, he turned to me and said, "Ronnie, this is sure different from what we've been doing, huh? I kinda like that sign, though . . . how much more does it cost?"

Uh oh. I knew that this question would be one of the first from Mr. Sam and knew it would require my best version of a politician; masterful evasion of a direct answer to the question. "I'll be giving you a complete recap of the costs when they're finalized," I gulped. "We're still waiting to get most of the bills. I think the sign will be about double the cost of the old one, though." He frowned as he headed for the entrance.

Entering the store, Mr. Sam just stood inside and scanned from left to right. I couldn't read him, couldn't tell what he was thinking. I would know soon enough. As we started down the spacious aisle, he stopped after a few paces and said, "Ronnie, this is a very pretty store. Maybe *too* pretty. It looks like we've spent a ton of money. I'll get with everybody when I get back to Bentonville, but I can tell you I don't like the fact we've done away with the 'ACTION ALLEY' displays."

I was ready for this one, sort of. "Well, sir," I said, "we have the features; they're just off the edge of the aisle in front of each department. We knew you'd want those tables and stack bases."

He wasn't having any of it. "Yeah," he shot back, "but they don't have the same impact. We've got to figure out a way to get our features back out in the aisle, going forward." He said this with certainty, in a way that left no room for further discussion.

As we examined each department and some of the expensive fixtures, Mr. Sam kept asking what this or that cost. He *did* like the merchandise on the walls and a number of other things about the store, but it was clear that it was too fancy for his tastes. We probably wouldn't be opening many stores exactly like this one. It was purely a matter of "culture shock" to Mr. Sam. And I understood why. This project looked more like a mid-tier department store than any discount retailer of that era.

The Pine Bluff and Moore Project 79 stores ultimately served their purpose. We incorporated many of the design elements and merchandising strategies from this effort into the new prototype stores that sprung up throughout the '80s. Other aspects were never repeated; for example, the 'ACTION ALLEY' promotional tables went right back into the aisles. I'll give you one guess why that decision was made. (Yep, good guess.) And it was the right call.

Today, as consumers and competition evolve, Walmart continues to test new store layouts, merchandise presentations, and programs. That is as it should be. I just hope that major changes are carefully tested and proven worthy before revamping the entire company, much as we did with this project. Had we moved forward with the Project 79 stores before "tweaking" them to meet our needs, we would have made a big mistake. This project reflected the company's willingness to try new things, even risking failure in an effort to improve the company.

> Changing the direction of a large company is like trying to turn an aircraft carrier. It takes a mile before anything happens. And if it is a wrong turn, getting back on course takes even longer.
>
> — AL RIES

The Buyer's Manual

After completing Project 79, I was prepared to go back to my regional manager responsibilities. But once again the company had different plans for me. Jack Shewmaker and Al Johnson decided that, since I was on special assignment anyway, I could spend a few months on another pet project — a Buyer's Training Manual. Though they never said it, I suppose they felt my experience working with the entire buying team during Project 79 would lead to the cooperation necessary to complete the manual ASAP.

Looking back, I believe our buying organization at this time was the best in the business. Much more about this in the next chapter, but as the company prepared for even faster growth, they felt the need to provide a training tool for new buyers, assistant managers, and hourly associates. They knew that building a solid foundation would create consistency throughout the buying group and clarify the role each group played within the organization. Nothing existed on paper at this time. In addition to procedures, forms, and mathematics, we needed to shed light on the corporate culture, philosophy, and policies. I had my work cut out for me.

So I set about tackling this new challenge. I had never been a buyer, so I had to start from scratch. I spent weeks gathering up every form in use for purchasing merchandise. I interviewed every buyer. I visited with the executive management team and all the support groups: data processing, advertising/sales promotion, accounting and finance, distribution center management . . . in other words, anyone and everyone involved with the purchasing and distribution of merchandise. That involved every area of the company in some capacity.

I completed the project in less than three months, and the resulting Buyer's Training Manual consisted of two huge tomes containing everything a person would need to know about buying merchandise for Walmart.

During the last few weeks of this assignment, the vice president of hardlines merchandising, Dave McClanahan, resigned from the company to work for a competitor. That position was still vacant when I completed the project.

Al Johnson called me into his office and offered that job to *me*. I was stunned and spooked by the offer. Walmart was quickly becoming one of the bright stars on the retailing landscape, approaching $1 billion in sales. And *I* was going to lead the merchandising team of the hardlines categories? It was an awesome responsibility. For the first time in my career, I was not at all confident that I was ready for it. I was thirty-seven-years-old.

The experience I reaped from these two projects was incalculable. I realized how fortunate I was to have been selected for these challenges. As a result, I met and formed personal and working relationships within every division of the company. Later in my career, and even after leaving Walmart, a number of retired executives shared the inside scoop as to how I came to be selected for these positions. Sam Walton and others saw me as a person who was "not a good maintainer," but one who "needed and relished a challenge." They knew that I would "bust my butt" to get a job done right — as quickly as possible. They also felt my ability to respect and get along with others would result in cooperation from the many folks throughout the company with whom these projects required coordination.

Today, as I write this section of the book, and think about Project 79, I pulled out and revisited one of the best business books I've ever read, *Thinking Inside the Box* by Kirk Cheyfitz, which should be mandatory reading for employees of every large company. I met Kirk some time ago in New York City, and not only is he a warm, friendly fellow, he is a very successful author. I shamelessly plug his book here, because he does a far better job of describing what I am attempting to say. As we "thought outside the box" in building a new and different store, Mr. Sam insisted on keeping the promotional merchandising and pricing image intact, the basic "box" of Walmart's image.

Over the years, and continuing today, Walmart has consistently "thought outside the box" while not forgetting the "planks" that built the "box," to borrow from Mr. Cheyfitz's terminology.

Two paragraphs from Kirk Chevitz' book, *Thinking Inside the Box:*

I began this book with the conviction that we can't think outside the box or even inside the box unless we have a precise idea of what the box is. A look at business past and present reveals the existence of certain unchanging, timeless rules — the rules that I collectively call "The Box." Among the planks that make up The Box, for example, are the millennia-old rules of organizational decision-making uncovered by Simon. Ignoring the established rules of The Box is neither innovative nor entrepreneurial nor revolutionary. It is, to borrow a word from Mel Karmazin's T-shirt, stupid. Plain and simple.

The welcome corollary of this premise is that there is no substance to the myth of the Oz-like CEO. Managing an enterprise requires neither genius nor constant invention (let alone reinvention). Rather, good management largely consists of paying attention to history and present reality while applying hard work and prudence. This is the gospel of business — that management is a set of skills to be learned, not a matter of divine inspiration or magical foresight, and that the list of requisite skills has been consistent over a long period of time. Given the right set of rules, we can all manage from one quarter to the next, providing something useful to society and making a reasonable profit in return, while avoiding doing too much that is stupid. That's what this book is all about.

> A committee is a thing that takes a week to do what one good man could do in an hour.
>
> — ELBERT HUBBARD

CHAPTER 11

Vice-President, Hardlines Merchandising — Dealing with Suppliers and Buyers

> **1979–1983**
> - Many "firsts" occur: IBM PC, CD player, the word "Internet."
> - Microsoft Word takes first step toward world domination.
> - Ronald Reagan is elected president.
> - Mt. St. Helens erupts.
> - John Lennon is assassinated.
> - Walmart buys Kuhn's Big K stores in Nashville and is now a multi-billion dollar company, ranked #1 discounter.
> - My family is now living comfortably, but problems arise.

Reporting to Al Johnson as general merchandise manager (GMM), with no prior working experience in the merchandising division, I began my new responsibilities with a high degree of trepidation. However, I had grown to greatly respect the existing buying team while working with most of them on Project 79. I devoted my first few days on the job to meeting with each of the divisional managers and their buyers. I made it clear that I was there to work with and support them, not to demand change or otherwise interfere.

In my opinion, the buying division during this period of Walmart's history was as strong as it had ever been, or possibly would ever be. I can't take any credit for this; it was already well-established before I moved into the leadership position. But I certainly benefited from a working relationship with this outstanding group. These folks knew their categories inside and out — either from their Walmart experience or from working in these categories with other retailers. I have listed the names of the buying team and other buyers who reported to me during my stint as GMM at the end of this chapter.*

Many changes took place during my three years in this position. People left, people got hired, people received promotions.

In conversations with our suppliers, I learned very quickly that they respected our buyers more than the buyers for the other dominant retailers of the time, particularly Sears and K-Mart.

An Education — Annual Business Reviews with Major Suppliers

Shortly after assuming my new position, we began annual business reviews with our major suppliers. In this process, the principals and our buyers sat down to discuss the current status of our relationship and share our plans for the upcoming year, all in an effort to achieve our mutual goals and budgets. Typically, three to six folks from a well-known consumer products company would come in for their scheduled appointment, dressed to impress and loaded with industry data, rankings, charts, graphs, new item introductions, and advertising/promotional plans.

The large suppliers pulled out all the stops to dazzle the new head of the division (me) during these meetings. I saw the process as an opportunity to learn a lot very quickly . . . and I seized that opportunity. Here are the key points I derived from these meetings:

Everybody is #1? Supplier after supplier started the meeting with some type of chart showing one of their brands rated #1 or #2 in market share. That's not a bad selling point, but the fact is, all their competitors claimed the same statistics. I suppose Neilson ratings, or whatever surveys they

Left: Connie and I with our dog Micky who was killed on the way to church in 1947. Right: My sisters and I with one of our cousins in front of our humble home. Note the bare feet. We only wore shoes in the winter, and had only one pair each.

Left: Little League Cardinals in Bentonville, 1955. Right: My mom, 1955, while a housekeeper for Sam and Helen Walton.

Left: Connie, me and Pat in Bentonville High School, 1959. Right: Me and Earl Bright, owner, Bright's Texaco on 8th and "A" Street Bentonville — where Mr. Sam interviewed and hired me, 1964.

All photos courtesy Ron Loveless, except as marked.

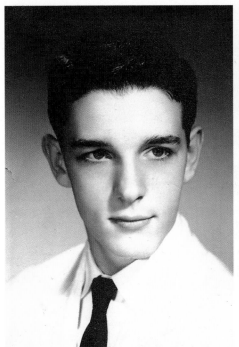

Left: My Bentonville High School Graduation picture 1960. Right: With my first love, Nancy Covey, the night we got engaged in Florida,1960.

Left: My official Air Force photo. Right: Stationed in St. Lawrence Island, Alaska, 1962. That's me on the left.

The Bentonville 5 & 10 location on the square — now a visitor's center and museum.
Below: An early Wal-Mart Discount City sign. Note the price of gas!

Bob Bogle, Sam's first store manager in Bentonville, my boss in 1968. Credited with naming the company "Wal-Mart" because the seven letters would be "cheaper than something longer."

Crowds line up for the grand opening of the very first Walmart store. Located in Rogers, Arkansas, it opened in 1962. (Courtesy Walmart, Inc.)

Three of the earliest associates of the company. (L to R) Merle Gilbraith, Variety Store Manager, Maxine Black, Walton's 5&10 store associate, Bob Bogle, the first store manager that Mr. Sam ever hired; to run his Bentonville Variety Store.

View of the very first Walmart store from the street. (Courtesy Walmart, Inc.)

The grand reopening of Walmart store #1 in Rogers, Arkansas after it was moved to a larger facility. (L to R) Tom Jefferson, Clarence Leis, store manager, Miss Arkansas, and Mr. Sam.

The Walmart analysts' meeting where I presented the "LIER" Report. At right is Sam Walton and Arkansas Governor, Bill Clinton.

Mr. Sam and me (left) getting in to the swing of our presentation with a rubber chicken. (Courtesy Walmart, Inc.)

Mr. Sam dances the hula on Wall Street in New York City. (Courtesy Walmart, Inc.)

One of the key people and "unsung" heroes in the success of Walmart, Mrs. Helen Walton with eventual CEO David Glass.

Mr. Sam asked many of the early management team to come in for a meeting to discuss ways to improve the company's business, 1989 Mr. Sam and Bud Walton kneeling in the front.

Front row (L to R) Don Bailey, Don Whitaker, Jr., Bob Lee, me, Ed Orr, Joe White, Phil Green, Bob Bogle, George Simpson, Bob Nelson. Back row (L to R) David Glass, Don Soderquist, Willard Walker, Claude Harris, Gary Reinboth, Theo Ashcraft, Ferold Arend, Darwin Smith, Dave Washburn, Bob Haines, Marsha Haines, Charles Cate, Ray Thomas, Tom Jefferson, Bob Thornton, Ken Kearney, M.I. Dillard, Charlie Baum.

The St. Robert team. (L to R) Me, Leland Huff, assistant manager, and Gary Reinboth, my boss, 1964

Being presented with our five-year service award pins in 1969. (L to R) Jack Brewer, Harry Green and me.

"Project 79"—My project, working with the Doody Company in Ohio, to redesign and up-grade the Walmart stores for the 80s decade. Though never duplicated, this project changed the look of our stores in a positive way for years to come.

Sam Walton speaks to the folks at my "retirement" party in 1987.

Jack Shewmaker, Walmart CFO, my boss, wishes me well at my "retirement" party in 1987.

"Mr. Sam" Walton

Bud Walton

David Glass

Jack Shewmaker

Al Johnson

Tom Jefferson

*Jim Dismore,
my first district manager.*

*M.I. Dillard, my D.M. while in
Mountain Home, Arkansas,
store #11.*

*"The Professor" Rex
Chase, store manager
in Walmart store
#4, Siloam Springs,
Arkansas*

Mr. Sam at the controls of his beloved airplane.

The Home Office sign with flag at half-mast the day Sam Walton passed away.
(Courtesy Walmart, Inc.)

Bud Walton

Sam Walton

Sign in front of Walmart headquarters today. (Courtesy Walmart, Inc.)

The first Sam's Club. (Courtesy Walmart, Inc.)

The first prototype, from the ground up, Sam's Club on Garland Road in the Dallas market. (Courtesy Walmart, Inc.)

A Sam's Club today. (Courtesy Walmart, Inc.)

My favorite Sam & Bud photo. Taking a break from bird hunting at their "fancy" hunting lodge.

Me in front of the Walmart Visitors Center.

My wife Cindy, with Kim and Ronnie in Mountain Home, Arkansas, 1973.

My Mom and her husband, Bernie at a Walmart truck driver luncheon.
Mom retired from the Walmart warehouse in Bentonville.

Receiving recognition for service on the Manco Advisory Board from Jack Kahl on left and his son, John Kahl, at right.

One of my many fishing trips. A peacock bass caught in Venezuela.

Current photo of my grandson, Kody Taylor, pictured at Lake Memphremagog in Newport, Vermont.

My daughter, Kim, just after graduation from HS in 1983.

Current photo of my wife, Robin, at right, and daughter, April Allen.

Preparing to tee off on hole #9 at Pebble Beach, with the famed cliff on #8 in the background. (L to R) Me, Ken Kearney and Bill Maas.

Ready for a golf outing in Branson, Missouri. (L to R) Ray Moss from Vermont, me, John Cote from Newport, Vermont., my brother-in-law, and good friend Bob Bronson.

Entrance at famed Pebble Beach Golf Course. (L to R) Ken Kearney, retired from Walmart, my son Ronnie, friend Bill Maas, and me.

My son, Ronnie, with his family, Debby, Morgan and Tripp on a recent vacation trip.

used, could be manipulated by region or some other category to show their brands in a favorable light. One fact was constant — we already knew what *we* were selling. With only one hour designated to discuss how we could improve our mutual businesses, I suggested they curb their marketing department's formal presentations, take off their "salesmen" hats, and get down to the business of talking about what was significant to our company's results. The challenge for both the retailer and the supplier is simple and can be summed up in one question . . . "What do consumers want and what will make them buy more of it?"

The advertising and price conundrum. The supplier presentation invariably included the introduction of a new item and the necessity to spend literally millions of dollars in national advertising to promote it. This was a negative for Walmart, but the suppliers didn't realize it. While no one would argue the need for marketing/advertising to create demand for a new product, Walmart was still a "regional" chain at this time. So one of the key questions our astute buyers asked was, "What marketing support are you going to give this item if we put it in our stores?" Most of the large suppliers were spending their advertising dollars in "Top 40" markets (big cities). With no stores in those markets, Walmart would realize no direct benefit from these advertising expenditures. Few suppliers had thought of that. As a result, Walmart developed its own "TV network," buying reasonably-priced airtime from smaller-market television stations in areas where we could best reach our stores and customers. We challenged the suppliers to use some of their national advertising budget to air their commercials on our network of stations, resulting in better sales of the new items in our store — a win-win for everyone. By participating in the Walmart television network, the vendors paid bargain rates for airtime, while getting more of their items on our shelves.

Pricing Advantage. During these meetings, on a number of occasions, I asked the simple question, "Are we getting the best price we can get?" After conversations with many of the chief executives and national sales managers of some of our largest suppliers, I learned a lesson I have never forgotten, one as pertinent today as it was then. They informed me that

Walmart was getting equal pricing, and in many cases, lower pricing than anyone in the industry. This not only surprised me, I seriously doubted if it were true. Sears and K-Mart were much larger and I couldn't fathom that we were the beneficiaries of better pricing. Thus, my follow-up question: "Why would you give us better pricing than K-Mart and the bigger companies?" The responses would vary a little, but in essence, the reasons were as follows:

▶ Walmart treats us with respect. It's a partnership. Many of the buyers in the other companies are arrogant and abusive.

▶ Walmart buyers are ethical. We've dealt with many buyers who are "on the take" or expect personal favors.

▶ Walmart asks for "net pricing." Other retailers demand "slotting allowances and other charges."

▶ Walmart keeps the focus on the customer. Many retailers are focusing on what's good for their numbers, but not necessarily their customers. They don't realize that if the customer comes first, the numbers take care of themselves.

One key executive from Lever Brothers said to me, "Mr. Loveless, all major suppliers know what it costs to do business with their biggest customers. If they're smart, they know exactly what it costs to do business with Walmart, K-Mart, Sears, or any other account for a given year. The price Walmart will ultimately pay is derived from that information. In other words, 'you never get something for nothing.'" That's an old adage, and rather elementary, but it certainly is one every buyer should keep taped on his or her desk in full view at all times. A good partnership with suppliers is one in which both companies respect one another and recognize that both must make a profit to stay in business.

When I think of the retailer/supplier relationship issues, I'm reminded of a conversation I once had with a retired federal judge. Although he was talking about ruling on contractual disputes between two parties in a courtroom, his comments could be applied to dealings between a retailer and supplier. He said to me, "Ronnie, I go to court and have to listen to numerous attorneys on both sides of a dispute argue incessantly about various obscure clauses in some contract, and point out why I should find in their favor. The truth is, there's no such thing as a contract that could cover every possible contingency. It would save everybody a lot of time and money to take a single page of paper and write on it 'both parties agree to treat the other fairly.' Both would sign it and the deal is done. Because, ultimately, my decision is to determine which party treated the other unfairly. Period."

I tell of this conversation with the judge, because I believe the buyer/vendor relationship should be that simple. Disputes with suppliers will inevitably arise, and rather than try to defend a position that is unfair, just do what is right and move forward. As general merchandise manager for Walmart, that is the way I tried to work with suppliers. As a result, I believe we received far more from the vendors than our competitors did.

Brand vs. Value

There's no question that name brands are important to a retailer's business. Walmart historically featured and sharply priced the leading brands for their EDLP (Every Day Low Price) pricing image. However, in many instances suppliers become so proud of their brands they feel the consumer will automatically pay whatever price they demand. Even though our country was dealing with a serious recession at this time, many of the major suppliers were asking for price increases. Rubbermaid and 3M were two of the worst offenders. With an obstinate stance and insistence that our customers demanded their brands, they stood their ground when we balked. We saw things differently, and in many cases, chose to offer lower-priced, high-quality alternatives to their branded products. It cost them a lot of business. I share one of the stories related to this issue in Chapter 19 of this book (Lessons for Suppliers).

The three years I served in this position were very rewarding and educational. Being in the retail business, I sum up this learning experience as follows: the operations folks represented the "heart" of our business and the merchandising team represented the "soul." Mr. Sam recognized the importance of maintaining a "balance of power" between these two divisions. It was not always easy to do. There were two issues I came face-to-face with from the get-go.

Budgeting. Our merchandising team was responsible for annual budgeting of sales, inventory, and markdown numbers. Simultaneously, the operations team was developing its own budget for the same numbers, but worked it from store-level management. At some point beyond my pay grade, someone had to make these numbers mesh. The wedding of the two budgets, a function of the CFO, posed an interesting challenge. He had to consider the expansion and contraction of departments from year to year in merchandising, while taking into account how store sales could change based on competition, remodels, relocation, and other factors. The details of the budgeting process, ultimately arriving at an acceptable corporate budget by the executive management folks, presented a new and daunting challenge for me.

Merchandise Meetings. The weekly Friday merchandise meetings always held our interest. The regional VPs from operations attended, after having spent the week in the stores, armed with merchandising suggestions and/or criticisms. The merchandising team attended, armed with whatever new programs they wanted to share and/or complaints about stores failing to properly execute their programs. All the top executives attended; no doubt to keep the peace . . . if they could. As a result of these meetings, reports were sent to the field, called "Priority Notes," which represented the most important actions to take in all stores for that week. This communication, in my opinion, was Walmart's single best program during the high-growth '70s and '80s. Still, while we all respected each other, it could get tough on buyers when six or seven operations VPs ganged up on them in such an open forum.

In my new role, I dealt with an abundance of issues having more to do with proper execution of merchandising matters and displays. I came up with an idea to also send out weekly "Merchandising Priorities," through a communication tool I dubbed COMAC (which came from the term "COMmunication and ACtion in Merchandising"). I understand this is still in use at Walmart today, yet no one knows what it stands for or how it got started. Now they do.

Manufacturer's Representatives — The "Third Party" Issue

Perhaps one of the most controversial and educational assignments I faced in merchandising came in 1981, when Al Johnson called me into his office and told me about an issue with our larger suppliers. He explained that Walmart wanted a "direct relationship" with them to improve communication and place a "decision-maker" in all buyer/vendor meetings. To this day, the subject remains one of the most misunderstood issues in our retailer/supplier relationships. I cover it in more detail in Chapter 19 of this book, sharing the exact story of how it became my assignment at this point in time.

In the '70s and '80s, when factories or consumer product companies were ready to sell to retail clients, they either staffed national or regional sales people, or they utilized "third parties," also known as manufacturer's representatives (reps). Unless a company was large enough to hire its own sales force nationwide, or in many cases even if they were, using reps became standard protocol; primarily because they worked a certain geographical territory and they knew, or had a business relationship with, the retail accounts in that territory.

Through the early growth years, Walmart had a difficult time attracting the attention of large suppliers. Mr. Sam, Claude Harris, Gary Reinboth and others who assisted in sourcing and buying products had to work very hard to find sources for the goods we needed. In many cases, we had to use distributors, the middle-men in the flow of goods. In other cases, manufacturer's reps who covered the Arkansas, Missouri, and Oklahoma areas became aware of Sam Walton's new company, and began calling on us, offering all sorts of goods and favorable promotional items. These reps are paid a commission on sales to the retail accounts and were fairly aggressive (their income depended on it). A number of astute reps made it a point to know Walmart — its needs and expectations — so well that they became an extension of our buying team. Many of them literally got Walmart better promotions and prices than we could have achieved ourselves. A number of the "rep firms" specialized in particular categories and were invaluable in educating our buyers on the nuances of their particular industry.

Conversely, a few reps simply wanted to make a sale (and a quick buck), with no consideration for selling us too much product, or for the merits or quality of the product they were selling. Those reps didn't last long; just long enough to create some of the problems "third parties" would face over the coming years. For example, they would represent items or factories which had "sales appeal" but didn't thoroughly "vet" the quality and/or manufacturer's ability to do business with a major retailer. This often resulted in large returns on products which the manufacturer could not handle financially. Yet the rep would have already received the sales commission. These reps were simply salesmen who appeared in our lobby day after day touting any or all items they could find to "make a sale." They were more a hindrance than a contribution to our success.

Frankly, "third-party" manufacturer reps were instrumental in helping the company get started, and because they earned a commission on sales, most of them made a nice living. In a few cases, they became rather wealthy doing business with the company. Most of that wealth came, not as a result of sales commissions, but because they were close enough to the company to realize they should buy Walmart stock.

While GMM, I came to know many of the early reps. In fact, over the course of my career I maintained direct contact with many of them — at store openings, in daily office activities, in conversation with the buyers, and even back when I worked in the stores. Many names come to mind. I remember Ernie Hall, Frank Fletcher, Kent Jenkins, Dick Berryman, Ray Murski, Charles Hanshaw, Michael Goldman, Don Brown, Paul Taske, Stan Kessler, Tony Romero, Stan Surlow, and Joe Bare. (There were many other good ones; I simply can't name all of them here.) Manufacturer's reps contributed a great deal to the growth of our company, and although the organization is huge today, the "good" reps continue to provide a valuable service to the retail distribution process and Walmart.

To understand my role and Al Johnson's directive to me in 1981 concerning the "third-party" issue, see Chapter 19 (Lessons for Suppliers).

The Buyer's Challenge at Walmart

During the first few months of my tenure as GMM, I came to see the buyers in an entirely different light. As I've stated earlier, I was as critical of the buyers as anyone when in the field. But now that I rubbed elbows with them on a daily basis, I came to appreciate even more the workload they endured and the difficult decisions for which they were responsible. And this was when we were approaching our first one billion in sales. I can hardly imagine that challenge with the size and scope of Walmart today.

A rule of thumb was that buyers were doing a good job if they were "seventy percent right" when buying merchandise. That sounds pretty low, but all things considered, it's a fair percentage. A good and aggressive buyer, while maintaining his/her basic assortment, is constantly looking for new, innovative items (always a risk); trying to buy just the right amount of merchandise for periodic sale circulars or seasons; and maintaining a mix of sales to achieve a particular gross margin, markdown, and GM-ROI (Gross Margin Return on Investment) budget. The list goes on and on — and that's just the *buying* responsibility. Consider the following, which was also part of the buyer's role at Walmart in 1981. Keep in mind this was before EDI (Electronic Data Interchange) and computer systems support:

▸ Write replenishment orders for the entire chain of stores.

▸ Write new item, grand opening, seasonal & circular orders for all stores.

▸ Return all phone calls from all stores.

▸ Attend daily meetings with sales promotion/advertising, data processing, accounting, supervisors, and operations.

▸ Attend trade shows several times per year.

▸ Satisfy Walmart's policy of visiting stores as often as possible.

- Respond to hundreds of calls from existing or potential suppliers.
- Attend supplier appointments three days per week.
- Attend Friday merchandise meeting (mandatory).
- Attend Saturday morning meetings.
- Review and know his/her department's sales and results on a daily and weekly basis.
- Know at all times his/her competitor's prices and "never be undersold."
- Never have too much or too little merchandise.
- Keep markdowns to a minimum.

This is just a partial list. Frankly, I can hardly imagine how buyers manage their responsibilities . . . then or now. I gained a great deal more respect for the buyers in my GMM position than I had as an operations VP. Now the company is so much larger and global in scope, but I also know everything is relative. Today's buyers have many more tools at their disposal. In 1980, buyers did not have computers on their desks. (No accoutrements such as cell phones, personal digital assistants (PDAs), or emails either; they didn't exist. Computerized data management tools were still in the early days of development.) However, we were quickly moving in that direction with the introduction of bar codes on merchandise. At the time, our success primarily depended on the experience and knowledge of the buying team — their ability to multi-task (before that term had entered the lexicon) — working long, hard hours with reliance on suppliers to help them achieve their numbers. Someone conducted a study toward the end of my stint as GMM and estimated that the average buyer in hardlines traveled twenty-six weeks per year, and in softlines, thirty-six weeks per year. That's a lot of frequent flyer miles and time spent away from loved ones. This itinerary included trade shows, store openings, store visits, corporate meetings, and trips to the Orient — all while juggling the tasks previously listed.

An innovative program for buyers and store managers of that era was "Job Appreciation Week," which we usually observed just after the Christmas selling season or in early January. Essentially a job-swapping scheme, it let participants walk a mile in the other person's shoes, requiring buyers to work in the stores while store personnel spent quality time in the buying offices. The program accomplished its goals, resulting in a far better understanding and appreciation for one another's jobs. Having spent the prior fifteen years in the stores, I didn't directly participate in the program, but was in charge of scheduling those who would. I put an emphasis on those buyers whom I believed needed to have this experience — those who seemed most critical of store operations. They needed to see the "other side of the coin," so to speak.

"Correction of Errors" was another beneficial company-wide program instituted by Walmart in its first two decades. Immediately following the Christmas selling season, everyone (and I mean everyone) was required to create a list of their most significant mistakes that, when corrected the following year, would result in improved sales and/or profits. This was a formal process with the results entering the employee's "permanent record" in the company files. Rather than mistakes or errors, we were taught to see them as "Opportunities." It's all about your point of view.

The last program I'll mention was called Volume Producing Item (VPI). Mr. Sam insisted on the designation of "merchant" for everyone in the company. VPI required that all store personnel, as well as management in the Home Office, select an underperforming item that held potential for much higher volume. We would then feature these items in our stores to see who could sell the most. I was amazed to see the volumes generated on items whose sales history had not reflected the potential. Of course, the contest didn't take place on a level playing field; when Mr. Sam chose his item, it received the best space, display, and attention in the stores. The store folks weren't stupid, ya know. But on the whole, when every department manager throughout the chain focused on his or her item, it resulted in unusually high sales volume and profit margins. This is another case for a quote I attribute to Mr. Sam in Chapter 19: "A computer can tell you what you have sold, but cannot tell you what you could have sold."

My Sister Pat and Women in the Workplace

In the past several years, I've seen occasional criticism of Walmart regarding the hiring and pay of women as a minority group in the company. Certainly, Walmart made its share of mistakes, and management will be the first to say that perhaps it took longer than it should have to make progress in the promotion and pay scale of women in the company. But it was never due to lack of effort. While GMM, I had occasion to work with many great women in the merchandising organization. Most of them served as assistants to the buyers. My sister Pat was assistant to Dick Mahan, the senior buyer in sporting goods. Dick developed our sporting goods distributor program called AIDCO. Other buyers in sporting goods included Tom Middleton, Jim Woodruff, and Ron Freidenberger. This group was, no doubt, the best in the business at that time. My sister, working as Dick's assistant, became highly respected by the supplier community, taking care of much of the detail work for Dick. Eventually, Dick wanted to give her the opportunity for promotion. She resisted for some time, having just given birth to twin boys. She didn't relish the thought of frequent travel that came with the position. Eventually, she decided to give it a try and was promoted to assistant buyer. As she had feared, after a few months, the travel requirements proved to be too much for her and she decided she'd been happier in her previous role. She gladly returned to serving as assistant to the buyer.

At the same time, another assistant to the buyer announced that she wished to be promoted and felt she wasn't being given the opportunity. She had occupied her position for many years, but still needed to improve in a number of areas before we would consider her for promotion. During our evaluation, we pinpointed those areas. She did not take the constructive criticism well. Subsequently, she developed a poor attitude and accused the company of not promoting women in the workplace. As a result, she remained in that job for the remainder of her time at Walmart.

I mention my sister Pat's situation and that of the second woman simply to point out that women have every right and should expect equal pay for equal work. But they also need to recognize that the demands of the job must also be equal. Pat preferred to be a stay-at-home mom (which I admire), and the second candidate lacked the necessary qualifications. We would have reached the same decision no matter the gender.

The truth was that we recognized and actively sought deserving women for promotion. Among others, Mary Ann Estes, Harryetta Bailey, Peggy Hamilton, Marcia Haines, Jane Mercer, Cherry Mills, Pam Sklut, Judy Garris, Lana Granger, Barbara Brown, Jane Marshall, and Vivian Dunnaway made great contributions in the early growth of our company. We considered many women as promotable, but like my sister, they preferred to forego promotion for personal reasons. Certain jobs in retailing require solid commitments, and equal pay requires an equal work load. Taking all this into consideration, I received marching orders in the early '80s to actively seek women for promotion and future leadership roles. I also know that Helen pushed Mr. Sam to recognize the need to hire and promote women for key positions in the company. Regardless, when Walmart grew large enough to gain national attention, the company was unfairly targeted for its hiring and promotion practices regarding women. We had been, in fact, giving this issue attention for many years. Did it happen fast enough or to the degree it should have? That is certainly debatable, but it wasn't for lack of trying.

Having Fun

While GMM, I liked to enjoy my favorite pastimes (as usual). We created a Walmart Bass Club that quickly grew to around sixty members, all of whom spent many hours competing in monthly tournaments on area lakes. Activities like this drew employees closer together and we gained an appreciation for other divisions as a result. In a bass boat, enjoying a few beers and pursuing a mutual interest, there was no distinction between a vice president of merchandising and a truck driver. Some of the real characters I worked with and who participated in our Bass Club included truck drivers Larry Fuller, Glen Bookout, and Bill Williams. From sporting goods we had Ron Freidenberger, Bill Woodard, Ron Rose (department manager in Store #1 in Rogers), David Gorman, who eventually ran loss prevention for the company, and Bob Hart, who served in many positions within the company.

In keeping with my affinity for baseball and softball, we also launched a Walmart softball team. Our team was a good one, and we successfully competed in numerous district and state tournaments. We won a number of them. Members of that initial team included Rick Russell, Clifford Young, Lonnie Burden, Buddy Carmichael, Mike Lewis, Jim Reynolds, Andy Schwerdtfeger, Rick McLintock, Bob McCurry, Parker Hunt, Steve Harig, and Bob Lee. Remembering the fun times reminds me of a good story relating to vendor relationship management and John Mariotti.

John Mariotti and Huffy Bicycles — Relationship Management

John Mariotti is one of the smartest guys I know, with an impressive list of credentials to prove it. He resides in Powell, Ohio, where he operates a consulting firm, The Enterprise Group, and sits on a number of consumer product company boards. He has become well-known as a business advisor, speaker, and author. He is a past-president of Huffy Bicycles and the Rubbermaid Office Product Group. He produces a weekly business newsletter to subscribers called *The Enterprise*. His latest book, *The Complexity Crisis*, is a fascinating read for anyone in business today. Now that I've given my good friend John his "plug," I'll share this story and its pertinence to the subject at hand.

I first came to know John in 1982 when he served as president of Huffy Bikes and was pitching our company to buy the new 20" BMX style bicycles, which were just beginning to take off. At the time, most bike sales were in the traditional coaster bikes, and 10- or 12-speed 26" adult models. We bought primarily from Murray. We hadn't yet decided to buy Huffy bikes when our Walmart softball team qualified to play in a world regional tournament in Oklahoma City. This just happened to be the location of Huffy's headquarters.

Our team lost our first game, won the second, and faced an elimination game against, who else, but the Huffy Bicycle team. The game was very competitive and we lost in the last inning by a run, eliminating us from the tournament. John tells the story this way:

"On Monday morning, I was in my office when one of my sales guys comes in and says, 'Boss, I have some good news and bad news.'

I reply, 'Okay, tell me the good news first.'

'We won our game yesterday.'

'Okay, great,' I say, 'what's the bad news?'

'Well, sir, the bad news is that we beat the Walmart team, and I know you're trying hard to do business with them. But there's even worse news. The coach and shortstop on that team is Ron Loveless, Walmart's VP of merchandising.'

'Oh, my God,' I say. 'Couldn't you have picked somebody else to beat?'"

John and I have shared a lot of laughs over this story, because it depicts the stress involved in supplier/retailer relationships and the way perceptions come into play. Without question, a softball game is not going to affect the purchase of merchandise that is good for the customers. But it surely entered John's mind at the time. We did buy the Huffy 20" bikes soon afterward, starting a relationship that generated untold millions of dollars through the years.

But, John, I'm still bitter that you beat us out at that tournament.

Culture Shock — Calling on Walmart

In the '70s and '80s, a trip to Walmart headquarters in pastoral Bentonville often resulted in "culture shock" for our suppliers. Once we were "on the map" so to speak, the larger suppliers from New York, Chicago, and other metropolitan areas began making the trek on a fairly regular basis. I became appreciative of the "ordeal" they endured to reach our neck of the woods.

The only commercial airport in the area was Drake Field in nearby

Fayetteville. This airport was nestled in a valley surrounded by hills on both the approach and departure routes, resulting in lower-than-normal landing minimums. Our geographic area receives a constant barrage of clashing warm gulf air mixing with cold fronts from the north, along with ensuing thunderstorms, fog, and low cloud ceilings. Cancellations or diversions to other airports are commonplace. The primary airline serving this airport at the time was Skyways, which flew the small commuter planes known as "puddle-jumpers." These were small turbo-props with very limited luggage/storage capacity. Considering the challenges, Skyways certainly did an admirable job. But often as not, suppliers arrived at the general office in a pale and shaky condition from the bumpy flights. They also showed up empty-handed, because their merchandise samples had been left off the plane because of weight restrictions.

Upon arriving at Drake Field, suppliers found very few ground transportation options. They could rent a car from one of the two companies offering such service (if there was even anyone manning the car rental booths, or if the three or four cars available had not already been taken). Or they could hire one of the two or three cabs available for the twenty-mile drive to Bentonville (arranging return transportation in advance, since Bentonville offered no taxi service). On occasion, an unsuspecting supplier would rent a limousine (very limited in number) and arrive at the office donning a tailored suit and expensive gold jewelry. This sort of behavior was discouraged after one particular incident. Sam Walton happened to witness a limo-renting-flashily-dressed-supplier exiting his ride in front of Walmart headquarters. Mr. Sam immediately commented on this ostentatious arrival, telling our buyer not to buy from that vendor because "he is obviously making too much money." Word quickly spread that it was wise to present a "frugal" image when calling on Walmart.

Another shocker to vendors was that Benton County was (and still is) a "dry" county. In Arkansas, the option to allow packaged-liquor sales (liquor/beer stores) is determined by public vote in each county. Counties are either "wet" or "dry." However, "private club" permits may be issued in dry counties. Private clubs are allowed to sell alcohol. A good friend of mine, Keith Dowell, owned the Holiday Inns in Rogers and Bentonville. The Holiday Inn was the only franchised motel in town. Keith also had the only place in town you could go for a drink, the Waterhole Lounge. Choices being limited, when suppliers came to town you could generally find them congregating at the Waterhole during the evening, or eating at Fred's Hickory Inn steak and rib house. Fred's continues to be a popular choice today.

Sam Walton didn't particularly like for his folks to go to the local bar, so it was considered unwise to hang out at the Waterhole. However, being the maverick I was, I liked to have a few drinks with friends from the softball team or bass club. Besides, I figured since it was "off-limits," I didn't run the risk of running into Mr. Sam there. In fact, I deduced that if anyone from the company spotted me, he or she was as guilty as I was.

I met a lot of suppliers in that place, but can honestly say that I always paid for my own drinks, as company policy required. Becoming acquainted and forming casual relationships with suppliers in a social setting benefited the company as well. While I was far from a "saint" when it came to company policies and political correctness (as my colleagues would attest), I can say that my shenanigans never put the company in a compromising position nor cost it money. Quite the contrary. I hope they don't mind me mentioning them, but two suppliers who became my friends through the infamous Waterhole Lounge were Gayle Graham with the Gillette Company and Ron Darby with Kimberly Clark. There were many more. But these two guys stand out as stand-up company men who, because of our personal relationship, gave me special deals on merchandise. The result? Happy customers and increased sales for Walmart. On paper, it's good company policy to insist that executives avoid becoming too close to suppliers. But in reality, this simply can't be avoided. Regardless of the level of management, these relationships will exist; whether rubbing elbows at big national meetings, social events, or industry pow-wows, people get to know and respect one another. Friendships begin, and in many cases, last throughout lifetimes. The important thing is the ability to separate the friendship from the business relationship when need be. Maybe there's a fine line there, but I can assure you that my vendor friends never crossed it.

Years after I left Walmart, I dabbled in the country music industry in Nashville and wrote lyrics to a song about the Waterhole and suppliers flying into Fayetteville. I hope the vendors will forgive me, because I don't intend to stereotype them in any negative way. Hopefully, folks will see the humor in this:

The Walmart Vendor (circa 1970s)

I'm a typical Walmart vendor
From Dallas or the big Northeast
I come in town on a Wednesday night
Every other month at least.
I head to the motel to meet my friends
At the famous Waterhole Bar
But I park in the back alley parking lot
So Sam won't see my car.

(Chorus)
I love to come to Bentonville
And eat Fred's Barbeque
Sit in a chair at the local lounge
And wait for girls to come through
But about midnight when I'm drunk on my butt
And I haven't seen a thing
I pay my tab, head for the room
And put on my wedding ring.

(Repeat Chorus)

The alarm goes off and I head for the office
To meet with the Walmart buyer
I make my pitch, quote my price
And he tells me I'm much higher
But I'm on my way out the door at eight
With an order on the way
But I can't figure out what I did and why
With the price they're gonna pay.

(Repeat Chorus)

So I jump in my rented economy car
And head to Fayetteville town
I stop by the Skyways service desk
To see what's goin' down
They had found my luggage from the inbound trip
And I checked it out at the scene
I said my prayers, got out my ticket
And took two Dramamine

(Repeat Chorus)

So, what do you think? This might have been a hit in the late '70s, when most Walmart suppliers were experiencing the trials and tribulations of calling on the company. Eventually, most suppliers with bulky samples figured out that it was better to fly into Tulsa (a bigger airport, serviced by larger planes) and make the two-hour drive over to Bentonville. Today, the new Northwest Arkansas Regional Airport (XNA) offers a more extensive selection of airlines and flight schedules, greatly improving the flying experience into and out of the area. Also, the area has grown substantially and practically every eatery in Rogers and Bentonville serves alcohol, though they are still considered private clubs (since the county remains dry). Transportation services are more readily available as well. Shoot, we're almost what you could call "big-time" now. (It's still not too wise to pull up in front of the office in a limousine, though. Some things never change.)

Preparing Walmart for the Future

During my tenure as GMM, Walmart began putting in place some of the most important programs in the company's history, setting the stage for the meteoric growth of the '80s. Jack Shewmaker and David Glass, in their respective positions as COO and CFO, pushed hard for programs that were very difficult to implement and costly to maintain (which made it hard to get Mr. Sam's approval), but instrumental to our growth.

Scanning. Though most grocery merchandise packaging at the time contained UPC "bar-codes," most non-food general merchandise did not. The company recognized that it would be beneficial to scan bar codes at our cash registers on all items, enabling us to eventually track all sales, keep a current computerized inventory, and ultimately replenish the stores electronically. This would also eliminate "under ringing" by dishonest associates (a major cause of internal shrinkage for retailers), the cost of applying price tickets to every item, and re-pricing items for sale events. The effort to get UPC codes on all items, install cash registers to read them, and set up the information systems to collect and report the data was a comprehensive, costly endeavor. But Walmart led the way among discounters to accomplish the task. This changed the industry forever. Jack Shewmaker and Glenn Habern pushed this initiative, which positioned Walmart for unprecedented success.

The Data Processing and Computer Evolution. For quite some time, the company had recognized the value of computerization in the industry. While I was GMM, we installed the first computer terminals on our buyers' desks. Royce Chambers, followed by Glenn Habern, led the data processing division (IS) at Walmart, which would become the envy of the industry. I'll never forget the first day computer terminals appeared in the merchandising offices. About 6:30 that morning, I saw Mr. Sam scoping out the buying office, which was mostly devoid of employees at that time of day. He strolled into my office and said, "Ronnie, I never thought I'd see the day we put TV screens on the desks." He went on to express his concern about the cost of our computer system. He doubted the reliability of the data compared to "good old-fashioned note pads and calculators."

Satellite Communications and Data Capability. Another of our keys to growth was the utilization of satellite transmission for communication and data processing. This was an entirely new "futuristic" vision at the time (and very expensive). But Jack and Glenn pushed hard for it. Jack said to me later, "I thought Mr. Sam would fire me over the initial cost" of getting that done. In retrospect, this was another of the crucial elements that helped Walmart get out in front of the competition and stay there. I recall Jack insisting we sell the early home satellite dishes and associated hardware in our stores. These were the earliest versions and the original supplier sold us some "defective" equipment. We had such huge refunds that I wanted to get out of that market for good, but Jack was adamant. He somehow saw a promising future in satellite technology and obviously his vision was right. (I was still mastering the calculator.)

As I've said, the company found it challenging to implement all of these major changes and innovations. I suppose it's human nature to resist change, particularly when it involves extra effort and seemingly impossible odds. I learned from Al Johnson, Jack Shewmaker, and David Glass the importance of keeping your RC Factor low, and the value of educating your people on the "whys" and "what-fors" of change. It's much easier to gain support and cooperation during change when people understand the needs and benefits. Informing, educating, and soliciting input and involvement early on ensures a smoother, quicker implementation process.

My Next Opportunity

In early 1983, Sam Walton opened a new "test" store in an old building in Midwest City, Oklahoma (Oklahoma City area). He called it Sam's Wholesale Club. I was aware of this test store, because a guy who reported directly to me, Rob Voss, assisted with the effort. But I didn't know much about it. That would change quickly.

A few months later, I became very familiar with the concept, because once again Mr. Sam had new plans for me. He walked into my office and said, "Ronnie, I think this Sam's Wholesale Club concept is going to work and I'd like to know if you have an interest in heading up the new division." You'd think by now I would have grown accustomed to these sudden pronouncements. You'd be wrong. True to form, I was floored. Here I was, the vice president, general merchandise manager for what was now one of the largest retail companies in the country. I'd become well-known in the vendor community. I felt like Steve Martin in my favorite movie, *The Jerk*. I love the scene when, after his daily disappointing visit to the mailbox, Steve (as Navin Johnson, born a "poor black child") opens the box and pulls out a telephone book. Frantically flipping through the pages, he finds his name in print and yells, "I'm somebody now! I'm somebody!" That was me at this stage in my career. Somebody.

So when Mr. Sam offered me this job, I was hesitant. Was this a demotion? Did Mr. Sam just offer me a position to supervise one dirty, rundown, old building in Midwest City, Oklahoma? That was my immediate thought. At that moment, I didn't much care that this store called Sam's Wholesale Club was producing unusually high sales numbers.

"Mr. Sam," I said, "I'm not sure that would be a good move for me right now. What do you think?" I didn't want to refuse Mr. Sam anything he asked, but this seemed like a giant step backward.

"Well, let me tell you how important I think this is. I'll double your salary if you'll take the position," he said with sincerity.

"When do I start?" I asked.

So in late 1983, the company announced that I was promoted to senior vice president, general manager of the new Sam's Wholesale Club Division.

Both in my career and Walmart's evolution, events that occurred during the 1979 to 1983 period were of crucial consequence, enabling Walmart to become the largest company in the world. We had topped the one billion dollar mark (back when that meant something), gaining the attention and respect of the best consumer product companies. We implemented point-of-sale cash register scanning systems, installed computer networks, pioneered satellite communication capability, and invested in the most sophisticated warehouse and distribution systems money could buy. Mr. Sam had assembled an executive management team second to none. With a continued focus on our people and customers, and a laser-like spotlight on the competition, we were now capable of growing the company at warp speed . . . which is exactly what we did.

A Tale of Two Decades:

In January, 1970, we were finishing a year in which our sales were $31 million and our profits were $1.2 million.

Sales for the year ended January 31, 1980 were $1.248 billion.

Reflecting upon the progress we have made in the '70s makes it apparent that there is even more opportunity in the '80s for your Company, and we are better positioned to maximize our opportunities this next year and in subsequent years than ever before.

— SAM M. WALTON COMMENTS FROM
THE WALMART ANNUAL REPORT, 1980

Surround yourself with the best people you can find, delegate authority and don't interfere.

— RONALD REAGAN

*The 1980 Buying Team in hardlines merchandising were as follows:

Al Johnson, Senior Vice President, Merchandise & Sales

Ron Loveless, Vice President, General Merchandise Manager (GMM), Hardlines

Don Bailey, Vice President, DMM

Bill Durflinger, Vice President, DMM

Gale Gore, Vice President, DMM

Bob Haines, Senior Buyer, Housewares

Bob Lee, Senior Buyer, HBA, Household

Dick Mahan, Senior Buyer, Sporting Goods

Jim Reynolds, Senior Buyer, Candy, Seasonal

John Bakelaar, Buyer, Stationery

Gary Broach, Buyer, Hardware

J. R. Campbell, Buyer, Toys

Gary Carver, Buyer, Horticulture & Patio

Ron Freidenberger, Buyer, Sporting Goods

Marcia Haines, Buyer, HBA

Ken Kearney, Buyer, HBA

Harold McGinnis, Buyer, Toys

Scott McVey, Buyer, Pet Supplies/Paint

Jim Sheffield, Buyer, Hardware

Mike Spear, Buyer, Automotive

Nick Traf, Buyer, Housewares

Rob Voss, Buyer, Automotive

Richard Ward, Buyer, Electronics

Jim Woodruff, Buyer, Sporting Goods

Other key personnel who played essential roles during my tenure include:

Ron Stover, Mary Ann Estes, Roger Gildehaus, Joe Craig, Joe Hatfield, Dean Sanders, Kent Reeves, and Bill Woodard. I worked closely with all these folks. Their positions in merchandising, along with their expertise and accomplishments played a crucial role in the company's success.

CHAPTER 12

Sam's Wholesale Club — Building a New Company

> ### 1983–1986
> ▸ Apple's McIntosh, Compact Discs, and IBM's first laptops are introduced.
> ▸ Space Shuttle Challenger explodes.
> ▸ Accident at the Soviet Nuclear Reactor in Chernobyl.
> ▸ "You've Got Mail" — Internet Mail Access Protocol arrives.
> ▸ I start up the new Sam's Wholesale Club division. My family falls apart, creating personal distress.

I was promoted to senior vice-president, general manager, Sam's Wholesale Club in June 1983. Unfortunately, Mr. Sam forgot he would "double my salary," but I wasn't complaining. I always welcomed a new challenge. This new opportunity resulted in both the most challenging and the most enjoyable time of my career. I reported to the Walmart CFO, David Glass, who was a pleasure to work with.

I quickly learned that Sam Walton was excited about this new concept for a number of reasons, but primarily I think he saw it as an opportunity to go back to his roots — item merchandising — buying and selling in high volume at extremely low prices. Plus, the division carried his name. He was personally involved from the beginning and attended every Club opening during my time there.

The First Wholesale Clubs

Sol Price introduced the club business concept in San Diego in 1976, when he opened his first Price Club. This was a "membership only" operation selling products to business owners, who paid a membership fee. Price (what a serendipitous last name) generated tremendous sales volumes but at very low margins. To increase profitability, he created another type of membership, allowing very select "group members" (individuals belonging to low-risk groups such as credit unions, banks, government employees, professionals, hospitals, and airlines) to join, subject to paying a five percent surcharge when checking out. This kept the regular "business members" satisfied, while increasing the profit margin on sales.

By 1981, Price Club was a growing, successful enterprise. Mr. Sam had noted the huge volumes, and typical of his character, flew out to visit with Sol Price. (He had admired Sol as one of the pioneers of big box retailing and had kept an eye on him since the days Sol operated his Fed Mart stores.) After his meeting with Sol, Mr. Sam decided to steal (he preferred the term "borrow") the idea. Eager to test the concept, he asked a team of four associates to develop and open a trial Sam's Wholesale Club in a suburb of Oklahoma City. In April, 1983, the first club debuted inauspiciously in an old dilapidated building (the rent was cheap) in Midwest City.

I'll always admire the four guys who got this first unit up and running. They did it very quietly, behind-the-scenes, with very little (or no) computer system support from the company. The merchandise mix, with multiple item packaging and larger sizes, differed considerably from that of Walmart, so the sourcing and distribution power of our company wasn't much help. Rob Voss led the merchandising effort, Dick Palmer the operations issues, and Mike Villines and Clyde Hulett assisted with merchandising and set-up.

That original club in Midwest City, managed by Carl Riche, was a physical disaster. An ancient 106,000 square-foot Woolco/Clark retail building, the floors featured bigger "chug-holes" than the parking lot.

This new concept required the use of forklifts and pallet jacks for receiving and slotting the merchandise, which broke up the thin concrete on the sales floor even more. The roof leaked. The fixtures and walls were all untreated wood, the cheapest available. The signs hung from wire over the counters. Much of the décor (if you could call it that) was intentional to create a "warehouse" atmosphere. The main reason Mr. Sam chose this particular building was the low rent. Though slow to get off the ground (the sales team still had to figure out how to market the memberships), the club started generating enough sales volume to convince Mr. Sam to proceed with two additional Sam's Clubs, which would open in late 1983. The word quickly got around that the prices at Sam's were unbelievably low.

The Pioneers at Sam's

Walmart's Home Office was already packed to the rafters, so our little group moved into space formerly occupied by an old skating rink on Moberly Lane in Bentonville. With two new clubs soon to open, I had no doubt the division would achieve the desired results. In fact, we were already planning for four or five additional clubs in 1984. To make this happen, we needed buyers and support staff immediately.

With Walmart store managers raking in nice bonuses, we couldn't find anyone willing to take a career chance in this unproven, upstart division. The same was true for the buyers' positions. We had no computer system (and no computerized merchandise ordering) and quite frankly, we flew by the seat of our pants those first two years. But it was exciting. Eventually, we staffed the office with what turned out to be a perfect mix of buyers ... some with needed grocery expertise, some pure item merchants, and a few genuine creative geniuses. As with any team, each member brought strengths and weaknesses, but collectively, we jelled. In 1983-84 the original Sam's Home Office (HO) team roster looked like this:

▸ General Manager, Ron Loveless; Merchandising Manager, Rob Voss; Operations Manager, Dick Palmer

- Buyers: David Jones, John Haney, Stan Moore, Larry King, Jim Branam, Mike Laney, Kent Reeves, Ken Hargis, Larry Courtney
- Rebuyers: Pam Houpe, Diana Mankin, Karolyn Cowherd, Cindy Frazier
- Buyer's Assistants: Gail Hopkins, Dona Owens, Nikki Higdon, Valerie McJunkin, Debra Sears, Lanna Myers, Sandy Yandell
- The early store managers included Jerry Oglesbay, Carl Riche, Gary Bilder, Bill Wagner, Russ Robertson, Joel Simon, Kent Rademacher, Hank Geerling, Jan Burd, Marvin Moxley, and Bill Campbell.

During the first few months, I knew we would need more support, such as a computer system, marketing/membership division, and construction. Individuals who played key roles in the early growth of Sam's Clubs included Bob Cheyne and Lori Swenson, Marketing; Jim Townsend and Randy Mott, Information Systems; and Steve Schwitters, Construction. We added many more folks over the next couple of years, and unfortunately I can't mention them all. However, all the people who came to Sam's early on contributed a great deal to the division's success.

The Club Concept and Basics for Success

A number of conceptual basics made these early clubs successful. I always defined the business as "very simple in concept," but "very difficult to execute." The idea was to eliminate or limit costs pertinent to typical retail operations and sell in higher volumes to make a profit on much lower gross margins. Simple, huh? The key elements of the concept included the following:

Limited Assortment. Limit the offering to 3,500 to 5,000 high-volume items, enabling the goods to be off-loaded and slotted in selling space on pallets. This saved labor costs by eliminating the need for individual handling and pricing.

Business Members. We devoted roughly half of our assortment to items appealing to targeted business members. These folks found the prices very attractive compared to the prices they typically paid their distributors. Because business members bought high volumes of product, we made sure we kept these items fully stocked at all times. We targeted restaurants, convenience stores, churches, hair salons, and other independent small businesses known to buy in large quantities.

Treasure Hunt. The balance of the merchandise would be "opportunity buys" of individual consumer items at noticeable savings. Recognizing that the clubs weren't intended to provide a complete assortment of everyday consumer needs and that there was a constant flow of new items, the members were excited to see what they could find on any given trip. It was imperative the items showed significant comparable savings . . . which made the "Treasure Hunt" moniker especially appropriate. We sought items or brands typically found in department stores or specialty shops, carrying a high profit margin. The members reveled in the recognizable savings and considered it a "privilege" to carry a Sam's Membership Card. Our most successful items were those packaged in a size that appealed to both high-volume business members and individual family buyers.

Average 10 Percent Profit Margin. Mr. Sam designed the clubs to operate on an overall average profit margin of 10 percent. A typical retail operation would find it impossible to make a profit on sales with less than a 25–30 percent profit margin. To make a profit, we needed to keep operating costs to less than 10 percent of sales. Not only would we have to keep a tight lid on every typical retail cost, the 5,000 items would need to generate extremely high volumes on a per-item basis. With these narrow margins a fact of life, some clubs would break even on the operating statement, but show a reasonable profit because of "membership income." Then and today, members pay an average of $40 to join a club. When you do the math, it's easy to understand that 100,000 paying members per club results in $4,000,000 profit if the club makes zero profit on sales. Thus the constant effort to attract and retain members. Properly merchandised and operated, members find this fee more than worth it.

Not a Retail Operation. One of the most difficult aspects of this new "wholesale club" concept was to avoid the temptation of carrying the typical "retail assortment and items." Because we used the most recognizable retail brands as "price loss leaders" by discount retailers such as our parent company, we could not give our members savings on items such as Crest toothpaste or Folger's coffee. So we chose not to offer them. When our members asked why, we instructed our managers to simply tell them, "We don't carry that because we can't save you money on the item." They found this explanation satisfactory, and we received few complaints. We understood that the only reason customers would pay us for the privilege of shopping in our clubs was their confidence that we would save them money. Any items that shoppers could find elsewhere for the same or lower price damaged our image. This philosophy, more than anything else, led to the development of private brands in the clubs. For example, a major and strong competitor, Costco, has developed their "Kirkland" brand to represent a competitive high-quality value option. Many of the competing warehouse clubs in these early days gave in to the temptation of carrying typical retail items and they began to fail. This increased their handling costs, created a lower-ticket average purchase, and eliminated their price advantage over typical retailers.

Early Success and Challenges

Although the early clubs' volume started slowly, the momentum quickly increased. Along with success came very real challenges. The original club in Oklahoma City, the second club in Grandview, Missouri (Kansas City area), and the first "prototype design," built from the ground up on Garland Road in Dallas, started generating tremendous volumes. Approaching $1 million in weekly sales (and then in Dallas, achieving $2 million a week), replenishing the merchandise required a great deal of manual work.

We had no warehouses; all shipments came directly to the clubs. We had no computer ordering systems. In fact, the business model was so new that most suppliers offered no items conducive to the club concept. Our team literally built the business the old-fashioned way: day-to-day from the ground up.

Johnny Haney and David Jones worked with major suppliers to develop items that had the potential to generate great volume. I recall the first "warehouse pack" of GE light bulbs containing four 4-packs shrink-wrapped on brown corrugated cardboard, with the words "warehouse pack" in black ink on the back. This became a super volume item for us, because the price saved the consumer approximately 30 percent. At first, GE shied away from making this item for us, because their assembly lines weren't geared for that type of production. I remember assuring them that if they decided to work with us, they'd have no regrets. I think it's safe to say they never did. This is only one example. All of our buyers went the extra mile to create custom items for the early Sam's Wholesale Clubs.

Stan Moore and Larry King became a resourceful team, pioneering the development of the grocery division for Sam's Club. At this time, Walmart had not yet entered the grocery business, so we had no experience or support in this area. Larry had worked for a grocery distributor and brought needed product and pricing experience to us. Stan Moore was an "item merchandising" guru. When the original team opened the first Sam's, they essentially copied Price Club. One item that stood out was a frozen 3-pack pizza, which was sold from a "coffin freezer" on an end cap. We replicated this display and we couldn't keep the item in stock. As we looked at ways to increase our business, we analyzed the grocery assortment offered by retailers and learned that frozen-foods produced higher than average profit margin. As a result, we blazed new trails in the expanded frozen-food and cooler offerings found in all the clubs today.

A Mix of Characters

I fondly recall one incident with Stan and Larry. They had developed and mastered a dance and lip-sync routine to the Blues Brothers — complete with the black suit, shades, briefcase, white socks, and dancing moves made famous in the movie. At a Walmart annual meeting at the Excelsior Hotel in downtown Little Rock, the first to include our new Sam's division, I delivered my LEIR presentation to the entire company. The "Blooze Brothers" followed me. The act brought down the house. It became so popular, the "Blooze" Brothers actually participated in a parade in downtown Bentonville a few months later. Immediately after the meeting, as Stan and Larry walked triumphantly up the stairs from the meeting room, Mr. Sam yelled for them to join him in the lobby eating area. He wanted to discuss topics related to Sam's Clubs. The boys sat down with him in the lobby and Sam ordered them some ice cream. Stan recalls thinking, *Should we take these sunglasses off?* People stopped and stared, but Sam paid them no attention. Picture this in your mind's eye; Sam Walton having a chit-chat with the Blues Brothers over a bowl of ice cream in the middle of a hotel lobby, oblivious to the thousands of Walmart associates walking by. To Mr. Sam, it was business as usual.

Jim Branam was another key merchant we were fortunate to bring in early on. Hiring him was one of the best moves we made. Jim had owned and operated the only large department store in Rogers, where I was living at the time. After Jim closed his store, Sam Walton hired him to work in our Rogers Walmart store to test wearables categories we had not previously carried, such as sports coats and dress slacks. When we started Sam's, we wanted to carry limited apparel, but items and lines that were more upscale than carried by Walmart. We were scouting brands carried by the department stores. With his department store background, Jim developed lines and items for us that generated huge volume. He knew where and how to source the merchandise and everything he bought we "blew" out of the clubs.

While I was GMM at Walmart, we decided to develop a new line of products that we had not previously carried, a 35-mm camera and photo line. I hired Kent Reeves away from Service Merchandise in 1980 to build that business for us. He exceeded my expectations, and I grew to appreciate Kent's abilities. He had since left the company, but I managed to locate him and lure him back to buy for us at Sam's. He, like the rest of our team, contributed a great deal to our early merchandising efforts.

Our merchandise team was led by Rob Voss. I must give most of the credit to Rob for developing the successful merchandise assortment for Sam's. By now you know my background; I am basically a self-described "Arkansas hillbilly." Rob, on the other hand, was more of a "yuppie." Hailing from Springfield, Missouri, Rob, for whatever reason, had an instinctive understanding and awareness of the brands and items that appealed to the higher-income classes. Whether canned pink salmon, Godiva chocolates, Polo shirts or fine wines, he put us into successful items I would never have considered. (Some I didn't even know existed.) It was beyond me why people would pay $79.00 for a box of salmon when I could go down to the banks of Beaver Lake and catch a nice mess of catfish. But Rob proved they would.

However, on one occasion Rob's talent for choosing "uppity" items backfired. This little snafu occurred during the opening of the original Oklahoma City club. Rob and his team decided to copy Price Club and place a stack of fine wines in the front of the store. Well, we didn't do so well with those wines. We soon figured out why. This club was close to the huge Tinker Air Force Base and it soon became obvious to us that our Air Force customers, plus the cowboys and "oil men" in this area, would rather drink beer any day. Another example of the importance of knowing and catering to your local customer base.

A Tough Job

We generated high volume in the start-up Sam's Clubs, but our buyers had to restock the clubs on manual "spreadsheet" order forms. (By manual, I mean on paper with a pencil, one club at a time, weekly). Before we could get the attention and help of the huge Walmart computer systems group, we had opened fifteen Sam's Wholesale Clubs, doing hundreds of millions in yearly volume. Our orders became so voluminous, we literally hauled them over to data entry in two-wheel carts. Once again, I was reminded of what can be accomplished through hard work and long hours.

The early data entry and re-buying group for Sam's was led by Larry Courtney. His support group included Shelly Flannery, Ronda Donald, Kathy Goodpaster, Gina Green, Sue Payne, and Kendra Phillips.

Our Club Managers and Stories

Our early club managers were certainly unique characters and the challenges they faced led to many funny stories. Again, we were "learning on the fly," but that was okay with us. Operations and merchandising guidelines lacked sophistication, to say the least. We gave each manager the creative freedom to get the job done. A few memories from that era stand out in my mind:

Sniper on the Roof. At the south Houston club (an old Gemco building on Gulf Freeway), our manager, Russ Robertson, averaged one car per day stolen from his parking lot. He was flustered and concerned, and that was before his personal car got stolen twice. That's when he decided to do something about it. On one particular visit to his club, I noticed an armed man with binoculars stationed on the roof. Entering the store, I asked Russ what was going on. He explained that he had hired a security guy to monitor the parking lot. I said, "What are you going to do, shoot him?" Soon after, the security guard discovered that the thieves were simply pulling a tow truck into the lot, hooking up the vehicles, and towing them away. Their arrest put an end to the car theft problem.

Better than Sex. We were always looking for ways to motivate our people in the new Sam's Club division. Two days before our Grand Opening in Birmingham, Alabama, I walked into the club and the manager, Hank Geerling, surprised me with the new T-shirts his associates planned to wear for the opening. With the Sam's Wholesale Club logo emblazoned on the front, the lettering on the back announced, "It's better than sex." Flabbergasted, I said, "Hank, they can't wear those! I like it, and it's true, but man, are you crazy?" The joke was on me. It turns out Hank had only made a dozen shirts to set me up. (Hank hung onto the shirts as a keepsake and we were going to display one at the Sam's Club Home Office during the twenty-fifth anniversary event in 2008. But even then, someone deemed it inappropriate and pulled it from the lobby display of memories.) I showed one of the shirts to Mr. Sam at the Birmingham Grand Opening, and he asked if he could have one. I never knew what he did with that shirt.

Location, Location, Location. We decided to build a second club in Dallas on a piece of vacant land. Mr. Sam was not accustomed to paying the much higher prices demanded for land in metropolitan areas, so he insisted on finding the least expensive location. In its infancy, the club business was successful without having to invest in prime retail estate. We opened many clubs in industrial areas. People would drive miles to shop at the clubs and the land was cheaper in these locations. Tom Seay, the Walmart real estate head at the time, bought some reasonably-priced land on Northwest Highway. Too late, we found out why that land was priced so low. As we were digging the foundation for that club, we discovered the property had once been a city dump. The junked cars and other trash made it all but impossible to find a solid foundation. This delayed our opening and caused us to store merchandise all over Dallas while we solved the problem. Eventually, they dug down to bedrock and installed "jacks" to support the floor of the club. At first glance (or even second), the location didn't look all that attractive, either. Two strip clubs and two beer joints were our neighbors across the street. But the members came to shop, and this was a successful club from the outset, with Bob Lamb as the Manager.

The Two-Million Dollar Week. In 1984, our first prototype club on Garland Road in Dallas, managed by Carl Riche, was enjoying an outstanding sales week. In fact, it had a chance to become the first operation in Walmart history to do $2 million in sales in a single week. When Carl and I spoke on the phone, I realized how sweet it would be for Mr. Sam to report in the "Saturday Morning Meeting" that our Dallas club sold $2 million in a single week. So I said, "Carl, whatever you have to do, make that $2 million number." As it turns out, late in the day on Friday with just a couple hours of business left, Carl knew he was going to be $10,000 shy of the mark. He called me at home late Friday night and announced he had just barely gone over the top. I was elated. The next morning, Mr. Sam made a big deal of it. I found out some time later that, in order to satisfy me and obey my demand, Carl had rung up sales on 26 riding lawn mowers just before the deadline expired. He had made a deal with another of our Clubs, which was reversed the following week. But it served its purpose. I chewed him out a little, but just for show. I actually appreciated his "maverick" ingenuity. After all, he was just doing what he was told.

The Jana Jae Story. In 1983, Mr. Sam and I stayed in a hotel in Tulsa while scouting a location for a club. Jim Powers, a sales executive for Handelman Records, who supplied most of the Walmart stores and all the K-Mart stores with music, had told me of an annual music "showcase" being presented that night by Jim Halsey. Jim owned a large country music agency in Tulsa. I asked Mr. Sam if he would like to go, since we had no plans that night. He said, "Why not? What's this country music thing all about anyway?" I paid for the tickets (Mr. Sam never carried much money) and we went to the show.

During the performance, which consisted of each new and/or popular act promoted by the agency, I noticed Mr. Sam constantly scanning the crowd, soaking in the loud, roaring reaction to each artist. One memorable talent was Jana Jae of "Hee Haw" fame, accompanied by her Hot Wire band. Clad in a blue sequined dress and putting on an outstanding performance with her blue fiddle, she received a standing ovation. Toward the end of the show, Mr. Sam turned to me and said, "Ronnie, I can't believe how these people are into this country music. They really get excited, don't they?" I could almost see the wheels turning in his head. Then he asked, "Is there any way we might meet some of these performers?" Of course, I knew Jim Powers could take care of that, so I excused myself and found Jim.

Following the show, Jim escorted Mr. Sam and me backstage, where Sam visited with a number of performers. He spent the longest time chatting with Jana Jae. We left and nothing much was said of the evening, other than Mr. Sam expressing how much he had enjoyed it. A few weeks later, I learned that Jana Jae and her band would be performing at the Sam's Wholesale Club Grand Openings. In fact, they performed at every opening from that point forward. We drew huge crowds. It worked. Sam Walton, ever the student.

Jim Powers has remained a close friend and resides in Punta Gorda, Florida. He served on the CMA Board for a number of years and is well known in the country music industry. I know him as a giving individual and a class guy.

Competition

I have many fond and amusing memories from the start-up days of Sam's Wholesale Club. However, on a serious note, people were noticing our early success. Joe Ellis, the analyst from Goldman-Sachs who had followed Walmart from the beginning, paid particular attention to this new Membership Club industry. He wrote some detailed research papers on Price Club and Sam's. With this attention, many pioneers in the big box retailing industry jumped into the wholesale fray, opening clubs in major metro areas in an attempt to "stake their claim" and "tie up" their respective markets. Following is a list of wholesale club start-ups at that time:

Price Club; based in San Diego, expanded on the west coast

Sam's Wholesale Club; expanded in the south central (Walmart country)

The Wholesale Club; Indianapolis, started by John Geisse (remember Project 79?)

Club Wholesale; Boise, Idaho

Pace Clubs; Denver, Colorado (eventually bought by K-Mart)

Costco; Washington, started by Jim Senegal, ex-Price Club executive

B.J.'s Wholesale Club; started on the east coast

There were other large boxes selling to businesses such as Metro in Chicago and Makro in Cincinnati. In the industry's infancy, companies avoided head-to-head competition if at all possible. But it wouldn't take long for the industry to "shake out." This was a very capital-intensive business, requiring tremendous buying power to succeed and staying power to survive. Plus, the clubs found it necessary to continue to increase the membership base, while refusing to give in to the temptation of carrying typical retail assortments. In just a few years, most of these start-up club operations had closed or were purchased, until only three major competitors survived. Costco bought Price Club, Sam's bought Pace Club from K-Mart, and B. J.'s remained successful on the east coast. The others simply could not survive financially. Costco today is the industry leader in volume. Although I naturally have a special affinity for Sam's Club, I have to admit a great deal of respect and admiration for Jim Sinegal, founder and CEO of Costco. I've never met Jim, but having studied his operation, and read many interviews and profiles, he reminds me of a "Sam Walton" for his company. He's a risk-taker who left Price Club, the pioneers, went up to Washington by himself, and opened his own club. Knowing the hazards and capital requirements of doing that and surviving while the business grew, he deserves much respect for his achievements. Lastly, his coup de gráce would have to be eventually buying his old company, Price Club. Suppliers and associates will tell you that Jim is involved in every detail of the Costco operation, appreciates his people and the suppliers, and understands what drives the success of a "Membership Club" operation better than anyone else in the business today.

The Right Place at the Right Time

I was very fortunate to be in the right place at the right time. By that I mean we had no club competition in the markets we entered in those first three years. As a result, the clubs chugged ahead producing great volume and above average profits. By 1985, rather than begging managers to come to Sam's, they were "standing in line." The Walmart folks now realized that Sam's Wholesale Clubs would become a significant new addition to the company, and they might be exciting places to work.

Greg Johnston, whose family lived down the street from mine in Rogers, grew up playing with my son. I hired Greg to work for Sam's when he was a young assistant manager in the Rogers Walmart store. He progressed through the ranks and became the executive VP of operations for Sam's Clubs in the 1990s. Greg likes to tell a rather humorous story about how I hired him to work for Sam's.

I called Greg at the Rogers Walmart store and asked how he was doing. He indicated that he was okay, but getting a little anxious and burned out. I told him he should come to work for me at Sam's. To make a long story short, Greg accepted my offer at an agreed-upon hourly salary figure of

$10.50, and reported as agreed to our Sam's Club in Tulsa. It was during this time that I had resigned from Sam's and "retired." Unfortunately, I hadn't bothered to inform the Tulsa manager that I had hired Greg. So when Greg strolled into the club and told the manager that "Ron Loveless hired me and said I would be paid $10.50 per hour in a management trainee capacity," the manager thought he was nuts. In no uncertain terms, he explained that he knew nothing of this arrangement, there was no way he would pay him $10.50 an hour, and besides, he had no openings anyway. Taken aback, Greg didn't know what to do; he'd already made living arrangements and was ready to go to work. He had no money to fall back on. So Greg rushed to a telephone, feverishly dialed the Sam's Club office and asked for Ron Loveless. By gosh, he would get this straightened out right now. When the Sam's receptionist answered the phone and heard Greg ask for Ron Loveless, she politely said, "I'm sorry, but Ron Loveless is no longer with the company, sir."

I can imagine what Greg thought at that point. He had made a career change, moved two hours away from his home, and had no job and no prospects. Dire straits, indeed. Of course, he did reach me at home, I straightened out the manager and everyone else, and the whole episode ended happily.Greg, as I've mentioned, moved up through the ranks and eventually became executive vice-president of operations for the entire Sam's Club division. I was so proud of Greg; the little neighbor boy down the street makes good.

This type of success story could be told of literally hundreds of Walmart and Sam's associates through the years. I can't think of another company in any industry that comes close to promoting as many hourly associates to long and successful retail executive careers.

Doug McMillon, the eventual CEO of Sam's Club's in the 2000s, started as an hourly associate in the Walmart stores, just like me and many others. I look back on these first three years of Sam's growth and get the greatest satisfaction from knowing how many lives our start-up operation changed for the better.

In early 1986, the Sam's division was poised to exceed $1 billion in sales. We were well-established with the necessary support functions in place, the supplier community offering an increasing number of items designed for the club concept, and the beginning of warehouse/distribution support to provide high-volume replenishment efficiencies. I was pleased with what my team and I had accomplished. Unfortunately, I couldn't say the same about my home life.

The Family and Personal Pressures

In 1983, I had an affair that ended in a divorce from Cindy the following year. Regardless of who might be at fault in the dissolution of a marriage, it's one of the most traumatic experiences a person can go through. Our children were still in high school. Watching what this did to them emotionally has been my greatest regret in life. Although once again happily married, I would counsel anyone to expend every effort to avoid divorce if humanly possible, particularly when children are involved. In the last chapter of this book, I will go into more detail concerning this period in my life. Not surprisingly, this situation spilled over into the workplace, creating a great deal of additional stress.

Also in 1983, while attending the Consumer Electronics Show in Las Vegas, I was overcome by an unknown illness that sent me to the hospital. After two bed-ridden days in my hotel room, Johnny Haney, my roommate and Sam's buyer, called the paramedics. They transported me to Humana hospital, where specialists ran every test in the book, only to wind up scratching their heads. I don't remember any of this because I was unconscious for two weeks. Sam Walton flew my family out, and assigned Joe Hatfield to stay in Las Vegas to ensure that I received the best of care. Joe was a great guy, a close friend, who served in many positions at Walmart. (He later became president, Walmart, China.)

Eventually, doctors diagnosed my condition as viral encephalitis (sleeping sickness), which is usually contracted from mosquito bites. I had been to the Northwest Territories on a fishing trip with Harold Ensley a few months before, where I was eaten alive by mosquitoes. This was most likely the cause of my illness. The malady results in swelling of the brain, which can be deadly if not treated appropriately with antibiotics. Memory loss is quite common. I eventually woke from my coma, saw my family sitting there, and didn't remember a thing that had happened from the time I arrived in Las Vegas. Like a character in a movie, I simply said, "What are you all doing here? Where am I?"

Following this medical problem, I recall having a much harder time handling the day-to-day stress of my job and family issues. I can't say whether the condition was a contributor or just an excuse, but the problem was real. Life was wearing on me, and when I had a particularly rough run-in with one of the Walmart management folks in early 1986, I decided it might be an appropriate time to do something I had always wanted to do . . . work in the world of entertainment.

My "Retirement"

Because Sam Walton had hired me, I felt I should resign only to him. I owed him that courtesy. I figured (or hoped) that he might try to talk me out of leaving, so I made sure in my mind that it was my final decision, regardless of what Mr. Sam might say. I could see the shock and surprise on his face. As expected, he did his best to convince me to stay. I know he was disappointed. But once he realized I'd made up my mind, he said, "Ronnie, I wish you the best of luck. I think you're making a big mistake. But we're the kind of company that when someone leaves, it simply opens up an opportunity for someone else. I hope you're not leaving because of any person in particular. We all have bosses. I have bosses — the board and the shareholders. It's not easy getting along with everyone. Just be sure you're leaving because you want to, and not because of some *one* individual."

I actually wasn't "retiring." That is the term the company used. But I can tell you, as life turned out, I left much too early and at far too young an age . . . forty-two-years-old.

My experience building the Sam's Wholesale Club Division was the most exciting of my career, excluding problems and difficulties in my personal and family life. All that I had learned, the associations within the company that I had made, and the support and trust of the executive management team culminated in a successful new venture for the company — an achievement of which I am very proud. I also recognize that a number of other folks within Walmart could have done that job equally well, given the opportunity. Any successful business becomes so because of the people involved. The leader is just the "coach." The team makes it work. So it was with Sam's.

> Here lies one who knew how to get around him men
> who were cleverer than himself.
> — ANDREW CARNEGIE

> The genius of a good leader is to leave behind him a situation
> which common sense, without the grace of genius,
> can deal with successfully.
> — WALTER LIPPMANN

> It's an unbelievable responsibility to influence decisions,
> shareholder value and, most important to me,
> people's careers and livelihoods.
> — ANDREA JUNG

PART THREE
UNDERSTANDING
WALMART'S SUCCESS

CHAPTER 13

Walmart's Top Ten Building Blocks for Success

ozens of books and thousands of articles have been written about Walmart. Nothing you are about to read here represents new or secret insights into the company's success. The points I make in this chapter come from my twenty-two years of experiencing first-hand the growth of the company from a little store on the Bentonville town square to the global giant of today. I have developed my own opinion of the key elements that made Walmart the largest company in the world.

Top Ten Building Blocks

In order of importance, these are the components I consider instrumental to Walmart's explosive growth and ultimate success:

1) Leadership

Sam, Helen, and Bud Walton were truly unique and charismatic leaders. Every successful company starts with a leader's vision that fulfills a need in the marketplace. The leader is filled with passion for the business, is normally a workaholic, and is driven by a desire to be the best at his/ her chosen pursuit. But Sam Walton's most important attribute was his uncanny knack for selecting the right people at the right time to manage the business. Mr. Sam "knew what he didn't know." He kept his eye on every detail. He empowered and motivated his management folks to do what was right for the company and ensured they were amply rewarded for the successes they achieved. Leaders in other companies exhibit many of the same attributes: Herb Kelleher, Southwest Airlines; Ingvar Kamprad, IKEA; Henry Ford; Michael Dell; Bill Gates; and Steve Jobs. These qualities aren't just limited to men; noted female entrepreneurs include the likes of Mary Kay Ash and Oprah Winfrey. These iconic men and women left their mark on the American landscape by revolutionizing their industries. The corporate culture and "servant leadership" exhibited by Sam Walton drove Walmart's success from the very beginning.

2) "Our People Make the Difference"

This company motto, officially adopted as our slogan in 1980 — our billion dollar year — was the foundation of Sam Walton's management philosophy. Long after we moved on to other slogans, Mr. Sam proudly sported his "Our People Make the Difference" lapel button. I've read every column Mr. Sam wrote for the intercompany newspaper, the *Wal-Mart World*. In every single one of those articles (some 300 issues), he mentioned the importance of the people in the stores and how we owed our success to them. In addition, he always mentioned the importance of taking care of customers. You see, Mr. Sam realized that if we took care of the associates, they would take care of the customers. In his opinion "Our People Make the Difference" served as the true catalyst for the company's success.

And he believed in that slogan. Many times I sat in executive meetings at the Home Office when we were feeling pretty good about ourselves. At these times, Mr. Sam took great pains to remind us, "You guys just remember that none of you would have a job and there'd be no need for a headquarters building without those wonderful people out in the stores!" That brought us down to earth very quickly. During the extremely competitive head-to-head competition with K-Mart in its heyday, the customer consensus was that they "felt a different atmosphere" when they entered a Walmart. Customers said our people were friendlier and conveyed an upbeat feeling. Much more than a slogan, our people "Truly Did Make the Difference."

3) Focus on Customers

Sam Walton founded the company with his favorite adage in mind: "Rule #1 – The customer is always right. Rule #2 – If the customer happens to be wrong, refer to Rule #1." Again, in every article he wrote for the *Wal-Mart World*, he always mentioned the importance of customers. My favorite bit of business relationship guidance is to "think like a customer." As business people, we make most of our mistakes when we forget to practice this simple step. The company created what they called the "Ten-Foot Rule." In a 1989 editorial, Mr. Sam wrote, "Let's renew our promise that 'every time customers come within ten feet of me, regardless of what I am doing, I'll look them in the eyes, smile, and greet them.'" Mr. Sam also said, "This is a proven fact — it costs five times more to gain a new customer as it does to retain a current customer. A dissatisfied customer is generally lost forever to us and probably with a host of their friends as well." The following note from an anonymous writer in the 1960s is as pertinent today as any time in history.

Ten Commandments of Satisfying Customers

▸ Our customers are our most valuable asset — and the most important people in our business.

▸ Our customers are NOT dependent on us — we are dependent on them. They don't owe us any favors.

▸ Our customers are the purpose of our work — without them there would be no jobs.

▸ Our customers are not just names, but flesh and blood human beings who have as much right to be satisfied as ourselves.

▸ Our customers are not outsiders — but a very necessary part of our business.

▸ Our customers do *us* a favor when they buy what we have to sell and we owe it to them to see that they are completely satisfied.

▸ Our customers are free to take their business wherever they wish — whenever we fail to satisfy them.

▸ Our satisfied customers are an army of AMBASSADORS OF GOOD WILL for our company.

▸ Our profits and our jobs depend not only on getting customers — but keeping them satisfied with everything we do on their behalf.

▸ Satisfied customers are the life blood of our business — and every business in America — for without them there would be no business.

My advice to anyone in business is to "think like a customer" with everything you consider doing. Whether it's designing a new package for a product, visiting a store as a supervisor, or planning a new store layout, if you're thinking like a customer you'll find you don't need a committee full of high-priced consultants and so-called experts.

4) Expense Control

Many companies preceded Walmart in the retail business and the discount-store industry. In fact, it seems Walmart should never have been able to achieve what it has, considering the head-starts by Sears, K-Mart, and others. Besides seizing the opportunity in smaller markets, an integral key to our success was the founder's obsession with expense control. Call it "tight-fisted, miserly, chintzy," or whatever you like, but the fact was we could sell merchandise at lower prices than our competitors because we spent less, and passed the savings on to the customers. Critics would have you believe that included under-paying the associates ... but that's simply not true. An hourly associate position in retailing has never been a high-paying position relative to other industries. Over the years, Walmart paid as well as anyone else in the business — above minimum wage, depending on the position. When you added the profit-sharing program, bonuses, health care programs, and other incentives, our people actually earned more than most retailers paid. It's not something anyone likes to face up to, but an hourly wage for a stock boy to gather carts from the lot, or to sweep the sidewalk or clean the restrooms, should not require the same wage as someone responsible for ordering the right merchandise, managing and evaluating people, or making management decisions. Pay is rightfully determined by level of responsibility. I can speak to this, because I was the stock boy, the department manager, and all of the above. I, too, made the low wages and struggled. But I never felt abused. I knew that if I worked harder and did a good job, I would reap the benefits later.

The expense control philosophy actually started with the cost of entry — land and buildings. The resulting lower overhead costs proved advantageous. In addition, Walmart utilized the following expense controls: keeping advertising costs lower than any in the industry, running one circular per month instead of one each week; limiting television advertising; maintaining a distribution system and strategy that enabled us to replenish the stores at a lower cost than anyone in the industry; not building a vanity headquarters such as the Sears Tower or KIH (K-Mart International Headquarters in Troy, Michigan); and keeping travel costs to a bare minimum. The list goes on and on. But the company philosophy and culture stemmed from the understanding that every dollar expended required fifteen dollars in sales to atone.

I'll never forget a meeting one of my fellow district managers conducted with hourly associates in one of our stores. He held up a one-dollar bill and asked the associates, "How many cents of this dollar do you think the company puts in the bank in profits?" The answers ranged from a low of thirty-four cents to a high of eighty cents. The correct answer was six cents ... before taxes. You should have seen their astonished expressions. His point was that every dollar lost for whatever reason — shrinkage, theft, errors, or expenses, could spell the difference between profitability and losses.

To understand how deeply ingrained the expense control culture is in the company, I must mention why the company name was chosen in the first place. The story goes that Bob Bogle ultimately decided on Walmart because it didn't have many letters and "would be cheaper to light up at night." This may indeed be urban legend … but it would certainly fit Mr. Sam's thinking and philosophy.

I hesitate to criticize the company today. Because my day-to-day involvement ended years ago, I have no right to do that. But I *do* know the company spends millions of dollars on input from agencies and consultants that could be obtained at no charge from very capable people within the organization. A Walmart pilot recently shared with me that they fly empty jets around the country to pick up one person. Not too many years ago, a company plane couldn't leave the ground unless every seat was filled. Walmart's ability to remain the "price leader" is directly dependent on saving every expense dollar possible. There's no longer a true price advantage from suppliers. They generally offer the same pricing to all the "big box" retailers. The only way to maintain price leadership is to sell at lower margins.

5) Communications

From the very beginning, Sam Walton knew he couldn't earn the trust and interest of the associates without sharing the business numbers with them. Through daily store meetings, all associates knew where their stores and/or departments stood regarding sales and budgets. Constant awareness encouraged them to do their best and take pride in their accomplishments. (And they were recognized when they excelled.) We were transparent when transparency wasn't cool. Walmart introduced programs through the years that ensured the steady flow of information: the Grass Roots program, the Open Door policy, and the *Wal-Mart World* newspaper, to name a few. At the management level, the Friday merchandise meetings, Saturday morning meetings, priority notes, weekly conference calls, and other intra-company programs facilitated communication throughout the company. *Managing by the Open Book*, by John Case, refers to this mode of operation as "Open Book" management. I believe Sam Walton epitomized this style (or maybe even created it). Author and consultant Tom Peters says, "The average employee can deliver far more than his or her current job demands and far more than the terms 'employee empowerment,' 'participative management,' and 'multiple skills' imply. The more open the company is with numbers, goals and results, the more an integral part the average associate feels."

6) Ethics

One of the first pages of the Buyer's Training Manual I developed in 1979 was devoted to the company's "Code of Ethics." This page clearly defined the expectations and importance of ethics in the conduct of our business. Over the years, Walmart became notorious for a very strict policy regarding the ban on accepting gifts, meals, drinks, or any favor from suppliers. The price of a cup of coffee was never the issue; rather, the concern was where it could lead. Through the years, many suppliers told me of cases with other major retailers where favors and gifts were *expected*, and many merchandising decisions were made based on how much the buyer could personally benefit from the transaction.

Promoting "ethics" within the Walmart organization went further than banning gifts and favors. Walmart's ethics (principals of conduct governing the organization) included values such as integrity, respect, trust, dignity, and responsibility. Walmart always strived to promote these qualities. Sure, mistakes were made; the company consisted of human beings. I admittedly made my share. However, we laid the foundation of ethical business from the beginning. I credit executives Don Soderquist and Paul Carter with championing the high ethical standards to which we aspired. The effort to be an "ethical" company was a key ingredient to our success.

7) Distribution and Information Systems

Without a doubt, the evolution of the Walmart warehouse/trucking distribution system gave the company an advantage over the competition that continues to this day. The philosophy of building warehouses that could service from sixty to one hundred stores within a day's reach of our trucks — called the "hub and spoke" concept — enabled our stores to rapidly and efficiently replenish inventories at a much lower cost than any competitor. We would build a new warehouse at the fringe of our existing trade territory; then add stores around that warehouse location.

Secondly, investing in and building out the information/data processing system well ahead of our major competitors positioned the company for rapid, limitless, and controlled expansion. The real-time gathering, processing, and reporting of item sales in every store every minute of every day boggles my mind. I've heard that the information capacity of the Walmart Information System is second only to the federal government. Today it may be larger. It's certainly more efficient.

8) Corporate Structure

Sam Walton's insistence on maintaining a balance of power between the operating and merchandising functions of the company, in my opinion, is of prime importance to Walmart's continued success. Many of the early competitors in the discount arena failed by being overly focused on operations at the expense of merchandising — or vice versa. A successful retail operation must be equally strong in both factions. Occasionally, during Walmart's growth, this balance might swing too far in one direction or the other. But we corrected it quickly before serious problems arose. That's not to say that maintaining balance was easy. With the need for a strong and experienced executive in either role, conflicts can and will arise. It's the supervisor's role to step in and make the ultimate decision when an impasse occurs.

A retail company that allows its merchandising division to plan every inch of space for every store, purchase and distribute every item for every season, with no input and prior information from operations, is asking for a host of problems. The result is sure to be fewer sales and higher clearance markdowns. On the other hand, if the operations division has final authority to determine what programs go into the stores, they will miss out on trends, new products, and shifting consumer demands.

9) Supplier Relationships

Walmart's buyers have long been recognized as "tough but fair." Most suppliers I spoke with over the years said that Walmart is, overall, more equitable to work with than most competitors. Some vendors will always believe they were mistreated and, frankly, there have been occasional buyers and management folks who failed to "do the right thing." But I have personally seen Sam Walton and other top management officers go out of their way to make decisions they felt were fair when conflicts did arise with suppliers. This was simply part of our company culture.

During the '70s and early '80s, we were still receiving orders and paying invoices on "paper." At one time it was said that Walmart's mail, in sheer volume, was greater than that of the Little Rock Post Office. We literally employed hundreds of associates to open the mail and match invoices to receiving documents. The sheer volume resulted in late payments to suppliers. This hurt our reputation at the time, but it was never intentional. Once we implemented EDI (Electronic Data Interchange) and computer invoice payments, our track record set the standard for the industry.

Most of the suppliers who have had bad experiences with the company did so because they were unaware of the complexities of dealing with a large retailer; many were simply too small to sell to the company in the first place.

10) "Profit" Is Not a Bad Word

As Walmart has become the largest company in the world, critics have loudly proclaimed its profits "obscene." As I write this, the liberal "left" in Washington and the media are generating headlines decrying corporate America's greed and profit. They espouse that profits should be taken away and shared with the masses. At the same time, they advocate job creation. This infuriates me. Most politicians have never started or grown a business, never created a job, and never understood how or why the free enterprise system drives the economy. Yet they are in a position to make decisions and enact laws which hamper the very companies that produce jobs and prosperity. I have a question for them. How many jobs will be created by companies that do not make a profit? Without a profit, companies fail. Without a profit, companies eliminate jobs. Without a profit, companies can't offer health care to employees. I believe this is called "common sense," something too many politicians lack. Walmart has always focused on making a profit. This is not only good business, it has enabled the company to grow, create wealth for associates, offer the shopping public a more affordable standard of living, and support communities in a myriad of other ways. Companies that make profits are also known for their charitable giving. Most charities are dependent on corporate donations to keep their doors open. This is another facet of the free enterprise system the politicians don't seem to understand. Those of us close to Walmart know the width and depth of their charitable activities through the Walmart Foundation. The media does little to point out theses positives.

These are my chosen Top Ten building blocks, gleaned from twenty-two years of experience with the company. I could write a book on any one of these key points. There's no shortage of business gurus who make a good living studying the successful companies in this country and sharing their findings with the business community. I've read many, if not most, of them. The authors use neat "buzzwords" and "acronyms" adopted for best business practices. Reading and learning all we can from these books and experts is good. We can always discover something new. But I once read a little adage that does a better job of summing up my feelings:

> The average man has five senses: touch, taste, smell, sight and hearing. The successful man has two more:
> HORSE AND COMMON.

Business school graduates enter the workplace with some useful and necessary book-learnin' (as we say in Arkansas), but I would challenge them to remember that retailing "ain't rocket science." You can't make it in the business arena on formal education alone. I believe successful and rewarding careers in retail combine formal education with the following: plenty of hard work, attention to detail, focus on the customer, experience, self-education, and common sense. Walmart became the largest company in the world thanks to a leader and a large group of ordinary folks with a strong work ethic and a healthy dose of common sense.

CHAPTER 14:

Sam Walton, a Unique Leader

Leadership is based on a spiritual quality; the power to inspire, the power to inspire others to follow.

— VINCE LOMBARDI

Just as the details of Walmart's success have been widely studied and published, so have the history and life of its founder, Sam Walton. Any of the executives and original managers could fill a book with his or her stories of Mr. Sam. As you've learned through this account of my career, he demanded performance. He was a tough taskmaster. Yet he was, in some ways, naïve. He mixed pleasure with business. He loved people. I always described Mr. Sam as an enigmatic personality. You never quite knew how he might respond to a given situation. He challenged you to try new things, yet wasn't too tolerant of mistakes. He challenged every dollar of expense, yet begrudgingly approved expenditures if you could convince him of their necessity. He was proud of others' accomplishments and quick to recognize them publicly, yet was just as quick to dole out punishment and criticism for something he felt was detrimental to the company.

As I stated early in this book, Mr. Sam became a father-figure to me. I was raised without a father, so I did not experience the elements of a father/son relationship from a son's perspective. To me, Mr. Sam was mentor, disciplinarian, and role model. I relished his praise, and felt crushed by his criticism. Most importantly, I knew that he supported me when others didn't. I suppose these feelings are similar to those felt by a son toward his father. At least I hope my son, Ronnie, feels the same way toward me today.

With this brief background, I offer my personal view of Mr. Sam garnered from my experiences.

Forever the Student

> The Only Thing I Know is That I Know Nothing.
> — SOCRATES

I often read this quote, posted on the wall of Jack Kahl's office in Cleveland. Jack, a good friend, was a Walmart supplier. (You'll read more about him in Chapter 20.) Every time I saw this sign, I thought of Sam Walton. He always sought to learn more about the business and recognized that he didn't know it all. Although I doubt he thought of himself as one, it was very clear to me that he achieved his success by "being a student" of retailing. From his days as a management trainee at J.C. Penny to his time spent building the largest retail company in the world, Mr. Sam was never satisfied with the status quo. He was forever studying the competition, asking questions of his associates, business colleagues, suppliers and executives — always on a quest for new ways to improve his business.

At Walmart, we copied our original checkout merchandising program from K-Mart. Many of our 1980s prototype stores evolved from Project 79, which contained merchandising techniques from the Target and Venture stores developed by John Geisse. The original Sam's Clubs were based on Price Club. The Supercenter concept driving the company today originated from Mr. Sam's exposure to the Hypermarche concept in Europe and evolved from the brief Walmart HyperMart venture. We like to think we improved on the original ideas lifted from competitors, but about the only concept unique to Walmart was how we brought "big box" discounting to small town America.

An example of Sam Walton's constant search for improvement and his charismatic charm would be the Cooperative Research Group he managed to put together in the 1970s. Walmart was still considered a small regional discounter, while other discount store chains operated successfully in their own larger metro markets. Having agreed to share mutual operating successes and strategies, the leaders of the companies participating in this research group did not consider Sam Walton's up-start chain to be a future competitor. Mr. Sam was able to convince them to help each other improve by conducting reciprocal meetings that in-volved store tours and a critique of one another's operations. The group included Ames Dept. Store, Inc., Fred Meyer Shopping Centers, Hart Stores, Inc., Shopko Stores, Inc., and Jamesway Corporation. Mr. Sam and the company learned a lot from this short-lived consortium. Of course, as Walmart went public and it became obvious the company was on the verge of becoming a significant player, this group disbanded rather quickly.

Jack Shewmaker tells the story of his trip to Europe in 1980 with his wife, Melba, and Mr. Sam. The purpose of the trip was to make presenta-tions to the investment community to promote Walmart stock. But as with any trip, Mr. Sam's primary interest lay in visiting all the retail stores he could find. They visited German stores such as MASSA and Vertkauf. They then went to Paris, touring several Carrefour operations, the largest retailer in France. Then on to England and Scotland, where they checked out retailers such as Asda, Marks and Spencer, British Home Stores, and Mother Care stores. Forever the student, Mr. Sam undoubtedly memo-rized everything he saw. Today Walmart owns Asda in Great Britain and operates Supercenters, a smaller version of the Hypermarches found in Europe. I would say it's not just a coincidence.

It's a known fact that Mr. Sam frequently went into competitors' stores to charm a sales clerk into opening up and sharing information with him. I hardly had the gall to do that, but it was just a part of Mr. Sam's makeup.

With his down-home manner and gregarious nature, people flat out liked him.

I learned a good lesson from him when I was a district manager in Kansas City. One of the best K-Mart stores in volume and profit was located on Metcalf Avenue in Overland Park. On one trip to my district, Mr. Sam had scheduled a meeting somewhere and told me, while he was gone, to visit that K-Mart store and report back to him. I went to the store and found it an overstocked disorganized mess. Later in the day, he asked me what I had seen in the K-Mart store.

I said, "Mr. Sam, I couldn't be less impressed. It was dirty, messy, and just plain awful. I can't imagine why it's one of their best."

We were in the parking lot of a McDonald's. Standing face-to-face, he looked me in the eye and said, "Ronnie, I don't know why I ever hired you. You're telling me that you were in the best store K-Mart has, and you came out of there without a list of items we could sell the hell out of? I'll tell you what I want from you. I want you to go back in that store and send me a report on what you find that they're doing better than us. And I want a list of items they're selling well that we don't have. Do you understand me?" I understood all right. I sent him that report and list lickety split. I learned a lesson that day I would never forget. Always be a student.

The Jana Jae story is another example of that philosophy. When Mr. Sam discovered how rabid country music fans could be, he immediately saw it as a way to draw people to his stores. So he tested the idea at his Grand Openings.

The noted "Walmart cheer" resulted from a trip to Korea, where Mr. Sam observed company employees participating in a cheer. He felt it was motivational then, and it still is.

Walmart was not always successful with its various experiments and formats. Savco (building supplies), Helen's (craft stores), Dart Drug, HyperMarts, and other brief forays into specialty operations all failed. But, like Thomas Edison, we learned from each effort. Mr. Sam kept trying because he was "forever the student."

Frugality

Mr. Sam was noted for his frugality and aversion to spending unnecessary dollars for anything, with the possible exceptions of bird-hunting and tennis. His 1984 pickup truck, torn up by his bird dogs, his old Chevy with crushed fenders and bumpers, his used airplanes and spartan offices, all served as examples of his belief that material things were just a necessary evil. He didn't understand why anyone felt the need to spend money on big homes, fancy cars, hotel suites, or expensive dinners. It wasn't just a façade — it was truly the way he felt.

"We're not ashamed of having money, but I just don't believe a big showy lifestyle is appropriate anywhere, least of all here in Bentonville where folks work hard for their money and where we all know that everyone puts on their trousers one leg at a time," he explained in his biography. When the media made a big deal out of Mr. Sam driving an old pickup, he said, "What did they expect me to haul my bird dogs around in, a Rolls-Royce?" Regarding the company, he said, "Now, when it comes to Walmart, there's no two ways about it; I'm cheap. On the road we sleep two to a room, although as I've gotten older I have finally started staying in my own room. We stay in Holiday Inns and Ramada Inns and Days Inns, and we eat a lot at family restaurants — when we have time to eat. A lot of what goes on these days with high-flying companies and their overpaid CEOs who're really just looting from the top and aren't watching out for anybody but themselves really upsets me. It's one of the main things wrong with American business today.

But sometimes I'm asked why today, when Walmart has been so successful, when we're a $50 billion dollar plus company, should we stay so cheap? That's simple; because we believe in the value of a dollar. We exist to provide value to our customers, which means that in addition to quality and service, we have to save them money. Every time Walmart spends one dollar foolishly, it comes right out of the customers' pockets. Every time we save them a dollar, that puts us one step ahead of the competition

— which is where we always plan to be." (These comments are excerpts from *Sam Walton, Made In America* by Sam Walton with John Huey.)

All of us who traveled with Mr. Sam could tell numerous stories relating to his thrifty persona. Most of them would be similar. Countless times, we'd pick up the tab for meals, because he would often forget to carry cash with him. As far as I know, he never rented a car when visiting his stores. He'd ask someone to pick him up at whatever small town airport he flew into or just hitch a ride into town with a complete stranger. We were careful to make sure we used a company car or an unimpressive family vehicle when we went to get him. We considered it a tactical error to pick him up in a Cadillac or Lincoln or some other fancy car he might think was "too big for our britches."

Jack Shewmaker — on his trip with Mr. Sam to Europe

On the European trip with Jack and Melba Shewmaker, Jack says Mr. Sam rented a Volkswagen Golf in Frankfurt, Germany. They loaded it down with the three of them, a ton of assorted luggage, and numerous boxes of presentation materials for their meetings with investors. They then drove the Volkswagen to Paris on the Autobahn, where the speed limit greatly exceeded the Golf's capability. They felt like they were standing still as Porsches and Mercedes-Benzes tore past them. On arrival in Paris, they made their way to the Plaza Athenee, a fancy hotel their host had booked for them. Most of the vehicles parked in front of the hotel were limousines. Jack and Mr. Sam got out of their rented Volkswagen and unloaded their array of mismatched luggage, tennis rackets, and cardboard boxes, much to the chagrin of the doorman in tie and tails. Mr. Sam said he would handle the tip — searched around in his pockets — handed the doorman a U.S. quarter — and said, "Gracias." According to Jack, the doorman never spoke to them again.

My Porsche Story

Without a doubt, my favorite anecdote about Mr. Sam and his frugality is my Porsche story. When people ask me to describe Sam Walton, it's the first thing that comes to mind. Because of Mr. Sam's iconic business status, people think his lack of attention to money and the finer things in life was just a "put-on." In fact, in some ways he was almost naïve. So I tell my story.

About once every two months at the Saturday morning meetings, Mr. Sam would give what some of us referred to as his "frugality speech." It was largely repetitive and always went something like this:

"Now fellas, I know I can't tell you how to live your lives, and wouldn't tell you what kind of car you should drive. But I've noticed lately a few more big Cadillacs and Lincolns here and there in the lot. But we're here in Bentonville, and I just don't think it would look good to our customers and associates to see a sea of big cars filling our lot. So I'd like for you to think about how this looks." We got the message, and most of us became hesitant to buy a fancy new car. We knew Mr. Sam considered it a negative.

In 1981, while running merchandising, I was doing okay financially and had always wanted to own a sports car. Rob Voss had a brother in Springfield who owned an exotic car dealership. Although I feared Sam Walton would find out I had splurged on a new sports car, I bought a brand new Porsche — solid black, gold wheels, moon roof — the "cat's meow," man. I was so proud of it, but for months I kept it away from work for fear that Mr. Sam might see it. I honestly believed it might get me fired or at least make Mr. Sam think less of me. One Saturday morning, I told my wife that it was silly to own this beautiful car and not drive it to work and show it off. Since Mr. Sam got to his office between 4:00 and 5:00 in the morning, and I didn't get in until about 6:30, I figured he wouldn't see me drive up . . . no problem. So that Saturday morning I drove my new Porsche to work.

Just as I pulled into the parking lot at the far right end of the Home Office building, the old red pickup truck parked right beside me. It was Mr. Sam. Just my luck, he was running late that morning. Busted! Oh, my gosh! I thought, *this is it; I'm in big time trouble now.* I got out of my car, ready to face the music. Mr. Sam glanced at the Porsche, then me, and said, "Morning, Ronnie, how's sales?"

"We had a great week, Mr. Sam," I replied. Neither of us said another word as we walked into the office.

The Saturday morning meeting started, and as usual, Mr. Sam led the way. Then, (coincidence?) he broke into his "frugality speech."

"Now fellas," he said, "you know how I feel about buying big new cars and how it might look to the public around here." Oh no, I thought, *he is going to single me out right here in front of everybody. I'm as good as gone.* He went on to say, "Now I saw Ronnie getting out of a new car this morning. I don't know if it was his, but it was one of those small economy cars. That's setting a good example."

You could hear snickers all over the room, as I went from shrinking into my seat to sitting up proudly, totally relieved — from a goat to a hero in just a few seconds. I love to tell this story on Mr. Sam. To him, big was expensive and small was economy ... simple as that. That Porsche cost twice what a Cadillac cost, but he didn't know enough about sports cars to understand the difference. I'm sure at some point someone might have told him, but he never mentioned it to me.

I like this automobile story, too:

Mr. Sam's wife, Helen, wanted to buy a new Lincoln Town Car. She made a deal with a local dealer to bring it over to the Home Office and have Mr. Sam write a check for it. The dealer delivered the car and Loretta Boss, Sam's secretary, escorted him into the office. Mr. Sam examined the invoice with a raised eyebrow and said, "How many cars is Helen buying?"

"One," said the dealer.

"One car can't cost this much," Sam said, incredulous at the price. He refused to pay and told the dealer to get out and take the car with him. Helen went back to the dealership the next day and bought the car anyway.

When Sam and Helen's house burned down as the result of a lightning strike in 1972, they moved a trailer house onto the property for temporary quarters. A local friend of the family told me that Sam was in no hurry to rebuild. He was perfectly content in the trailer. After all, his tennis court wasn't damaged. I honestly don't know if that's true or not, but I was told that Ferold Arend, the president of Walmart at the time, helped Helen handle the details of designing and rebuilding their home. Mr. Sam simply didn't have time and it wasn't that important to him. Knowing him as I did, it wouldn't surprise me one bit.

An Infamous Driver and Pilot

Those of us who knew or spent much time with Mr. Sam have all experienced "white-knuckle" times with him when he was flying a plane or driving his vehicle. He may have been a good pilot, but he did some stupid things. As for driving, let's just say he was very lucky. With his obsession for business and his inquisitive mind, it's no wonder he found it hard to focus on the tasks at hand.

Through the years, Mr. Sam spent many, many hours at the controls of his various aircraft. His original plane, an Ercoupe, he purchased for $1800, and the plane is still maintained in Bentonville as part of Walmart's history. He went on to a second plane, a Tripacer, and eventually a Piper Navajo, in which I experienced personal time with Mr. Sam.

My first-hand experiences are limited, but hundreds of similar stories could be told by anyone who flew with him. The first time, he put me in the right front co-pilot seat and we took off from the Bentonville airport. As soon as we lifted off, climbing toward altitude, Mr. Sam unbuckled his seatbelt and said, "Ronnie, take over for a minute, will you? I want to get the P & Ls (Profit and Loss Statements) out of my briefcase." With that, he climbed out of the seat and disappeared into the rear of the plane. In terror, I grabbed the "steering wheel" and just hung on as tight as I could, trying not to push it forward or pull it backward. I had flown considerable hours in the right seat with our Walmart pilots, and did understand the basics. But climbing out of a takeoff and not knowing where or what I was supposed to be doing made me break out in a cold sweat. Mr. Sam may have been gone only two or three minutes, but it seemed like hours to me. Still, I managed to act as if nothing was wrong. Besides, the plane was still upright.

I experienced yet another example of Mr. Sam's impatience in an airplane when I was a regional VP over parts of Kansas and Missouri in 1979. That was the year our Arkansas Razorbacks went to the finals of the NCAA regional basketball tournament and played number one-ranked Indiana State with their star, Larry Bird. The big game took place in Lawrence, Kansas. My assignment was to pick up Sam Walton and his entourage at the private airport there. This airport was way too small to handle the influx of private aircraft coming in for the big game, which included Mr. Sam with a planeload of folks and his son, Rob, with another.

I waited and waited in the FBO. The congestion in the approach pattern messed up everyone's schedules. With only an hour left before game time, I overheard two men coming out of the FBO, ranting about some S.O.B. who almost caused a mid-air collision. I didn't think much of it, until I ventured inside to ask about the status of an inbound flight from Arkansas. The harassed FBO manager informed me that the aircraft had just landed. The bad news? The pilot had done so by cutting directly in front of two other planes ahead of him in the landing order. About that time, in walked Mr. Sam, apologizing profusely, but managing to avoid any repercussions by saying, "Ronnie, let's hurry. Hope we're not too late for the start of the game." (Calm as you please, as if nothing out of the ordinary had happened.)

While serving as district manager in 1976, I was told to pick up Mr. Sam at the Manhattan, Kansas airport. Once again, his plane was considerably past due. Finally, the FBO manager handed me a phone. It was Mr. Sam, who said, "Ronnie, we had a little mix-up. Could you come get me at the military airport in Junction City?"

I came to find out that Mr. Sam had landed at an "off-limits" air strip on the Fort Riley army training base, a restricted runway used for helicopter training exercises. Mr. Sam, it turns out, had gotten a wee bit confused. When I arrived, the authorities made me wait for some time. The sergeant in charge told me that when Mr. Sam landed, a convoy of emergency and MP vehicles "escorted" him to the parking ramp, where he was still being questioned by authorities. (He's lucky they didn't shoot him.) About thirty minutes later, Mr. Sam walked out, completely unruffled, and said, "Ronnie, I got delayed here a little bit, but we should be able to visit at least a couple of stores today." Business as usual in Mr. Sam's world.

The airplane stories told by the early management team could fill another book. Though funny after the fact, I consider Mr. Sam and many of the folks who flew with him pretty darn fortunate. I could tell of the time he took off out of Memphis and didn't want to be bothered by the radio (so he turned it off). After he failed to maintain the altitude assigned him, causing a near-miss by a private jet crossing his path, he arrived in Bentonville and found an FAA agent waiting for him . . . resulting in a temporary suspension of his license. Or I could mention the time Mr. Sam needed to take his pilot's instrument rating flight down in Florida. He failed that one, so he "hired" the instrument instructor who failed him. Mr. Sam made him the "chief pilot" of our Walmart aviation department. Shortly after, Mr. Sam passed his instrument test, but the instructor didn't last long as "chief pilot."

As I said earlier, I do believe he must have been a good pilot to have survived all the mental lapses while at the controls. On the other hand, any pilot will tell you that a good pilot does not have mental lapses.

Mental lapses alone can't explain Mr. Sam's driving habits; they were simply atrocious. The many dents and crushed fenders on his car and truck offered testament to that fact. Although none of us would ever admit it to his face, no one relished the thought of riding with him.

Perhaps the most notable incident occurred when Mr. Sam spoke at a gathering of our truck drivers in Bentonville. Ironically enough, the primary purpose of this get-together was to give out "Safe Driving Awards." Mr. Sam presented a particular driver with his "One Million Mile Accident Free Award," a fine-looking custom belt buckle. Upon leaving the event and driving to nearby Rogers to visit a store, Mr. Sam became distracted and rear-ended a Walmart truck. Yep . . . you guessed it. It was the truck of the driver who Mr. Sam had just recognized for safe driving. So

I guess the guy made it one million and *four* accident-free miles before he had to start all over (thanks to Mr. Sam). At least he got to keep the belt buckle.

I suppose to those without a sense of humor, these stories of his flying and driving escapades may have a serious side, but in my mind, they just served to endear him to us. The man lived, breathed, and ate work 24/7. Transportation was simply a necessary evil to him. Planes, trucks, and automobiles held no particular value other than to get him to the next store or bird-hunting location. We won't tell the story of the time he left his bird dogs in his plane for a few hours in hot weather, resulting in a $100,000 rewiring and repair bill.

The Bird Hunt

I was raised hunting squirrels, rabbits, and other game for dinner. But I had never become a bird hunter. I could knock the eyes out of a squirrel with a .22 rifle, but couldn't hit the broad side of a barn with a shotgun. On one occasion, Mr. Sam invited me down to Texas to hunt quail with him and the management team. When I started asking about what to take with me and what to wear, one of my buddies said, "Aw, Ronnie, wear anything you want. It'll be warm, and there ain't much to huntin' birds down there. We have these four-by-four vehicles, with bench seats up high. We ride down the road, let the dogs out, wait 'til they point some birds, get down off the truck, shoot 'em, then get back on the truck. Nothin' to it." Sounded easy to me. So going to Texas to ride around in a four-by-four truck, I took my only pair of snakeskin cowboy boots, a couple of T-shirts, jeans, and my first brand-new hunting vest.

The night before the hunt, the guys sat around the cabin, had a few drinks, and decided who would hunt with whom. Turns out they hunted in two-man groups. I was lucky, because I was chosen to hunt with Mr. Sam himself the next morning. Wow. Pretty neat. I'm sure everyone else was jealous, what with me getting to hunt with the man himself and all.

The next morning it was raining . . . hard. Mr. Sam jumped in a pick-up truck, loaded up two of his dogs, and said, "Let's go, Ronnie." We drove a couple miles away from the cabin into some scrub and he parked the truck. "Okay, Ronnie, you take the left, I'll take the right," and with that brief instruction, he let the dogs go. That was the beginning of what would be one of the most miserable days of my entire life.

I found out eight hours later that I had been "set up." No one wanted to hunt with Mr. Sam, for a number of reasons. One, he never used his truck to follow the dogs. Two, it seems he was always "training" a dog or two rather than using well-trained dogs. This usually resulted in running after them all day long. Three, he never stopped to rest or eat. You did it on the go.

From the time Mr. Sam parked his truck that morning, I jogged or ran non-stop in high-heeled snakeskin cowboy boots for eight hours in pouring rain, chasing dogs that wouldn't stop, no matter how many times Mr. Sam blew on his darned whistle. And when we did occasionally find some birds, I couldn't hit one . . . which I think disappointed Mr. Sam no end. That was the last time he extended the invitation to bird-hunt the lease. And frankly, I was awfully glad. (To add insult to injury, I had to buy new boots to participate in the "Urban Cowboy" dance craze.)

Sam Walton, the Free Enterprise System and Politics

Mr. Sam became an icon of the business world. He'd be the first to tell you that he was able to do so because of the free enterprise system that built America. He loved this country and always worried about our government and potential laws that would burden or limit free enterprise and business. He admittedly never aspired to politics, though many encouraged him to do so.

In early 1980, our country was going through a deep recession, with extremely high inflation and job losses nationwide. As I write this book, we are again experiencing a deep recession with a government that has no clue how to combat it (that's just my opinion). Mr. Sam explained his position on the situation with this excerpt from an editorial he wrote. "We must become involved politically, individually, and corporately. And I'm talking about each of us throughout our company. Taking more interest in the business of politics — at all levels — city, state, and national. Unless we do, all 22,000 of us, and really work to have the best possible people represent us, who believe in our free enterprise capitalistic system — unless we work hard to elect these kind of representatives — I can assure you we'll all be facing a very limited future, with little or no economic security for any of us. Our profit-sharing and future job security — everything we've all worked so hard for — would be out the window — washed away — as this great country of ours becomes crippled and helpless. We're in the grips of the worst skyrocketing period of inflation this nation has ever seen. We do now have good options, and I'm convinced we're not in a hopeless situation. And I'm also convinced that our leaders and politicians will listen if we sound off and become involved. So this is one of my pleas; that we crank it up, individually, and learn what the candidates stand for."

As I read these comments from Mr. Sam, I felt the need to include them in this book and sensed the appropriateness of these words for America in 2010, twenty-one years later. He was challenging 22,000 associates to get involved. Today, Walmart has in excess of 2 million associates. To use a flip on Mr. Sam's favorite company slogan — what a difference our people could make.

Sam Walton was a champion of the free enterprise system. In 1977, one of our hourly associates wrote an essay which won her a scholarship at the University of Missouri, Columbia. I think it timely to share it here. It was written by Mary Maher, an associate in Walmart store #44 in Eldon, Missouri.

The Free Enterprise System

America's economy depends on the free enterprise system. We have led the world economically through a strong home-front belief in this system. It is not merely an ideal, but a reality that private businesses can operate freely and for a profit with minimal government interference. It takes full participation on everyone's part to keep this system running, or to face the downfall of America through its economy. Participation in the economy is the heart of success. The stimulation of the economy does not come from the government, but from the people. We must constantly serve as watchdogs of ourselves to correct any slippage in maintaining free enterprise.

To begin promoting free enterprise, it is important to think in long-range terms. America is synonymous with free enterprise and it should be taught in our schools. This education would not evolve into passive indoctrination, but would be presented as an objective course such as math or history, or even integrated into these courses. The point would be to present free enterprise early as an important subject that will be of constant use to future adults.

The basis of free enterprise is not political, or for special interest groups, or for world manipulation. Free enterprise is the way American people make a living in a democratic society. That is the benefit free enterprise should provide first. How does one ensure that the economy will not become dependent upon government? In a democracy the people are the government. That is one insurance that keeps the government from becoming too powerful. Basic freedoms of speech, press and vote are in the people's hands to use. The majority's influence should be readily apparent in government. The failure of the government to maintain free enterprise would stem from the people. It is important that the people do not shove the responsibility into the hands of a few legislators.

To ensure awareness of the people's responsibility one may refer to the basic freedoms mentioned above. They are not merely idealistic jargon, but truths. They have taken America from the Revolutionary War to the present prosperity and that is strong evidence of their success.

Freedom to speak, write, and vote opinion keeps the people's needs as first obligation. We as Americans must look at legislation through these medias. Free enterprise is an American right. As long as the American people are aware of their rights and power en masse, free enterprise will never be endangered. We of course do not have a patent on freedom, nor can we be sure that total freedom will not result in the infringement on other's rights. The key to a balance in this problem is proper and practical legislation. Legislation that involves the economy should always be geared to meet the obligations of the American people first and in the general best interest of the people. If anyone finds this democratic system too slow, it is best to be reminded that careful consideration is always in his favor.

Promotion of free enterprise is a worthy cause deserving of everyone's

consideration. Again, it is necessary to stress the people as a force in education, legislation, and personal attitude.

Free enterprise is not a walking personification that feeds on itself. It
manifests itself in the people's needs and actions. It is difficult to predict
the success of any economic system and the extent of benefit to the people,
but the past record of free enterprise assures Americans' financial security
as a nation and promotion will assure free enterprise.

Education and legislation are good directions to emphasize. It may seem
as if the individual is inactive. Actually the individual has his own personal
responsibility in promoting free enterprise. It comes from his attitude and
endeavor. A healthy and optimistic attitude will keep free enterprise flour-
ishing.

Any transactions and choices in business affect the individual immediately. Absolutely nothing is wrong in being bullish on America and consumer and producers must appreciate the system.

To demonstrate the meaning of attitude, stress would be put on the law
of supply and demand. The demanders make their needs known to suppliers. In turn the producers provide the demanders' need at a personal profit.
This system is fair and legal. They are the guardians of each other with the
option of approval or rejection. The question is how to promote the individual attitude. The answer comes through in the realization of their mu-
tuality. Laws concerning producer misrepresentation and consumer abuse
discourage dishonesty. Both parties benefit from honesty and it is this benefit that a faith in a free enterprise emerges.

— BY MARY MAHER

What a great essay. I believe it should be required reading for every
politician in Washington . . . including the president of the United States.
(Maybe *especially* the president of the United States.)

The Servant Leader

My good friend, Jack Kahl, authored a book entitled, *Leading from the
Heart, Choosing to be a Servant Leader*. It's a good read. Jack built and
operated his company, Manco, with the passion and servant leadership
qualities that he credits to Sam Walton. In Jack's view, Mr. Walton was
the embodiment of servant leadership. I agree wholeheartedly. Mr. Sam

exemplified the qualities of a servant leader, which were penned in a 1980 article I found, author unknown:

The Twelve Qualities of a Good Leader

1. Sets a good example.
2. Gets results through other people.
3. Treats everyone as individuals. Lets them know they are important.
4. Suggests or requests rather than commands.
5. Asks questions before reprimanding. Criticizes in private.
6. Leads rather than bosses.
7. Gives credit where credit is due.
8. Welcomes suggestions for improvement.
9. Explains why. Lets people know in advance about changes that affect them.
10. Lets people know how they stand. Suggests ways to improve.
11. Praises good performance rather than criticizing the bad.
12. Keeps all promises.

Sam Walton passed away in 1992. It was like losing a large part of my life or a close relative. I toyed with the idea of writing this book for a number of years, but was not compelled to do so until I read *In Sam We Trust* by Bob Ortega. Mr. Ortega portrayed Sam Walton as a ruthless, uncaring, cunning businessman solely out to create wealth. He proffered that all the things Mr. Sam did for associates, the hokey cheers and hoopla he created, were a front — all geared toward "increasing the bottom line." On the book jacket, Mr. Ortega stated that he was assigned to write his book by the *Wall Street Journal*, and that he "was an expert," since he had spent five years doing his research. Well, since Mr. Ortega wrote his opinion, I feel the need to share my opinion: he was dead wrong. I believe I'm more of an expert on Sam Walton and Walmart than Mr. Ortega. I'm sure the *Wall Street Journal* continues to be a viable business because they pay attention to their own "bottom line." Rather than a negative, I would hope that everyone in business has a focus on profitability.

Sam Walton was a driven, passionate man. He had a desire to be the best at his chosen profession. Surely, he relished the thought of taking his company to the top of the retailing industry. That, in my opinion, is admirable; however, personal money and power had nothing to do with it. He desired profits to grow his company. People who knew him knew that, if anything, he was embarrassed by his personal wealth. Sam Walton never drew large salaries for himself. He received the same salary for more than twenty years, and it was extremely low compared to any other CEO of comparably-sized companies. He believed executives should be paid modest salaries, but incentivized through stock options, thus ensuring performance-based compensation. And it worked well.

A servant leader truly serves his people. Sam Walton didn't like the necessity of staying in his office. He much preferred to be out in the stores, visiting with his folks, and looking at competition. He would arrive at the office very early, read the reports, go through his mail, dictate necessary responses, and attend any necessary meetings. But then he high-tailed it out of there at the earliest opportunity.

To see Mr. Sam at his happiest moments was to watch him interact with the people in the stores. He truly loved them. As he would visit with these folks, he'd jot down many notes. Hardly a Home Office meeting occurred that he didn't bring up some comment or suggestion from a store-level associate. And when he did, it most usually was not a suggestion, but rather a directive to change policy or merchandising strategy as a result.

I recall on one occasion when Mr. Sam came into a meeting and reversed one of his own policies based on a simple conversation with a stock clerk. Mr. Sam himself had insisted that Walmart truck drivers should help unload their trucks once arriving at the docks. But while visiting a particular store, a stock clerk told him that these truck drivers drove half the night to ensure their freight arrived at 7:00 or 8:00 a.m. It wasn't right to make them unload the trucks, too, and then drive all the way back to the warehouse. Besides, they'd get so tired they could cause an accident. This associate's comment in hand, Mr. Sam announced that no longer would our drivers help unload the trucks. They could take a nap in their trucks or go to the associate lounge and rest. Servant leadership.

Occasionally, this approach would result in something we knew might be the wrong thing to do company-wide, a suggestion that came from an upset or problem associate. But overall, this "bottom-up" approach set a tone and culture for the company that "we listened and we cared."

I recognize my good fortune at being in the right place at the right time in coming to know Sam Walton and his family on a personal basis. I have continued to watch Walmart evolve and grow. The company still operates with Sam Walton's "Rules of Business" as its guidelines. But it hasn't been an easy road. Some management folks feel the rules are passé. I've heard people say "It's a different company today." I even heard one individual state, "We should take down the Sam Walton signs. That's past history" (This gentleman is now gone).

These people miss the point. Every manager in a business should strive to be a "servant leader," as was Sam Walton. Success will follow.

Two quotes attributed to the founder of IKEA, Ingvar Kamprad, could have been uttered by Mr. Sam himself, because they exemplify his management philosophy:

How the hell can I ask people who work for me to travel cheaply if I am traveling in luxury?

My answer is to stay close to ordinary people because at heart I am one.

I'm gratified that Sam Walton's legacy lives on. And I say, "Rest at peace, Mr. Sam; we miss you."

Chapter 15:

How We Beat the Competition

Contrary to popular belief, when Sam Walton started his Ben Franklin variety store operations in small towns in Arkansas and Missouri, he faced a great deal of competition. In most communities, variety stores already existed as entrenched national or regional chain stores. In addition, most downtown areas also offered shopping in other franchised store operations such as Western Auto, Otasco, and others. Before Mr. Sam opened his first store, many of the towns already provided expanded variety store operations or even early discounters like TG&Y, Gibson's, Pamida, and Sterling stores. Sam Walton succeeded against these larger downtown chain store competitors because of his natural bent for merchandising and promotion, and a lot of hard work.

Discounting caught his eye, though, and it appealed to his "merchant" instincts. He started studying the big operators in the large cities around the country: Ann & Hope, Zayres, Arlans, Korvettes, and Two Guys. In Sam's northwest Arkansas region, Gibson's was opening a number of discount stores. Then, in 1962, the real discounting race heated up. F. W. Woolworth opened its Woolco store, S.S. Kresge the first K-Mart store, Dayton-Hudson the first Target store. And Mr. Sam, his first Walmart store.

Backed by huge existing companies, Woolco and K-Mart expanded widely and rapidly in the larger metro markets. K-Mart represented the best of them all, and Mr. Sam greatly admired Harry Cunningham, the Kresge executive who pioneered their rollout. As more Walmart stores sprung up throughout the '60s and '70s, they succeeded against smaller or poorly-operated discounters in small towns. The first head-to-head competition with K-Mart occurred in Hot Springs, Arkansas. It was a real battle, with pricing wars on key items, but ultimately Walmart held its own and Mr. Sam became unafraid to compete with them.

Over the years, Walmart grew to become a formidable competitor. But frankly, they should never have been able to beat the likes of Woolco and K-Mart with their huge parent companies and deep financial pockets. As many of the early retailers and discounters went bankrupt or closed their doors, we studied the reasons we felt they failed. Like squirrels scavenging for acorns, we looked for nuggets of wisdom pertaining to these defunct operations. In many cases, we traced the cause to an imbalance of the merchandising and operations divisions. (I discussed this dilemma in earlier chapters.) For example, TG&Y was a strong competitor in small towns in our market, but weak in operations. Woolco ran a first-rate operations division, but fell short in merchandising.

Perhaps the best study, or at least the one I am most familiar with, is how we ultimately outperformed K-Mart. This story, better than anything else, illustrates the "building blocks for success" I pointed out in a previous chapter. Just before K-Mart declared bankruptcy, they were attempting to turn the company around, and I was privy to a consulting group's study of the steps K-Mart needed to take to accomplish that task. I found it to be a revealing study. K-Mart must not have seen it the same way. When interim management chose to ignore most of it, bankruptcy ensued.

Beating K-Mart

t's reasonable to think that K-Mart, with its size advantage and established markets, should have been able to undersell Walmart in the 1960s, '70s, and '80s. It seems, because of the sheer strength of numbers, they should have commanded better pricing from suppliers, which would have enabled them to outlast the competition in discount pricing wars. A number of reasons cost them the battle, and ultimately, the war. Therein lie the lessons for all of us in the retail business.

▸ Cost of Entry: K-Mart grew initially in larger metro markets, while Walmart chose to concentrate on small towns/cities. Building and lands costs were much lower for Walmart, resulting in a lower rent charge for the store operations. Whether a small business or a large one, the "cost of entry" or occupancy overhead should be the very first consideration in the pro forma to determine whether a business has a chance to be profitable.

▸ Expenses: Led by Sam Walton's own tight-fisted control, the Walmart culture questioned the need for every expense dollar. From the spartan Home Office (an old warehouse) to accommodations in lower-cost motels (two to a room), Walmart enjoyed a built-in advantage for under-selling the competition. K-Mart, on the other hand, built extravagant headquarters in Troy, Michigan. With Walmart's total SG&A expenses running as low as 16 percent of sales, compared to K-Mart's expenses of 21 percent, Walmart had a built-in 5 percent advantage in the selling price of any given product.

▸ Advertising Costs: Early on, both Walmart and K-Mart printed weekly sale circulars, mailing millions of them to customers. The cost of printing and mailing was high and buying a large number of items in the right quantities weekly was next to impossible. This often resulted in either out-of-stocks, and therefore, upset customers, or overstocks on advertised items, creating higher clearance markdowns. We made the decision in the late '70s to publish only one sale circular per month, while K-Mart continued the weekly program. Eliminating the costs of circulars and inventory issues enabled us to lower everyday prices and eliminate much customer dissatisfaction. K-Mart could not meet our everyday low prices while continuing to offer hundreds of items weekly on their sale circulars. There simply was not enough profit margin to do both. Our strategic decision separated the two companies and proved to be a key to our ultimate success.

▸ Merchandising: As they suffered gross profit margin problems during the '70s, K-Mart clearly began to offer more private-label and imported merchandise. Meanwhile, Walmart held true to course, choosing to reemphasize our name-brand products. From the beginning, our company had identified the most recognizable brands/items in each department, and priced them aggressively with narrow profit margins. We called this the "Image Item Program." As a result, in the minds of the consumer, Walmart truly offered the lowest prices. Initially, K-Mart fought us on pricing. In the first head-to-head competition in Hot Springs, Arkansas, we were determined not to be undersold. For a short period of time, we sold Crest toothpaste for six cents per tube. K-Mart eventually gave up the price wars. Toward the end, in an effort to limit losses, K-Mart allowed its merchandising and distribution system to build up excess stale and seasonal inventory. This caused more problems than it solved. Ultimately, they didn't have the cash on hand to purchase needed inventory.

▸ Updating Stores: From the beginning, Walmart believed in keeping its stores updated as much as possible. We had an unwritten policy to "touch" a store within six years, meaning we would remodel the existing store or build a new, larger store. K-Mart, on the other hand, allowed most of their stores to become old, dreary, or outdated. They eventually recognized this issue and spent hundreds of millions to remodel and/or build new exciting stores, but by that time they had already lost their customer base.

▸ Zone Pricing: Perhaps one of the biggest reasons we were able to conquer K-Mart was their zone-pricing philosophy. K-Mart created multiple retail pricing levels for their stores. In locations perceived to have no competition, merchandise was priced significantly higher than in locations where competitors were strong. In markets where they competed directly with Walmart, prices were at their lowest levels. This became most evident when Walmart entered new states during expansion. For example, when we opened our first stores in Florida, it forced K-Mart to slash their prices to "Walmart competitive" levels. The customers recognized this, and basically said, "Hey, now that Walmart's here, you're dropping your prices. You've been ripping us off." We heard that from many customers as we grew our business in new markets.

▸ Diverting Attention: With the success of their K-Mart stores, the company succumbed to the pressure of growing their overall empire by acquisition and expansion into specialty operations that included Waldenbook stores, Builder's Square home improvement stores, Payless Drug stores, SportsAuthority stores, Office Square stationery stores, and Pace Wholesale Warehouses. Notice that most of these operations are now defunct or have been acquired. Walmart, meanwhile, invested their focus and cash on improving and expanding the core Walmart stores. In keeping with our company's desire to test new ideas and store formats, we also tried some similar ventures — but very carefully and a couple of stores at a time. We found that, although other formats held possibilities, we would be better off focusing on our successful core competencies.

▸ People: As we grew our company and battled K-Mart, most customers would say, "When you walk around in a Walmart, you just get a better feeling. The people are friendlier and there's a more up-beat atmosphere." In the study conducted by the consulting group that I referred to earlier (about turning K-Mart around), researchers interviewed thousands of store-level personnel within the K-Mart organization. Unanimous feedback indicated three major problems that had to be corrected. (1) The employees detested KIH (K-Mart International Headquarters), because they felt their headquarters people did not care about them. (2) One particular individual, who headed up operations, was perceived to be the biggest problem in the company and deserved to be fired (but never was). (3) The stores were often out-of-stock on the best-selling items, yet full of merchandise that would not sell. These three key points should represent a lesson to any and all corporations today. As I stated earlier, K-Mart did not embrace the changes recommended in this study and as a result, declared bankruptcy.

Over the years, Walmart hired a lot of good former K-Mart employees. That company had many great managers and associates. The problems arose when management ignored the importance of those people, stopped listening to them, and managed dictatorially from the top down. What a tough lesson.

Too Much, Too Late

Once K-Mart's leadership recognized they had to significantly up-date their stores and make the changes necessary to survive, it was too late. They sold off some divisions to acquire cash to make the necessary changes. I will cite one example of the fruitlessness of their efforts. I have owned a condo outside of Punta Gorda, Florida since 1986. K-Mart built a brand new prototype store there in the '90s. Walmart ran a small older unit in the same area. The new K-Mart store was truly one of the nicest, best-merchandised stores I had ever seen. Frankly, it put our little store to shame. I visited that K-Mart shortly after opening and again a few months later. As the old saying goes, "You could shoot a cannon down the aisles and not hit anyone." The lesson here is that once you've lost your customer base, you just can't get it back. The huge investment K-Mart finally made in the attempt to turn their fortunes around simply hastened their demise.

When looking at a list of the top performing department stores and discounters in 1977, I'm struck by how many of them don't exist today. A January 1, 1977 article in *Forbes* Magazine lists them in order of growth and profitability, not total sales, for a five-year period prior to publication:

Department Stores

Mercantile Stores
Federated Dept. Stores
J C Penny
Carter Hawley Hale
Gamble-Skogmo
Garfinckel Brooks Bros.
Sears, Roebuck
Allied Stores
May Dept. Stores
R H Macy
Dayton-Hudson
Associated Dry Goods
Carson Pirie Scott
Marshall Field

Alexander's
Goldblatt Bros.
City Stores

Discount Stores

Wal-Mart Stores
S.S. Kresge
Fed-Mart
Household Finance
F W Woolworth
G C Murphy
Rose's Stores
Zayre
Vornado
Sav-A-Stop
Cook United
Rapid-American
Arlen Realty Dvpt
Daylin
Hartfield-Zodys

Today's retail landscape looks much different. The few large discount chains that remain are dominated by Walmart, Target, and Sears holdings. Sales have become fragmented between "category killers"(large stores specializing in a particular merchandise category) such as Best Buy, Lowes, Home Depot, Toys R Us, PetSmart, Office Depot, Cabela's, and Bass Pro Shops, a variety of successful specialty stores, and aggressive mid-tier department stores such as Kohl's and Gap. Discount drug stores such as Walgreens and CVS continue to perform well. Catering to the lower-end consumers successfully are Dollar General, Fred's, and Family Dollar. In addition to the Walmart Supercenters, a number of regional grocery chains are holding their own, such as H.E.B. and Publix. The membership club business has evolved into only three major players: Sam's, Costco, and B.J.'s. Large regional malls have seen better days, while "lifestyle" open-air malls are pushing them out. The retail industry has always reinvented itself and will continue to do so. Walmart must continue to adapt, change, and renew, while maintaining the culture and philosophy that enabled it to become the top player in the industry.

> You cannot renew a company without revitalizing its people.
>
> — CHRISTOPHER BARTLETT

> When a business goes wrong, look only to the people
> who are running it.
>
> — MICHAEL DELL

> Sometimes it is the men "higher up" who most need revamping —
> and they themselves are the last to recognize it.
>
> — HENRY FORD

CHAPTER 16

Right People, Right Time

The highly-educated pundits who write about and teach human resource recruitment, management, and training cover all the bases, offering a wide variety of recommendations they deem to be the best. Many successful companies both recruit outside talent and promote from within. My experience and observations of Walmart reveal that Sam Walton and his team utilized both of these approaches without the benefit of professional guidance. Mr. Sam had an uncanny gift for finding and hiring the right people at the right time, from competitors and outside companies alike. But Walmart has also been recognized as a company that grew primarily by promoting talent from within its own ranks.

Much recognition has been given to the early top-level management people who helped lead the company, people recruited by Mr. Sam out of necessity from other retail operations. These folks brought the immediate expertise needed for growth. The company evolved from a small-town, insignificant start-up retailer to a public entity that out-performed and out-grew everyone in the industry with the help of talents like Ron Mayer, Ferold Arend, Jack Shewmaker, and David Glass. Joining later were Don Soderquist, Bob Martin, and Lee Scott.

These men, in turn, recognized the need to bring in specialized outside talent to continue to grow the business. People such as Bob Thorton, to build a warehouse/distribution system; Royce Chambers and Glenn

Habern, to create a Data Processing Division; Jim Dismore, the first advertising/sales promotion head; Ray Gash and Jim Henry, finance; Jim Rountree, the first PR man; Rob Walton, the first official company attorney (counsel); Claude Harris and Al Johnson, merchandising; Bill Fields, merchandising; Jim Elliot and David Washburn, personnel; Paul Carter, Special Divisions; and George Simpson, transportation dispatcher. These were just a few of the early management folks who played key roles in the development of the company.

David H. Maister, author of *Creating Value through People*, summarizes his guidance with this statement, "A person doesn't build a business. A person builds an organization that builds a business." And that is so true in the case of Walmart.

Allow me some indulgence here as I mention many of the early pioneers in the Walton organization. I am somewhat reticent to mention folks by name because many will go unrecognized who were just as instrumental. However, I feel I must give credit to some of the people with whom I worked and maintained a friendship with over the years. All of these folks were great contributors to the early success of the company in their respective areas.

Some of the earliest Ben Franklin store managers included: Bob Bogle, Claude Harris, Charlie Baum, Jack Carmichael, Norm Buchanan, Ray Stephens, Larry Woods, Charlie Cate and Merle Gilbreath.

A few of the earliest hourly associates included: Wanda Wiseman, Inez Threet, Maxine Black, Josie Wolfe, Ruby Parish, Dala Peeples, Grace Hopper, Belle Kuebler, Ruth Jones, Vern Linde and Wanda Nichols. And, of course, Mr. Sam's personal assistants: Becky Elliott and Loretta Boss.

The managers of the very first Walmart store in Rogers were Don Whitaker and Clarence Leis, respectively. Two of the early assistant managers in that store who I worked with for many years were Larry English and John Jacobs. A few of the early hourly associates in that first store included Lucy Mayfield, Imogene Sweeten, Clara Evans, Garneta Smith, and Merle Martfield.

Keith Binkelman developed the company's original Modular/PlanO-Gram program and Joe White started the New Store Planning group.

As the company grew in the '70s and '80s, I worked with the following people who played key roles in their particular areas: in Warehousing/Distribution, Ernie Lundy, Gary Smith, and Ross Rodden; in Advertising/Sales Promotion, Tom McCoy and Bob McCurry; in Personnel, Von Johnston; the *Wal-Mart World* editor, Betty McAllister; in the finance area, Charles Rateliff and Jim Walker; Loss Prevention, Dave Gorman, Richard Wells and Nick Shepherd; Attorney Robert Rhoads; and with Insurance/Benefits/Audit, John Sooter and Jim Von Gremp.

Company pilots Bill Creech, Jerry Turney, and Bill Mansker — what a crew! I would be remiss in not giving more "ink" to this group. Each had his own personal traits. Jerry and Bill Mansker were a little more laid-back and "by-the-book" in their flying habits. Bill Creech, on the other hand, was noted for liking to "hedge-hop," regardless of how uncomfortable it might be for the passengers. Most of us who have flown in small private planes know that the lower a pilot flies, the rougher the ride, and Bill was infamous for flying just over tree-top level so he could "truly fly the plane" rather than just put it on auto-pilot — thus the term "hedge-hop." It was hard to keep lunch down when flying with Bill Creech. These guys put in countless hours, flying in all weather conditions, and played an integral part in helping our company succeed. All of us, at one time or another, endured some "hairy" experiences in our Walmart aircraft. But we were blessed with these very talented pilots and always survived to tell the tale.

The pilots shared with me a humorous little note back in the early 70s that they clipped from a newspaper in Dallas. It read:

PILOTS NOT AWARE OF FIELD RULES

Airline pilots flying in and out of Love Field may not be aware of all the rules that they have to contend with. Among these U.S. Air Service rules, laid down in 1920, but still on the books, are:

▸ Don't turn sharply while taxiing. Instead, have someone lift the tail around.

▸ Pilots should carry handkerchiefs to wipe off their goggles.

- Hedge-hopping won't be tolerated.
- Pilots will not wear spurs while flying.
- Don't trust altitude instruments.
- Don't leave the ground with your motor leaking.
- And last, but not least, if an emergency occurs while flying, land as soon as you can.

Duh! (My comment)

The Walmart truck drivers are among the most unheralded but valuable groups of associates in the company. They are dedicated, proud of their role, and deserve all the recognition they can receive.Early truck drivers and dispatch included: George Simpson, Bob Clark, Frank Doss, Larry Fuller, John Hall, Leslie Jensen, Bob Lloyd, Francis McNelly, Donnie Marsh, Lee Noah, John Renfroe, John Reynolds, Lester Sparks, George Steele, Herbert Townsend, Joe Bob Wilson, and my stepfather Bernie Ritchey.

And once delivered, the store set-up team kicked in: Larry Capps, Tom Clifton, Dale Pool, Oscar Stotts, Bob Pemberton, and Bob Erickson. From the Hong Kong and Taiwan Merchandise Office: Bob and Marcia Haines, J. R. Campbell, and Bill Woodard.

In the early days, several departments were actually leased operations owned by outside companies. Eventually, we bought these leases and they became company-operated divisions. Early developers of these special divisions included: Clarence Archer with Pharmacies; Bill Hutcheson with Shoes; Dave Rogers in Photo Processing; Lowell Kinder with Tire & Battery Centers; Greg Guthrie for Food Services (Snack Bars); and Dick Mahan with AIDCO (Sporting Goods Distributor).

While I have noted outstanding contributors here, I apologize for inadvertently leaving out deserving people. My intention, to the best of my ability (and memory), is to recognize colleagues instrumental in Walmart's growth who may not have received proper acknowledgment up until now. Those of us who lived the experience are proud of what we accomplished and continue to support the company. While many others have followed since my tenure, rising through the ranks or joining from outside the company, the folks mentioned here worked tirelessly to create the foundation that exists today. Others who contributed a great deal to Walmart's growth are named at the end of this chapter.*

No Clones — Lessons on Human Resources

When I think about my career and the people with whom I worked, what stands out in my mind are the diverse qualities and abilities within the group. There were high school dropouts and college graduates, equally capable. There were creative people, renegades, detail freaks, workaholics, politicians, administrators, delegators, motivators, and partiers. We worked hard and played hard. But we all aspired to a common goal — that of achieving personal and corporate success.

Perhaps above all, we employed an ideal mixture of young workers and older veterans. There are merits to hiring both. Henry Ford is quoted as saying, "A company needs smart young people with the imagination and the guts to turn everything upside down if they can. It also needs old figures to keep them from turning upside down those things that ought to be right side up." I find a lot of wisdom in that.

Harold Geneen, who turned ITT into one of the world's giant conglomerates, shares this quote, "Every company has two organizational structures: the formal one is written on the charts; the other is the everyday relationships of the men and women in the organization." That describes Walmart. We all had titles or job descriptions, but we generally wore many hats and did everything necessary to make our business work.

I get concerned today when I hear how companies make prospective employees jump through hoops to get a job.

A friend recently showed me a test and some sort of psychometric form that supposedly determined whether I could be a good hire for a company. (I won't mention the friend's name here. Whew.) For kicks, I took the test. I failed it. Another retired executive friend took the same test with identical results. This gentleman successfully helped run Walmart. I sincerely hope the company did not pay anyone for this so-called human resource "tool."

Philip Sadler, in his best practice treatise, *Finding and Keeping Top Talent,* wrote, "The 'nursery' approach; recruiting young people straight from high school or college, nurturing or developing their emerging talent and bringing it to fruition is clearly a long-term approach and one fraught with obvious risks, one of which is the difficulty of predicting ultimate success."

He goes on to say that psychometric tests are weak in predicting creativity and entrepreneurial ability; that the "nursery" approach tends to put too much weight on academic qualifications. He states that motivation and drive may well be more powerful determinants of performance than sheer ability. This is not meant to say a company should never hire folks straight from school. Obviously, that is necessary and important. But today, a retail giant like Walmart must have literally thousands of potential "winners" who can serve very important roles, with or without a formal education. If nothing else in my career, I found that experience in the stores is far more valuable than book-learnin' when it comes to merchandising. If it was good before, why wouldn't it be good today?

The last element of people management that I observed within the Walmart organization, beginning with Sam Walton's approach to people, was that every person possesses strengths and weaknesses. Our key to successful management involved recognizing those traits, and putting people in positions to capitalize on the strengths and minimize the weaknesses. For example, you may have a person with good merchandising skills who is not a "people person" . . . or vice versa. I've seen good talent terminated when they might have been allowed to succeed in a different function. Why would a company place someone who doesn't manage people well in a position to do just that? Mr. Sam excelled at recognizing certain abilities and strengths, and wouldn't hesitate to move people to areas better suited to them, even though they may have performed poorly in their previous duties.

At Walmart we believed in "cross-pollination." A good talent could be assigned to any particular position and perform well. This philosophy doesn't necessarily conflict with the issue I mentioned in the previous paragraph. A capable manager recognizes his or her own weaknesses and can change or improve in those areas. Problems arise when no attempt is made to address a person's weaknesses and/or if a person's inherent personal traits are so ingrained that correction is impossible. The key is to recognize mistakes when they occur and quickly correct them before the organization is negatively affected.

Studies have proven that salary is third or fourth on the list of items that motivate people to perform well. Appreciation, recognition, and empowerment all take precedence in creating a satisfied and productive employee. I learned over the years that the single biggest mistake managers make is to handle all people the same way. The successful manager maximizes production by understanding when and who to coax, ask, thank, praise, kick in the rear, or privately chastise. And the worst mistake any manager can make is to publicly reprimand an employee. This not only has a negative effect on that employee but on the entire organization. I have seen that done so many times during my career, and I remember every single incident as damaging.

So, yes, Mr. Sam and the Walmart organization achieved great success by hiring the right people at the right time. But they also *managed* people right at the right time. If and when the company begins to falter, it will more than likely be due to a failure in hiring the right people and/ or managing people the wrong way.

> The man who views the world at fifty the same as he did at twenty has wasted thirty years of his life.
>
> — MUHAMMAD ALI

> Professional management is an invention that produced gain in organizational efficiency so great that it eventually destroyed organizational effectiveness.
>
> — HENRY MINTZBERG

Human resources are the greatest asset of any company.
— NARAYANA MURTHY

*Other Walmart employees instrumental in our early success:

Key Operations People	Key Merchandising People
Jack Brewer	Harryetta Bailey
Jack Mackey	Terry Tucker
Bob Hart	Don Rolle
Richard Cudd	Brent Berry
J.W. Hyde	Jim Kachellek
Steve Bailey	Roger Gildehaus
Melvin Acree	Rick McClintock
Bob Thomas	Dick Jalosky
Wesley Wright	Dean Sanders
Bill Smith	Tom Sharp
Steve Furner	Ray Wilson
Harry Miller	Bob Sherba
Quent Dixon	Peggy Griffith
Charles Russell	Ron Stover
Lolan Mackey	Ned Irving
Kendall Schwindt	Mike Smith
A.R. McDonald	Pete Metzger
Clyde Hulett	Clifford Young
Tom Stockdale	Bill Fields
Darwin Smith	Steve Tiernan
Chuck Webb	Don Bailey
Lew Skelton	Dick Tucker
Mike Campbell	Larry Dimmit
Larry Francis	Joe Craig
Bill Adams	David Dible
Harry Green	Dick Mahan
John Tillman	Dave McClanahan
M. I. Dillard	Tom Middleton
Nick White	
Tom Coughlin	

CHAPTER 17

The Challenge of Retaining the Corporate Culture

The bulk of the metro-market area of Northwest Arkansas (Benton and Washington counties) is comprised of the cities of Bentonville, Rogers, Springdale, Fayetteville, and Siloam Springs. The Walmart Home Office and approximately one thousand supplier/vendor offices, which support their largest customer, are located in this area. All told, the area is home to roughly 20,000 Walmart associates and their families, the vendors, and the employees who staff their offices, and hundreds of retirees who have left Walmart over the years (including me). This all adds up to close scrutiny for current Walmart management folks. It's like working under the world's largest microscope.

On any given day, I hear concern from fellow retirees about Walmart "losing the culture" that built the company. I've engaged in discussions with members of the Walmart management team who voice the same concerns and work hard to address the issue. Many associates comment that the old culture is disappearing, even though Walmart holds leadership classes and culture training as part of its ongoing activities. This has become such a hot topic around the area that I decided to learn what I could about Walmart's corporate culture to be able to comment on it intelligently in this book. It was always just a term to me that meant "how we do things around here." And yes, much of how we did things around there is changing. Is that good or bad? I contend it is some of both.

Definition of Culture

The Merriam-Webster Open Dictionary defines culture as: "(5c) the set of shared attitudes, values, goals, and practices that characterizes an institution or organization." In his book, *Culture Clashes,* Tim Hindle says that Geert Hofstede, a Dutch academic, defines it as "the collective programming of the mind which distinguishes the members of one organization from another." He credits Edgar Schein, a professor at MIT's Sloan School of Management as saying it is what a corporation "has learned as a total social unit over the course of its history." Hindle goes on to write that some just refer to culture as "the way we do things around here" (sound familiar?). Others prefer to call it the set of values that the company holds most dear. I really like the sound of that last one.

Should it Change?

As I continued my research in preparation for commenting on Walmart's corporate culture, I ran across excerpts from a book which gave me cause for pause and thought. A book by the aforementioned Edgar Schein entitled, *Organizational Culture and Leadership,* is considered to be the catalyst for many additional studies on corporate culture. He contends there are three stages in the development of a corporate culture:

Birth and early growth. The culture may be dominated by the business founder. It is regarded as a source of the company's identity, a bonding agent protecting it against outside forces.

Organizational and mid-life. The original culture is likely to be diluted and undermined as new cultures emerge and there is a loss of the original sense of identity. At this stage, there is an opportunity for the fundamental culture to be realigned and changed.

Organizational maturity. Culture, at this stage, is regarded sentimentally. People are hopelessly addicted to how things used to be done and unwilling to contemplate change. Here the organization is at its weakest, as the culture has been transformed from a source of competitive advantage and distinctiveness to a hindrance in the marketplace. Only through aggressive measures will it survive.

A couple of other books and articles address the fact that large multinational companies (Walmart?) today face challenges with culture due to diversity in the workplace, changing lifestyles of today's employees, and the globalization of business.

My Conclusion

The question of Walmart's corporate culture has occupied the forefront for quite some time. And it has been a personal concern since the beginning. In the early days of my employment (when I had never even heard the term), we all recognized the values and goals Mr. Sam embodied and we always strove to adhere to them. While the culture was "tacit" at that time, it was nonetheless developing. This was the "birth and early growth" phase Edgar Schein noted.

Now that I'm an expert (tongue-in-cheek) on corporate culture, I admit that it is harder to be critical of my former company when I hear the culture is changing. I think the matter is twofold.

First, decisions may need to be made regarding what elements of the corporate culture should be changed and what should remain the same. Second, the company may need to determine the difference between elements of culture and general operating practices. I certainly don't have those answers, only opinions. I have, admittedly, been away from the company for too long to make those determinations. I left long before the company grew to international prominence — long before such a diverse culture became part of the company.

In 1997, I was invited to speak at Walmart's annual manager's meeting in Houston. I addressed store managers with a presentation on "Keeping the Culture." The list I shared contained ten items that should be of concern when attempting to maintain Walmart's core values. If I worked there today, faced with the current challenges of size, diversity, and international concerns, I am not confident I would present the exact same list.

I now see things through the eyes of a twenty-three-year company veteran who served at every level of employment, from hourly associate to senior officer, and participated in the acquisition, defeat, or surpassing of many competitors. In addition, I continue to follow the evolution of the industry today, watching new competition and growing rivals as they emerge. As a result, I have identified a few elements of the Walmart culture that I believe are absolute musts for continued success, as well as some that perhaps should change. I offer my opinions constructively, not critically. I am also cognizant that most of the Walmart management folks I speak to on a regular basis are like-minded. Please note that some of the following components are included in the "Top Ten Building Blocks" for success that I shared in Chapter 13.

Five elements of the Walmart culture that, in my opinion, should remain:

1. **"Our People Make the Difference."** From the very top, down through the various management levels, the executives absolutely must believe in, not just give lip service to, the importance of the associates in the stores and clubs. If associates reach the point they believe management does not care about them, Walmart will survive for some time, but will become just another company — with increasing problems and declining profits. Other than poor management, most companies fail because they do not understand the importance of a satisfied and motivated team of people.

2. **Open Door Management.** Treating people like partners, sharing all the numbers, seeking suggestions and improvements from the bottom up and hearing complaints without retribution are often difficult tasks, but are parts of the Walmart culture that are as essential today as they were at the beginning. Although this cultural element is related to item one above, the size of the organization today makes it a separate challenge. Unless management continues to develop communication tools, actively seeks input from all echelons of the organization, and most importantly, acts on this input, they will lose the trust of their people.

3. **Treating Others with Respect.** Walmart is the largest company

in the world. But this must not lead to the arrogance of its employees, as that would result in a gradual loss of respect throughout the industry. Humility, as a part of the culture instilled by the founder, should be constantly emphasized in all supplier, shareholder, and intra-company relationships. Every time a Walmart associate exhibits arrogance in his or her approach with others, mutual respect erodes. Perhaps the most visible and important area of concern is the buyer/supplier relationship. Walmart is the largest company in the world, but should be humble and act as if it needs everyone's help (because it does).

4. **Who's Number One?** The Customer. The ending of the Walmart cheer is more important than ever. Appreciating the customer is a major part of the culture. The competition today is more formidable than when I worked for the company. It's becoming more difficult to ensure the customer is taken care of and treated properly, but no less crucial. Many managers determine what they want to accomplish or dictate "from the top down" the direction they plan to take the company. That's not necessarily wrong, but prior to doing so, they had best determine what their customers want and let that dictate what they do. The acronym TLC means different things to different people, from Elvis Presley to nurses. I use it as a reference to "Think Like a Customer" or "Think Like a Client." If you apply TLC, no matter what your business or position, you'll be astonished how much easier and how much better your decisions, interpersonal relationships, and success will be.

5. **Low Prices.** I'm not sure this is as much a part of the culture as it is a business strategy, but the ability to offer the best prices is largely due to the level of expenses. It's a fact that Walmart faces tremendous expenses today. As a customer, I will say that Walmart no longer represents the clear choice on low pricing. That worries me. The category killers and specialty operations create great pressure on competitive pricing. This brings to mind the lesson I learned from working with major suppliers: "you don't get something for nothing." The more Walmart asks of suppliers, the more they will pay in the end. The nature of our litigious society increases the likelihood that every negative in-

cident and lawsuit will result in yet another requirement in the item sourcing and approval processes. There is a similarity in how the federal government and large corporations tend to build more and more bureaucracy, regulations, and paperwork into their processes. This eliminates "speed to market" and builds in costs at every step, whether for the company or the suppliers. To maintain price leadership, Walmart must occasionally back up and take a hard look at the complexities and costs they have slowly built into their business.

In addition, as I see increasing input from ad agencies, television advertising, and overall expenditures (without a commensurate improvement in sales), I wonder about the wisdom of these expenditures. Actually, if a company doesn't have its merchandising and operations right in the stores, all advertising dollars designed to attract customers are simply a waste of money. Customers have always considered Walmart the place to go for savings (now, "to live better"). This promise is an integral part of the Walmart culture. It can only continue if Walmart controls expenses better than its competitors.

What Elements of the Culture Should Change?

The elements of the corporate culture that I no longer deem applicable in today's environment include the following:

1. Lifestyle and Associate Retention. Walmart is a huge, global company and as a result must attract and/or retain very talented people. Unlike the early years, if someone wants a nicer home, a Cadillac or Lincoln (or maybe even a Porsche), so be it. People today demand more workplace satisfaction and more time with family. In the old days, some people measured the dedication of associates by how early they came in and how late they stayed, rather than what they accomplished. So the "old way" may not be apropos today. This is one area of the culture that has already undergone a change and rightly so.

2. Diversity in the Workplace. Today the Walmart workforce consists of more female, Hispanic, African-American, and Asian associates. Hiring and retaining a diverse group of people from

Walmart's global subsidiaries is a natural progression. This creates the need to understand the various cultures and challenges. In addition, the young people entering the workplace today think and respond differently than those of my generation, and must be trained and motivated differently. The company needs to consider those cultural elements that traditionally may have been acceptable only to aging white males. The challenge is complex and may be overwhelming at times. But Walmart's ability to satisfy and motivate this new cadre of associates is dependent on changing these elements.

In 2008, Greg Johnston, head of operations for Sam's Club, invited me to attend the twenty-fifth anniversary meeting in Kansas City. While there, I sat in on some breakout sessions about corporate culture that all club managers attended. Each of us received a small book entitled, *This We Believe,* which Walmart created to outline the company's cultural cornerstones. The project manager/editor for that book was Sheri Hottinger, the copy editor was Gina Webb, and the designer was Jill Dible. They produced a high-quality publication that explained the basics as well as anything I've ever seen. Here's a particularly relevant excerpt from the introduction:

> As you know, our Company's Culture has always been a topic of interest for us and thought to be one of our competitive advantages. But what is our Culture? Culture is what we do and how we engage others. It's how we act with Members (Customers) and Associates, and even how we behave when we think no one is watching. It's how we treat each other and the habits we exhibit in our business. Culture is to our company as an operating system is to a computer. It's what keeps us going; it's the lifeblood of our organization. It determines results.
>
> Sam Walton, our Founder, established and operated the Company on a foundation of three simple, yet very important, beliefs:
> **Respect For The Individual**
> **Service To Our Members (Customers)**
> **Strive For Excellence**
> Our Culture is a result of the behavior that is demonstrated when we support these core beliefs. This behavior includes: being friendly to people,

attentive listening, face-to-face communications, demonstrating caring for those in need, delivering results through performance, teaching and training others, eliminating waste, and supporting the Open Door. As we interact with each other and our members (customers), we should strive to protect and preserve these beliefs today and for future generations.

— Doug McMillon, CEO, Sam's Clubs

When I was on stage being recognized as the first leader of Sam's, I told the audience and Doug how much that book impressed me; that it was a great guide for not only the company and associates, but for living our individual lives. I also told the group that I would keep that little book on my desk for the rest of my life. That may sound hokey, but it still sits on my desk three years later. I believe it should claim a spot on everyone's desk at Walmart and Sam's Club, lest they forget what their corporate culture is all about.

The more time I spend with our people, the more I find out about our business.

— Herb Kelleher

The worst disease which can afflict business executives is not, as popularly supposed, alcoholism; its egotism.

— Harold S. Geneen

CHAPTER 18

A Rebuttal to the Critics

Let me warn you in advance, this will be the most impassioned chapter of my memoir. Walmart has not expressed support or participated in any way in the writing of this book. I am expressing only my personal opinion regarding the negative publicity and comments many have made about the company. In fact, the scope of negativity actually spurred me to write this book. I sometimes feel like sticking my head out the window, like Howard Beale in the movie, *Network*, to rant, "I'm mad as hell and I'm not going to take this anymore!" That classic line most closely represents my position.

The publicity Walmart receives creates a true conundrum. On one hand, writers would have you believe Walmart and the "Walmartization" of the country is the ruination of America as we know it. On the other, Walmart has consistently been identified as "The Most Admired Company" and one of the "Best Companies to Work For." Which is it? How can it be both good and bad? Obviously, it depends on the perspective of the writer and his or her agenda.

People who have no clue about business, capitalism, and free enterprise (which enabled this country to become the greatest on earth — at least so far), have tried to paint a picture of Walmart as a retail monster. They blame the company for ruining small business, driving jobs offshore, abusing employees, bankrupting suppliers, and creating the trade deficit.

(They've stopped just short of advocating public hangings, but that might be next.) I've researched the origins of most of the negative publicity, and have identified three major factions that seem to be consistently critical of Walmart.

▸ The Politicians. A number of politicians have publicly criticized and "bad-mouthed Walmart. John Kerry (even though his wife owned millions of dollars worth of Walmart stock), Howard Dean, John Edwards, Richard Gephart, and George Miller have all spoken publicly and negatively about Walmart. Curious, isn't it, that the Democrats' largest contributors are the unions?

▸ The Unions. And speaking of unions, this is the second group that spends an exorbitant amount of behind-the-scenes money describing Walmart as the enemy of the entire nation. I wonder why. Could it be because they are an antiquated, disruptive group of money-grabbers whose membership has declined so badly in the U.S. that they are threatened with extinction? Walmart is their last big target (no pun intended), now that they have ruined every industry they have touched; i.e., automobile, textile, steel, airlines, and the government. Unions have never created a job in this country, but they have caused the loss of many. There was a time in history that unions were a "good thing." In the early days of the twentieth century, companies and industries that consistently abused employees set the stage for unions to flourish. Simply put, the unions helped level the playing field, giving workers a degree of clout. Over the years, however, union leadership became overly aggressive, without an understanding that their unrealistic demands would make the industries themselves uncompetitive, resulting in their own members' job losses. In addition, through notorious pension fund scandals and violent organization activity, unions became their own worst enemy. I realize many members are pleased with their union membership, and I'm sure there are some good locals that understand how to effectively deal with management. But overall, they have harmed the economy and destroyed the manufacturing industry in the U.S.

▸ The Left-Leaning Media. With all the good Walmart does, the mainstream media will take any mistake they can find and blow it up into a full-scale news story. The *New York Times* has done just that on a number of occasions. As an example, I will reference Jane Pauley and Brian Ross with their *Dateline* story later in this chapter. But where are the headlines when Walmart does good things? Maybe that's just not "newsworthy."

I would be the first to admit that Walmart has made many mistakes. When human beings are involved, mistakes are sure to follow. The company has hired or promoted a few bad store managers, bad buyers, and even some bad upper level management folks, but on the whole, these are rare exceptions. Walmart has been quick to correct problems when they recognize them. I'm not pointing a finger here, as I've never been confused for a saint. (If you've gotten this far in the book, you know that already.) I wasn't perfect and neither was Walmart. But the good certainly outweighs the bad by a large margin.

The media have paid much attention to the thousands of lawsuits filed against the company at any given time. Part of the reason is the sheer size of the company and the huge number of associates and customers involved; however, many of the cases represent opportunists looking to make a quick buck at Walmart's expense. Unfortunately, some suits are valid and Walmart settles them, as they should.

You just don't seem to hear about it when Walmart "does the right thing." Mr. Ortega's book, *In Sam We Trust,* while predominately negative, probably served a good purpose by forcing the company to take a close look at itself and correct some ongoing issues. Another book, *The Wal-Mart Effect,* by Charles Fishman, is a good read. Although it points out faults, it offers a more balanced view of how Walmart affects the marketplace. At least Mr. Fishman doesn't obviously despise Sam Walton and his success, as does Mr. Ortega. Mr. Fishman, undoubtedly and rightfully, also inspired Walmart to examine itself critically, again resulting in a positive outcome.

I am just an Arkansas boy with a high school education. I may not write with the talented flair of a professional journalist nor am I as learned as a liberal college professor (who has never worked in or built a business). But I'm not trying to impress anyone. I'm just a man who has lived and experienced the opportunity our free enterprise system affords each of us — the chance to make something of ourselves and succeed in life and business through hard work and self-education. So having established that background, the following are *my* opinions in response to the Walmart bashers.

Wal-Mart Ruins Downtowns and Small Businesses

Sam Walton himself, lest ye forget, was a small-town businessman. He just happened to be one who loved his chosen profession and aspired to be the best in that business. In studying his industry, he discovered that discounting was the future of retailing. He also, along with his wife, Helen, liked the small-town life and people. He thought, *why shouldn't people in small towns be able to buy discounted merchandise just like the people in large cities?* Is that a bad thing? I don't think so.

As he slowly grew his chain of Walmart Discount Cities, Sam fell deeply in debt. He fought and scratched for suppliers to sell to him. He worked nonstop and didn't spend money foolishly. He was building his dream. He liked and respected downtown merchants and still considered himself one. But he also knew that eventually someone would succeed at what he was trying to do. There were Gibson stores, TG&Y, Duckwalls, Alco, Pamida, and others taking similar paths in smaller communities. So had it not been Walmart, it would have been some other company that built large discount stores in small towns. People commonly refer to this as "progress." Whether or not folks liked the idea of strip centers and "big boxes" popping up on the outskirts of downtown areas, it was going to happen. Walmart did not cause it. In fact, other companies led the way before Walmart grew to prominence. Large regional malls, strip shopping centers, and lifestyle malls appeared on the scene throughout the '80s and '90s. Big box specialty stores such as Lowe's and Home Depot, Circuit City, and Best Buy, Sears, Target, and many others built facilities in the same areas as Walmart. I find it strange why those companies have escaped criticism for "hurting" small towns' downtown areas.

Certainly, some businesses feel the pain when Walmart comes to town. There's no doubt that small-town grocers and others lose customers or perhaps even close their doors. I've read all the negative comments and stories the critics like to point out, but I have yet to read a story or book that portrays the positive side — consumers in those small towns prefer the option of shopping at Walmart. I would like to share what it might be like if Walmart never existed.

My hometown (Hiwassee) is not a good example, because nothing ever prompted any growth in that community and the businesses are boarded up (without a Walmart there). Other than the Hiwassee Hilton, downtown is a ghost town. On the opposite end of the spectrum, Bentonville is not a good example either, because it's the home of Walmart. But I must say that little town square remains vibrant, although it has undergone much change. More professional offices and various types of businesses fill the spaces, and the square is beautiful. In fact, while Arkansas boasts as many Walmart stores per capita as any state in the country, most of the towns continue to benefit from thriving downtown and small business communities.

And what of the stores that go out of business? Is it because of Walmart or were they simply outdated and destined for the scrap heap? I don't propose to answer that question. You can decide. But if you insist on blaming Walmart, I will repeat: had it not been Walmart, it would have been another major discount chain. Whether or not Walmart becomes a good corporate citizen in any given community determines the amount of "bashing" it receives. K-Mart's history proved they often took the low road. Properly managed, a Walmart store can be a good local citizen. When managers fail in this regard, negative criticism results. But critics fail to take into account that many consumers in these small towns live paycheck to paycheck. If a company such as Walmart didn't create a competitive environment, these folks would pay much higher prices on every purchase. Most of the detractors are the business owners themselves, or wealthy people who never have to worry about the cost of basic goods.

Allow me to share a good example of a town with no Walmart. Robin, my wife of nineteen years, and her family hail from one of the prettiest places I've ever seen — Newport, Vermont. I love this beautiful small town. Newport is located on the Canadian border in northern Vermont, settled around Lake Memphremagog. Half of the lake is in the U.S. and half is in Canada. Nearby Jay Peak is a wonderful place for skiing. The downtown area features a number of unique shops, although some are barely eking out a living. Robin and her family have shared their views with me. They love their state and their town, but they say that Vermont is one of the most notorious states for restricting capitalistic growth. Jobs are scarce. Retail sprawl is very restricted. That's not necessarily a bad thing, as the state is well known for its beauty. Vermont was the last state to allow Walmart to build. I'm not privy to ongoing discussions between Walmart and Vermont officials. But I do know that the town of Newport had an Ames store, the only option for purchasing general merchandise at any sort of discount. This store closed and nothing has replaced it. My wife's family and many others have no choice but to drive to Burlington to shop at Costco and Walmart or Lowe's. They also make the one-hour plus trek to Littleton, Vermont, to shop at the Walmart store there.

Newport has one of the highest unemployment rates in the state. Jobs are especially scarce for younger and older people. The small shops, if and when they need employees, generally pay minimum wage and certainly can't offer health care to their staff. So I venture the question, "Why would a Walmart be a bad thing for that community?" You can decide. A Walmart in Newport would attract many customers from across the Canadian border. This would help the local economy, rather than the citizens crossing the Canadian border to shop at a new Walmart in Magog, Ontario. The point is not that Walmart might come in and destroy a small town, but that Walmart could come in and help a small town; with 200-500 associates earning more than minimum wage, with health care and the opportunity for advancement, plus sales tax revenue for the community. Hmmm . . .

Towns attempting to stop Walmart from building have received much publicity, from Inglewood, California to Chicago area communities. I won't delve into all the details, because the stories have been told many times. I think it is important to note that the proposed sites in Chicago and some in California are located in distressed and challenged areas. California, admittedly a beautiful state, is currently billions of dollars in debt and hoping for a government "bailout." It has one of the highest cost-of-living ratios, huge government-subsidized programs, high taxes, and is heavily unionized and losing companies and businesses daily to other states. I find it strange they believe a Walmart, providing jobs and additional taxes, would be a bad thing. Again, hmmm . . .

In the case of one particular Chicago area site, the issue was discussed at a city council meeting. The largest anti-Walmart voice happened to be a union man. When he was through making his case against Walmart, a city councilwoman asked him one question: "If the council voted to keep Walmart out, what would the union do on that site to provide jobs for the citizens of the area?" Of course, he was dumbfounded and unable to answer. The council then approved Walmart for the site. I believe that says it all, and should be a question asked of all those towns that want to impede progress in their communities — whether it is Walmart or any another company that is attempting to build. Walmart now has a store in Austin and has been approved for a location in Chatham (Chicago area).

At one time, a group of pharmacies in Conway, Arkansas, sued Walmart for "predatory pricing." The case went to court, with Walmart eventually winning. The case was thrown out primarily because the pharmacies' records revealed that their sales and profits were greater after Walmart arrived.

Many studies have been conducted by so-called experts and many articles have been written about Walmart's effect on small towns. They conveniently leave out two facts: big regional malls were already being built on the outskirts of cities/towns and strip centers would have been built in the suburbs with or without Walmart. These are simply examples of evolution in the retail industry. I enjoy the small-town atmosphere and nostalgia of the past as much as anyone. But the days of waiting for a parking place, dropping a dime or two in the meter, paying higher prices, and/or working for the 9:00 to 5:00 local proprietor with no hope for advancement are long gone. Anyone can point out negatives about "Walmart coming to town." But they are ignoring the positive aspects of the issue . . . and there are plenty of them. In most of these debates, the average consumer is pro-Walmart, but he or she is drowned out or ignored by the company's adversaries.

I know of numerous stories of downtown associations and small business owners who adopted the attitude: Okay, Walmart is coming, so let's get to work. They revitalized their downtown areas, reinvented their offerings, opened competitive businesses, and took advantage of the additional traffic drawn to the area. The press rarely covers these stories. I understand why the owner of an existing business would be less than overjoyed by the prospect of a Walmart coming to town. If I were a business owner, I'd be right in the middle of the fight. But that's not the point. You will recall I worked at a gas station and a Western Auto as a young man growing up in Bentonville. I was also one of those "underpaid, abused, and over-worked" (as defined by the critics) associates working for Walmart for many years. But I will always defend the company. Had my only option been to work for a small business, I would probably still be toiling away for minimum wage, with no health insurance and no future. I certainly wouldn't have had a chance for advancement, because small businesses were "family-owned and operated." I could have been a union member, possibly earning a couple more dollars per hour, but would never have had the opportunity to rise through the ranks, much less retire at age forty-two. Again, there are two sides to the argument. I'm simply pointing out the side that never gets media attention (which also happens to be my side).

Walmart is Driving Jobs OffShore

Long before Walmart became the dominant company in retail — while still a small regional powerhouse in four states — its large competitors were importing boatloads of merchandise from the Orient. One of the strategies that helped Walmart outperform K-Mart in the '70s was recognizing K-Mart's ever-growing reliance on imported merchandise. Walmart emphasized top name brands, mostly U.S. merchandise. Largely because of unrealistic union contract demands, the U.S. textile industry had practically disappeared before Walmart had begun to buy direct imports. We didn't know much about that aspect of the business. When we started sourcing offshore, either because we couldn't compete with our competitors' lower-priced imports, or the goods simply weren't readily available in the states, we primarily sought out the factories already making goods for all of our large competitors: J. C. Penny, K-Mart, Woolworth, and other top retailers. Isn't it odd, unlike Walmart, these companies have never been targeted or criticized for importing goods?

We finally opened our own offices in Hong Kong and Taiwan in 1980. This enabled us to more easily inspect factories supplying our goods, hire ethical Asian agents, and control shipping costs, rather than go through domestic importers. Unfortunately, in the beginning, we didn't know enough about the serious issues of child labor, prison labor, and other abuses that existed in some factories in the Asian market. Initially, we trusted that these factories were reliable and ethical. However, even before critics brought abuses to light, Walmart recognized the need to avoid factories which exploited those workforces. Without fanfare, we started this process long before we were large enough to attract attention.

In the early '80s, as the country was going through a severe recession, Sam Walton expressed concern about the U.S. unemployment rate. I don't know how or exactly when this thought came to his mind, but he issued an internal company announcement that he wanted to create a "Buy American" program. He felt if we identified items that could be produced by American manufacturers close to the same price and quality found offshore, our company could truly make a difference by increasing the number of jobs. The critics touted this as nothing more than a PR gimmick. I assure you it was not. We lived by it and Mr. Sam was so serious about it that he insisted we should close our Orient offices, which we had only opened a year earlier. Every buyer in the company was challenged to participate and all rose to the challenge. It was not an easy task to find suppliers for items or categories that often no longer existed in the United States. When we were able to find some goods, the extremely high prices put us at a severe disadvantage with our competitors and alienated our customers. However, over the next few years we made great headway. Conversions from direct importation of foreign goods to American manufacturers improved. At one time, the program was credited with $1.9 billion in sales that created 42,400 American jobs. Two leaders in developing items for the Buy American program were Ed Clifford and Wally Switzer, two of our buyers at that time.

The company featured the American-made products with signs in the stores that read, "Bring it Home to the USA." Manufacturers and customers throughout our trade territory told us it was the best program the company ever instituted. Mr. Sam was so proud of that program and its benefits. Sure, he knew it was good for Walmart, well-received by the customers, and generated positive publicity. But that certainly wasn't the reason he started it. He truly wanted to help the American workers. He told me personally, "Ronnie, by helping the people keep their jobs in the factories, we're helping our own customers." The program was still growing in sales and job creation when Mr. Sam passed away on April 5, 1992.

Eight months later, NBC aired a *Dateline* show hosted by Jane Pauley and Brian Ross, which is one of the best (or worst) examples of underhanded, deceptive, "ambush" journalism I have ever seen. I have not watched an episode of *Dateline* since, knowing how the producers mishandled this one. Before he died, Mr. Sam had finally acquiesced and allowed Ms. Pauley to interview David Glass for a positive story on Walmart's success. She assured Mr. Glass more than once that the interview would be "positive." Unknown to anyone, she assigned crews to go into a store with a hidden camera to film a rack of clothing made in Bangladesh, with a sign hanging over or adjacent to the rack touting the "Bring It Home to the USA" theme. They had also filmed some factory in Bangladesh that was making clothing for Walmart using "child labor." None of this was known to David Glass at the time of the interview. The interview started and after a few run-of-the-mill questions, the ever-so-knowledgeable Ms. Pauley and Mr. Ross blindsided David with the issue of public deception. Mr. Glass was so dumbfounded, so unprepared for this surprise, that he was simply tongue-tied, as anyone in that situation would have been. A few questions later, the damage already done, Pauley and her cohorts were escorted out of the room, cameras still rolling. The repercussions from this incident changed Walmart in many ways. Those changes are still evident today.

Perhaps the saddest part of this incident was that the company immediately took down their "Bring It Home" signs, stopped driving the program, and no longer made a push to convert import purchases to American purchases. They continue to favor sources in the U.S. if at all possible. But to spend countless hours making it happen, only to be depicted as charlatans, simply wasn't worth it. All I can say is that if Jane Pauley and NBC's *Dateline* are proud of themselves for this sorry excuse for investigative journalism, then I truly feel sorry for them as human beings. (I savored an incident later on when the same show was exposed for staging "fake" explosions of vehicles for another investigative news story.) And people wonder why Walmart doesn't like to cooperate with the media? I would suggest that everyone avoid *Dateline*, because there is absolutely no certainty that what you see is the truth. They sensationalize stories and call it journalism. (I will say the Walmart episode on *Dateline* may have had some positive impact by exposing abuses in Asian factories. So some good came of it.) However, that story could have been told without being misleading and lying about what the "interview" would include. I worked for David Glass. He is one of the most honest, ethical, and outstanding CEOs in the company's history. In my opinion, that interview could have been handled in a way that would have told the truth about the Buy America program. Instead, the *Dateline* people came into the interview close-minded, did all they could to make Mr. Glass and Walmart look bad, and basked in their successful "investigative journalism."

Books critical of Walmart like to relate stories of companies that were hurt or went out of business because of unrelenting price pressure. I do feel sorry for those businesses and regret the jobs lost. But the company does have a business to run, which means it is constantly adding, dropping, and changing items based on sales history. With the size of Walmart today, I have hopes that a more understanding position might be taken by the company. We are again going through a major economic recession and I believe Walmart could make a difference.

In a recent retirees' meeting with Walmart's management team, we discussed the impact Walmart could have if they again made a push to create jobs by assisting factories in the United States. It raised some eyebrows on the management team and I can't blame them. Let's suppose for a moment they reinstated a Buy American program. The reality is that any retailer has to sell the merchandise it buys. When Walmart takes on an item from a new supplier, the item may not sell well, or may sell well initially and then decline to a point where it must be dropped in favor of another item. Based on the history of media treatment, I could foresee headlines about Walmart dropping a supplier who had geared up with capital investment and hired a lot of people. Oh my, big bad Walmart strikes again. In the meantime, they would ignore perhaps another hundred suppliers benefiting from the program. That's unfortunately the nature of the critics. People and groups who hate Walmart would continue to find fault with a few examples instead of giving Walmart credit for what they do well. But is that a reason not to "do what's right?" Who knows; perhaps something may evolve in this arena.

Many journalists have written stories on the pressure Walmart puts on its suppliers. Yes, they are tough negotiators. That's their job. We used to say, "No one knows what the lowest price is unless you ask." Good suppliers know their bottom line. If they agree to sell their product at a price they can't afford, that is their fault. Suppliers have to know when to walk away. I've been approached by hundreds of companies so small they have no business selling to Walmart. The company never wants to bankrupt a supplier. That's why they have such strict requirements and ask for so much information before assigning a "vendor number." They take these precautions to protect the potential supplier as much as themselves. Yet Walmart still receives criticism for wanting financial information on a company before doing business with them. This is another issue which prevents the company from dealing with some domestic small factories — not because they don't want to — but because Walmart's sheer size creates more demand than these smaller entities can provide.

Another major criticism is that Walmart puts so much pressure on suppliers that it has forced them to move their manufacturing offshore. I can't say that has never happened, but there are two sides to that story. When I was involved, we had a policy of keeping at least two suppliers of key items or categories. Our reasoning was twofold: to "keep them honest with pricing" and/or to offer a low-price option for those customers who simply couldn't or wouldn't pay for the top brand or highest quality item. I think that's simply good business. Too often, we couldn't find a domestic supplier to provide the lower price point item. So importing became a necessity.

Buyers challenge their larger, leading consumer-brand companies to "keep their pencils sharp." Suppliers know their "market share" is at risk to lower-priced imports, and in many cases they aren't willing to give up market share. Many of them reduce their profit margins in an effort to compete with other lower-priced goods. It's their call to make. Instead of accepting that they could be successful selling their brands side-by-side with the lower-priced options, they decide they want it all and open offshore manufacturing in an attempt to get it. Is that Walmart's fault? I don't believe so. Walmart may be a factor, but critics blame Walmart entirely. I'd say there's plenty of blame to go around.

I'd like to point out, if we constructed borders around our country and eliminated imports or slapped huge tariffs on imports, as some union-backed politicians would have us do, half the people in this country could not afford to satisfy their everyday needs. In turn, our domestic exports would shrink to nothing. Large suppliers are monopolistic, too. Without competition, there would be nothing to stop them from charging far more than reasonable for their products, effectively pricing ordinary folks out of the market. But you won't hear about that from the critics. In

Chapter 20, I discuss this issue in greater detail. Today, I believe both the critics and defenders of Walmart make good points.

It's no secret that our manufacturing jobs continue to disappear. There are many reasons for this. Walmart may be a small contributing factor, but no one is writing books about the large role played by the unions, or the globalization of commerce exacerbated by the Internet and multinational conglomerates. And lastly, no one talks about how our federal and/or state governments have created such burdensome regulations and taxations on American businesses that companies are forced to move offshore to keep their doors open. This, perhaps, is the biggest cause of all for our declining manufacturing jobs . . . but I have yet to find a book about it (not to mention a *Dateline* segment).

California is a textbook example of a state overrun by prohibitive regulations . . . and businesses are moving out of the state. All of the previously booming industrial cities of the northern U.S., such as Detroit, Cleveland, and the New England area, are now in dire straits. In some areas, shuttered factories outnumber going concerns. They were all heavily unionized and now lead the nation in unemployment and poverty. Rather than produce more regulations and make it easier for unions, our government needs to recognize the real reasons we have lost our industrial base. That's the first step in working with American businesses to create jobs.

Walmart Underpays and Mistreats its People

I'm sure you've heard this one. Critics tend to compare Walmart associate wage and benefit scales with those of any other enterprise in America, rather than with other industry retailers. My daughter currently works for Gap, and she is happy there. I have relatives who have worked for every kind of retailer over the years. These companies offer no better pay and benefit packages than Walmart. But I don't see critics publicly criticizing these companies. Where are the studies of fast food and other retail chains that pay even less than Walmart? Just curious, but could it be they're not such a potential "cash cow" for the unions? We beat a union organization effort, which I mentioned in this book, simply by obtaining a union contract which showed no better salary package. In other words, Walmart generally pays as well or better than other retail operations. There are exceptions of course, and critics are quick to point them out in an attempt to make splashy headlines (often backed by union funding). By now, you're probably getting the idea that I'm not a big fan of unions.

Walmart runs its stores efficiently; that's an essential component of business success. All retailers experience a natural ebb and flow; sales are more concentrated in certain hours of the day or week. Management must staff each store with more people during the high-traffic hours than the slow ones; part-time associates provide the needed flexibility to fill in during those busy times. These part-timers may be high school and/or college students who wish to have a job that fits their availability, retirees who need to supplement their Social Security income, or housewives who want to earn extra money while working around their children's schedules. To me, these part-time positions are a positive thing to offer a community. However, part-time positions turn over rapidly (not because Walmart is a bad place to work), but because people move on or no longer need the supplemental income. It's not feasible for the company to handle the paperwork involved with offering the same benefit packages and salaries that full-time associates receive. I don't find it unreasonable that the company requires employees to work there for a period of time before receiving benefits. The associates in these part-time situations don't generally complain, but the critics surely make an issue of it. From the time I began working for Walmart as a stock boy, I had a health insurance program, and it was a good one.

I was always satisfied with the benefit programs Walmart offered. The alternative is terrible. I found out how terrible after I left Walmart and had to pay for private insurance. Critics who make an issue about Walmart not offering health care don't know what they're talking about. Some Walmart associates do access state-assisted health care for their children and families. Typically, these are part-time people or associates who choose not to participate in the company's insurance program. That should not be blamed on Walmart.

While with the company, I served on a profit-sharing/benefits program committee for a short time. We looked into providing dental insurance for associates, because it was an oft-requested benefit from our grass roots program. We discussed the issue at length with a number of potential dental insurance providers. After all was said and done, we couldn't offer the benefit — primarily because of unrealistic requirements. For example, to qualify for reasonable premium costs, seventy-nine percent of our associates had to "sign up for the program and stay on the program for a minimum of two years." That sounded okay except that, historically, when people sign up for dental insurance, they immediately go out and get everything "fixed" — and once that is done, they drop the insurance rather than continue paying premiums. So you see, there's much more to any issue than the critics want to tell you. They should blame insurance companies rather than Walmart, but no books have been written about that either. (Cue violin on shoulder, bow gently, stroking the strings.)

Having worked in the stores for most of my career with Walmart, I can tell you without question, we were never allowed to work people "off-the-clock." Critics cite class-action lawsuits against Walmart filed by a few associates who claim they were regularly made to clock out and then work. If that occurred, it was because some manager violated company policy on his or her own. No reasonable person could imagine a company like Walmart dictating or condoning such activity. Frankly, when I was running my stores, many associates literally asked to come in on their own time in an effort to increase their opportunities for advancement. Never did we make them work for no pay. Yet, articles and books are written in such a manner to make readers believe Walmart condoned or even promoted this kind of activity. That is simply not true.

One incident about big, bad Walmart "hiring illegal aliens" to clean their floors at night made the headlines. In this instance, Walmart had brought in an outside contractor to clean floors. The "illegal aliens" worked for the contractor. Walmart fully cooperated in the investigation from the beginning, but this fact didn't get much press coverage. In my opinion, if government officials were doing the jobs we elected them to do, there would be no illegal aliens to hire. Touché.

As you can see, I get pretty emotional about all of this. I owe my success in life to Walmart, as do thousands of others. We get tired of all the negative publicity. However, Walmart, somewhat because of all the criticism, has continued to learn along the way. When Lee Scott became CEO, he made needed changes. He increased the staff at the Home Office to take a more proactive approach to PR and to develop our Washington connections. He also recognized the merits of some criticism and launched an initiative to help Walmart become a better corporate citizen. I credit some critics with exposing certain problems that the company continues to address. My main concern, if not evident by now, is that these same critics fail to write follow-ups about how the company responded by "doing the right thing." I feel that's because most of the criticism is funded by union money. We should all be aware of their end-game. It certainly isn't concern for the associates or American business. They want those dues coming in.

My mother retired after working as an hourly associate in the Walmart warehouse. My sister worked as a buyer's assistant until she passed away far too early. Her twin sons, Dave and Doug, work for Walmart in information systems. My niece is the personal assistant to a Walmart executive. My stepsister is an hourly associate in a Walmart store in Missouri. Another nephew works as a supervisor in a company warehouse. My stepfather drove a truck for Walmart. Two other nieces currently work as hourly Walmart associates. My other sister worked for the pharmacy area in a store in Missouri. Another one of my nephews started as an hourly associate with Walmart in Missouri, and eventually managed stores and became a buyer for the company. Another nephew managed stores for Walmart. Many of these folks had sons or daughters who are still working for Walmart. This list could go on and on, as I have already determined that I have a huge family. The point is — if big, bad Walmart is so harmful to America, how could just one family have this many members dependent upon their jobs with the company . . . in some cases because of their benefits and health care program. (Many other families could tell you the same kind of story.) Again, you won't see books written about these people, because they generally have positive things to say about the company.

In closing this blatant, yet ardent, defense of Walmart, I think of the liberal element in our country today, including Washington leadership who espouse that large corporations, banks, and Wall Street are the problem with America and that "profits" are obscene. They wish to impose heavier tax burdens and share any wealth with those who have nothing. They wish to control the pay of corporate executives. Basically, they wish to control everything. I will be the first to say that there are corrupt corporations. I believe they "mean well," but these very people who sit in Washington with degrees in law and politics profess to know how to manage businesses and the economy. They are wrong. Business and free enterprise are the engines that drive our economy.

The Wall Street motto at one time was "Greed is good." I vehemently disagree with that statement. Greed is not good. Greed creates corruption. Should some regulation and oversight be in place? Yes. But America's free enterprise system does work. It is what allowed this nation to become the best in the world. But the system also polices itself. Some critics have described Sam Walton and Walmart as greedy and only in business to create wealth. Not true. Sam Walton was anything but greedy. He wanted to be the best and largest retailer, yes. But wealth mattered not to him. He never paid himself an inflated salary. He was proud that he was creating wealth for his associates, colleagues, and shareholders. The truth is, taking a company public should be the last desirable route to take. Once done, a company is no longer its own boss. Pleasing Wall Street becomes a pervasive thought in the minds of management level personnel, and many make wrong decisions to ensure that short-term numbers make the stock look good. ENRON and many others have made these mistakes. Smart companies will continue to make decisions and operate with the long-term success of the company in mind. The stock performance will ultimately be determined by long-term success, despite the occasional bad quarter or year.

Corrupt companies eventually fold. The shareholders and customers see to that. Smart companies know they must take care of their people and shareholders. If they don't, they will no longer exist. The question really is, "What kind of company is Walmart?" Are they run by a team of crooks? No. Are they bad corporate citizens? No. Are they abusive to their people? No. Are they single-handedly driving manufacturing off-shore? No.

Walmart makes mistakes. They don't do everything right. A company of two million people can't possibly control every single decision by every single individual. So the real question is, "Do they try to do what's right? Or, do they intentionally try to abuse people, customers, and sharehold-ers, as some other companies have done?" I believe the answer is emphati-cally yes, they try to do what's right. And, no, there are no intentional abuses.

I'm sure this chapter will be controversial. Anyone can debate any-thing. While I was writing this memoir, well-meaning people often told me that readers do not like to be preached to; that I should avoid politics and religion. Perhaps so, but it is my memoir. It is my story. And I feel strongly about these things (in case you haven't guessed). I may have only a Bentonvillle high school education, but I have also experienced first-hand one of the greatest (if not *the* greatest), examples of the American free enterprise system. What else could I believe?

PART FOUR
LESSONS FOR
SUPPLIERS,
ASSOCIATES AND LIFE

CHAPTER 19

So You Want to Sell to Walmart?

I left Walmart in 1986. Along with many others in northwest Arkansas who left the company or retired, I've been approached by literally hundreds of suppliers who wish to take their products to Walmart and seek insight or help in doing that. I've chosen not to become directly involved with selling products to the company. When I hear of something that could be a good fit, I like to think they will listen. However, I understand they must be careful not to allow past relationships to influence merchandising decisions. I can attest that personal relationships have little or no bearing on selling to Walmart, and that is the way it should be. As suppliers visit with me, I caution them about being ready to call on Walmart or question whether they even should.

When I think back through my experiences, and consider the situation today, the contrast is dramatic. It might go something like this:

A supplier call — circa 1962

Buyer: "Oh, man, thanks so much for coming in. We need merchandise badly. You really will sell this to us, huh?"

Vendor: "Well, maybe. How many do you want? Are you sure you can pay us for it?"

Buyer: "Well, we're only buying for two stores right now, but we're going to grow, so you could get in on the ground floor here. If you'll sell to us, it could be the start of something big. We need a good price, though.

We really want to show the customers a bargain. Maybe you have some discontinued models or something? The main thing is to show a real deal for the customers."

Vendor: "Sure, I'll sell you the goods. Here's the price, right here. That's it. Take it or leave it. By the way, I'll need to be paid within ten days. If you can do that, we have a deal."

Buyer: "Thanks, man. We're gonna sell the heck out of this. Mr. Sam likes to stack it high and sell it cheap, ya know?"

A supplier call — circa 1982

Vendor: "Thanks so much for seeing me. We've wanted an appointment with your company for so long. Our company would be so proud to be a supplier to Walmart. These products would sell well in your stores."

Buyer: "What makes you think so? We've already got similar products in our stores. Why should we change?"

Vendor: "Well, ours is better. And we have a better price. I think."

Buyer: "Have you been in our stores? Convince me why I should drop my existing supplier for you. And if I did, will you take back all the products from the supplier I'm dropping? I can't afford the markdowns to get rid of them."

Vendor: "That would cost me a fortune."

Buyer: "Well, you're asking me to buy your products. It costs me to make a change on our modulars. If I'm going to invest in a change, then you're going to have to invest, too."

Vendor: "Well, I don't know if we're prepared to do that. I'll have to get back with you."

Buyer: "Okay, and while you're at it, if we have another meeting, I want you to bring me the information on your industry, showing the market share each of your products has in comparison to your competitors' products. I'll also need to know what accounts you have today. And if I buy from you, what percentage of your business would Walmart represent? You need to understand that we would be establishing a partnership here. It isn't just a matter of you selling, me buying. There's much more to it than that. So give me a call in a couple of weeks when you've got all your ducks in a row, and we'll discuss it one more time. I like your product, though."

A supplier call — circa 2010

Prior to meeting with the buyer, a company must provide information which might include: Sales volume for the past three years, number of employees (including minorities), top three accounts, EDI capability, a list of all direct and indirect similar competitive products, an explanation of their products' advantages and disadvantages for Walmart, and promotional plans. A company should come to the meeting prepared with answers to questions such as: Where will growth in your item or category come from? How will Walmart benefit from this growth? Who is the customer for your product? What is the size of that target market? Who are the direct and indirect competitors in your category? How will your product impact products Walmart already carries? How does your packaging impact the environment? Have you studied the sustainability factors of your item's manufacturing process from beginning to end? Are you authorizing Walmart to inspect your factories? Have you tested the product in our testing laboratory? Do you have adequate product liability insurance? What are the shipping points, terms, defective disposition terms, allowances, and dating? And the list goes on.

Once a company is ready for the meeting, it must be prepared to discuss estimates of sales, inventory, in-stock percentage, turns, shipping at retail and costs, initial margin, maintain margin, net maintain margin, markdowns, average lead time, fill rate percentage, on-time shipping percentage, co-op amount, MABD compliance, EDI pick-up rate, GMROI estimate, and myriad other details.

After learning of the expectations and preparing for the meeting, the conversation might go something like this:

Buyer: "Thanks for coming in. Our Product Development Group said your product might be something I would be interested in."

Vendor: "Thank you. Yes, I believe it could be good for Walmart, but

I've decided I'm just not ready to do business with you. Our company isn't structured to deal with your company's demands. Maybe at some point in the future we can come back and take a look at it again."

Buyer: "You mean you don't want to sell us?"

Vendor: "Yes, I want to sell to you, but I realize now that we're just not ready to do that. I'm sorry I've wasted your time here."

There was a time when selling to Walmart was every vendor's dream, and understandably so, considering the potential sales volume. However, the complexities associated with doing business with Walmart today must be thoroughly understood prior to calling on them. Their distribution and information system requirements have created the need for a level of sophistication and knowledge from suppliers which many simply can't provide. I don't believe Walmart has intentionally made doing business with them a difficult endeavor. It has been an evolving process made more complicated by government regulations, negative media exposure, and better customer data mining.

As a result of the complexities involved in adding a new item or supplier, the buyer simply does not have time to "teach" the supplier how to do business with them, and is averse to going through the process. Walmart challenges large existing suppliers to bring new and innovative products to the company and is constantly seeking acquisition possibilities. New, truly ground-breaking product developers might consider taking items to a large supplier rather than to Walmart directly. This is not to say, however, that it is unwise to sell to Walmart. It is a matter of becoming aware of and prepared for the challenges involved.

Think Like a Buyer and a Customer

While I was GMM for Walmart, I was surprised by how many suppliers came into meetings with what I called their "salesman mentality." They presented their products, dutifully pitching the merits and costs, and then waited to see if the buyer was interested. The most common mistakes suppliers make when calling on Walmart could be avoided if they would simply "think like a customer" and/or "think like a buyer." Niall

Fitzgerald of Unilever was quoted as saying, "With every decision we make, the last question we ask is 'What does the consumer think of this?'"

Common Mistakes Suppliers Make

▸ **Unfamiliar with Walmart stores.** Vendors should visit enough stores to know exactly why, how, where, and when their item or line of products would increase the buyer's sales and profits.

▸ **False claims regarding their product or industry.** The meeting could be over before it really starts if the vendor makes a claim that is false, due to a lack of knowledge about the industry or category. Too often I heard the claim, "We're the only one with this item." In reality, we may have just come out of a meeting with a competitor claiming the same thing. When calling on Walmart, you must keep in mind that the buyer visits with all major competitors on an ongoing basis, and should assume he/she knows as much about the industry as you do. In addition, the buyer expects you to be an expert in the category in which your item falls.

▸ **Poor Packaging.** Countless times I sat in meetings and listened to suppliers make a compelling case about the selling merits of their product. For example: "It is superior to competitive products because of 'its eco-friendly features,' 'better quality,' or 'one-of-a-kind innovation.'" Yet the package itself doesn't play up these features and is not designed to capture the consumer's interest at a glance. This always floored me. If packaging designers would "think like a customer," picture the product sitting on the shelf, and ask themselves if the package called out to them to buy the product, their jobs would be much easier and the products would sell so much better.

▸ **Lack of respect regarding the buyer's time.** Again, if suppliers would "think like a buyer," they would develop a better understanding of what's important and what's not, and better utilize their limited "face-to-face" time. Buyers at Walmart are inundated with responsibilities and time pressures. While a supplier's meeting with a Walmart buyer may be the most important and critical thing on his/her schedule, it's just one of hundreds of tasks for the buyer. Recognizing this, I always appreciated a supplier who asked the simple question, right up front, "How much time do we have today?" The answer would dictate what key information we would discuss and what needed to be in a "leave-behind-package." Literally hundreds of suppliers have commented to me that they can't get a response from the buyers at Walmart. "They won't return phone calls." I point out to them that they should "put themselves in the buyer's shoes." He/she has hundreds of current suppliers requesting meetings and three or four times that number of potential suppliers trying to get an appointment. In addition, buyers field thousands of intra-company e-mails and calls, attend countless internal meetings and make scores of required trips, all while trying to manage personal lives. Honestly, I don't know how anyone could ever return a phone call.

▸ **Not Knowing Your Bottom Line.** Every supplier calling on Walmart knows the company's buyers are "tough negotiators." They are demanding. They want the best price. Critics are quick to cite cases where suppliers got hurt or went bankrupt dealing with Walmart. There are undoubtedly cases where Walmart buyers treated suppliers unfairly, but more often than not, problems arise because of the suppliers' failure to understand the ramifications of selling to a company the size of Walmart. Walmart manages its business down to individual item performance. They make changes any time they realize sales and profits can be improved. It's that simple and suppliers should be aware of that when they decide to sell to Walmart. If, in an effort to make the sale, suppliers price merchandise too low to absorb unknown costs and still maintain the ability to survive in the event Walmart drops their items, they have no one to blame but themselves. There are many options today for selling products to consumers. As large as Walmart has become, they only represent 10 to 12 percent of retail sales in most categories. Suppliers simply have to educate themselves on the pros and cons of selling to them and know their "bottom line" price. Sometimes, knowing when to say "no" and walk away is the smartest decision they can make.

Buyers: Respect the Suppliers/Learn From Them

I always found that a smart buyer will show respect to and utilize the knowledge of their suppliers to maximize sales and performance in their categories. During my term at Walmart, I was fortunate to work with experienced "merchants" responsible for buying the various categories of goods. They were knowledgeable as a result of store-level experience, longevity, and expertise in their assigned areas. This resulted in a mutual respect in supplier relationships. It should go without saying that both Walmart and their suppliers have the same goals. Both sides want to increase sales and make a profit while doing so. An unprofitable supplier does not benefit Walmart. We constantly counseled the buyers to treat our suppliers with respect, whether telling them "yes" or "no." Frequently, major suppliers informed me that we received better pricing because our competitors' buyers were arrogant and overly-demanding. Those are conversations I've always remembered.

Key Points for buyers:

"You never get something for nothing." That quote, made many years ago by the key executive from Lever Brothers, is still pertinent today. Buyers and companies that continually demand more and more concessions from suppliers, while simultaneously demanding the same or lower pricing, are simply positioning themselves for long-term problems. Suppliers know what it costs to do business with each of their accounts. They have a responsibility to their company and shareholders to make a profit, just as Walmart does. They must recoup any costs through pricing. Buyers always resist higher pricing caused by increased costs of raw materials, manufacturing, transportation, inflation, concessions, etc., but in a true "partnership," both sides must be conciliatory. Ultimately, the consumer pays for the increase. The supplier must control expenses wherever possible to avoid a price bump, and the buyer must understand the supplier's situation for a mutually profitable partnership to thrive. As I stated in Chapter 11, Walmart received better pricing than larger competitors in the '70s and '80s, because we didn't ask for concessions or slotting fees,

treated suppliers with respect, focused on the customer, and behaved ethically in our actions and relationships. Smart buyers will try to make their suppliers "partners" rather than adversaries.

Target pricing. I believe this term and buying approach should be eliminated from the buyer/supplier relationship. When a buyer demands that a supplier meet his "targeted" price on an item, it often results in a sacrifice in quality. A key electronics supplier shared this fact with me in 1980 when we sought a particular price point on a tape player for our sale circular. We obtained the target price, but ultimately experienced heavy returns on the item. In an effort to meet the pricing demands, the supplier had substituted cheaper plastic components and switches. Selling poorly-made products to your customers is the last thing any retailer or supplier should do.

Staying humble. The successful buyer is one who does his/her best to stay humble. Suppliers can help or hurt Walmart now and in the future. I learned this long ago. I admit I sometimes lost my temper with suppliers and occasionally the meetings turned negative; that's part of the nature of the business. When suppliers are wrong, they must be corrected. However, it can be handled in a respectful manner. Buyers should make an earnest attempt to remain humble. Although Walmart is the largest company in the world, they will receive better pricing and achieve more success in the long-run by behaving in a fair and respectful way with suppliers. When a twenty-year veteran principal of a large consumer product company is verbally abused or treated disrespectfully by a recent college grad in his/her twenties (who has been buying for perhaps six months), what do you suppose will happen? That supplier will favor the competition. I've personally seen this many times.

On-the-job education. Successful buyers educate themselves in their categories by every means available. In addition to visiting their stores, their competitors' stores, and trade shows, they listen and learn from every supplier meeting they attend. Computer reports and data are great for knowing what is selling and what is not, but do not portray what buyers should be doing that they are not. Peter F. Drucker said, "I find more and more executives less and less well-informed about the outside world, if only because they believe that the data on the computer printouts are ipso facto information." I will also repeat the quote attributed to Sam Walton; "A computer can tell you what you have sold, but cannot tell you how much you could have sold." If executives aren't allowing time for the buyers to be out in the marketplace and in the stores, they are making a big mistake.

Innovative and new products. It is a fact that most truly new and innovative products are developed by small startup suppliers — the very companies perceived to be too small to sell to a company the size of Walmart. This presents a challenge to a buyer. Where and how does a buyer find or source these products? This question is not easily answered. But it does relate to the "education" mentioned above. Because of Walmart's sheer size, most new products are sold in competitive stores first. The competition welcomes these new products because they do not have to compete with Walmart on price. This is all the more reason for smart buyers to get out into the marketplace. In the 1980s, I went with the buyers to many of the large trade shows. Typically, we would meet with our major suppliers, which would consume most of the day. Realizing these meetings took place at the Home Office anyway, I wanted to get a first-hand feel for the trends and new items. So I cancelled meetings with our major suppliers and set aside two days for "just walking the floor." I found numerous items and new exciting trends in various categories, which resulted in improved sales and profits for our company. The buyers who simply sit in their offices and visit with existing large suppliers will severely limit their category's potential.

Risks in being too large. A key lesson I learned as GMM in the 1980s relates to the dangers for both Walmart and its suppliers regarding "percentage of business they represent." For several years, Walmart, in an effort to protect their suppliers, wanted to know what percentage of the supplier's business our company represented. Today, with the leading large consumer brand companies, Walmart represents from 15 to 40 percent of their business. Usually, the smaller the supplier, the higher the percentage. There's no easy solution. In 1980, for example, Roper, a manufacturer of lawn mowers with the Craftsman brand for Sears, asked for a meeting. They disclosed that Sears represented 67 percent of their total business, and that Sears dictated what price and how much profit margin they were "allowed" to make. They begged us to buy some mowers from them to reduce their reliance on Sears. At the time, we were buying MTD and Murray mowers, and chose not to do business with Roper. But it brought to light the potential problem for suppliers to Walmart as they became much larger. Conversely, if Walmart limits their business to just the large suppliers, the company will become more susceptible to whatever price they demand. Over the years, we always felt it a safer practice to purchase from at least two suppliers in all major merchandise categories.

To summarize my thoughts: I recognize how difficult it is for a company the size and scope of Walmart, and the suppliers who sell to and service it, to manage their mutual businesses. There must be a constant effort to enforce a culture of "mutual respect," as well as train buyers in the "supplier/buyer partnership" approach.

I suggest both buyers and suppliers remember this ancient proverb:

Best is to know — and know you know. Next best is to know that
you don't know. Third best is to know, but not realize it.
Worst is not to know that you don't know.

CHAPTER 20

Brand vs. Value and Merchandising

O ne of the big issues I contended with during my term as GMM at Walmart was the brand/value equation. That conundrum is as important today as it was then, maybe more so. No one, including me, could question the significance of brands (brand name products). A brand is built through a combination of quality, trust, promise, and consistency in the offering. The Walmart brand, for example, was built on the promise of saving customers money — period. Value, on the other hand, is represented by a price and/or a brand, plus a perception on the part of the consumer. I've seen the formula described as Quality + Price = Value. You could replace Value with Brand in that equation.

Most large supplier accounts at Walmart become so through brand recognition. Perhaps the biggest and best example is Proctor & Gamble. They get it. They know how to build and maintain their brand relevance, but also understand that the consumer demands value. They maintain their number one position because they understand how to market their brands.

The challenges to recognizable brands are the low-cost alternatives such as direct imports and private-label merchandise. In some cases, quality is sacrificed for price, but the true winners are those items or lines of equal quality, yet priced well below the leading brands. Therein is the lesson I wish to point out in this chapter.

The 3M/Manco Story

During the deep recession of the early '80s, the cost of raw materials was escalating. In this situation, Walmart's suppliers justifiably requested price increases, with production costs rising beyond what they could absorb. Price increase requests ranged from 3 to 6 percent. It was normal practice for Walmart buyers to resist these increases, since we had to, in turn, increase retail prices to the customer. In one case, we received a very unusual request. The 3M Company requested a 16 percent increase on their masking tape and duct tape items, and slightly less on their line of Scotch transparent tapes. We were stunned. No one had ever requested such a large immediate increase. The buyer and I agreed that it just wasn't going to happen. We took the case to our superior, Al Johnson, and up the chain of command all the way to Sam Walton.

When 3M learned of our refusal, they requested a meeting. Their six-man team stormed in and insisted that we had to accept the increase, because we could not do without their "brand." They were arrogant and demanding. We offered them an increase, but more in the range of what we gave other companies: 4 percent. They stood their ground.

Just prior to this incident, I had taken a meeting with a small company, Manco, based in Cleveland. The company owner and CEO, Jack Kahl, had asked to do more business with us. We carried their duct tape in a few of our stores. This company also offered masking tape. When 3M dug in, I instructed our buyer to call Jack to issue a challenge. I told him I wanted to prove a point to 3M. I contended that tape was a "commodity" item; if the quality was equal, the customer would not consider the brand more important than the price. We told Jack that if he sent samples that equaled 3M in quality, we would give him the business in half of our stores. Jack couldn't believe we were offering him this opportunity, and eagerly accepted the challenge.

We called the 3M team back for another meeting. I actually enjoyed telling them that I had good news and bad news. The good news was that we were offering them a 4 percent price increase. The bad news was that they were losing half of our stores to a competitor. They were irate and insisted on seeing Sam Walton personally, which we allowed them to do. After Mr. Sam explained to them in no uncertain terms, "You are crazy if you expect us to increase the price to our customers by 16 percent," they left unhappy, but with their arrogance intact.

Making this significant change left me feeling uneasy. I thought I was right, but what if customers complained because we didn't offer 3M or Scotch-brand masking tapes? The retail price on Manco's tapes was approximately 30 percent less than that of 3M's.

My misgivings were short-lived. After the change, our sales in the stores offering Manco tapes immediately jumped by more than 30 percent compared to stores selling 3M tapes, a significant difference. We considered giving all the stores to Manco, but still recognized the value of carrying the Scotch or 3M brand. Eventually, we offered both, but 3M came to realize the limits of their brand, and subsequently became far more reasonable. I believe they learned a lesson as well. By the way, to my knowledge we never received a single customer complaint about replacing 3M with Manco tapes.

Manco went on to become a valued supplier to Walmart. The company ultimately was bought by the Henkel Corporation, who then sold the operation to the current owner, ShurTech Brands. Several years after this incident, they became the first supplier to win vendor of the year awards in three merchandise categories: stationery, hardware, and housewares. Jack Kahl had long been an admirer of Sam Walton and patterned his company's culture on Mr. Sam's "Rules of Business." Jack, out of loyalty, demanded his team focus on meeting his largest customer's needs, and as a result, experienced the same growth curve as Walmart. Their brand is highly recognized today, as Jack literally developed and trademarked the little yellow duck on his packaging, along with the "DUCK" tape name. Their dedication to the consumer (and to their largest customer, Walmart), makes it easy to benefit from a long-term business relationship.

This story points out a couple of important lessons. First, brands are important, but how important? At what point does perceived value enter the equation? Can a company be too proud of its brand? Second, if suppliers are comfortable and have no real competition, will they take advantage by offering uncompetitive pricing? I believe that the Manco/3M competitive situation has been good for both companies. It was certainly good for Walmart. The competition made both Manco and 3M better suppliers.

During that same recessionary period, Rubbermaid also issued significant price increases. This was when they introduced their "flip-top" trash can, which instantly became a hot item. Although they demanded a hefty price increase, we believed it to be a realistic one. Over time, however, Rubbermaid extended this price increase to all of their products, because "people want our brand." Rubbermaid products were (and are), without question, of high quality. At that time, Walmart maintained that many of its customers simply could not afford to pay $6.00 to $7.00 for a trash can or laundry basket. While touring the Chicago Housewares Show, the buyers and I sought an alternative to Rubbermaid. We found a company called SteriLite, whose products were of comparable quality at half the price. We bought SteriLite and promoted their line extensively in our stores. The program was highly successful. We continued to carry products from both companies. The lesson here is that brands should be cautious not to over-value their products. Furthermore, if they wish to do business with Walmart, they should consider offering lower-cost alternatives.

Evolving Brands

When I worked in merchandising, some of the leading electronics and appliance brands included household names such as JVC, Panasonic, Pioneer, Sylvania, Samsung, Black & Decker, Sunbeam, GE, and Emerson. In today's marketplace, many older distinguished brands no longer represent existing companies, but are simply brand names that have been purchased or licensed and applied to a line of products made by someone else. You also see retail shelves full of brands that have appeared only recently, such as Haier and Vizio. Why this constant shift in brand awareness?

This is a result of the "value" equation. Haier and Vizio began as the low-cost alternative to some of the major brands. As a result, they received shelf space. Today, they are recognized as brands — good ones. They achieved this success by offering products at a lower price while matching the quality of many of the leading brand name products, whose high marketing costs are recovered in retail pricing. All suppliers must keep in mind that a large segment of the consuming public simply cannot afford to pay the price for top brands. There will always be a need for lower-cost alternatives.

When I was involved with Walmart and Sam's, we recognized that Sony represented the upscale brand. We wanted to carry Sony for the image it portrayed — Walmart offers quality merchandise. Truth be known, we sold very few Sony items. They were simply too expensive for our customers. We found that many other brands also offered high quality, but at a much lower cost. Our customers shopped at Walmart because they had confidence in our brand — Walmart. They also knew they would be taken care of if they had a problem with the merchandise, no matter the cost of the item.

Some Thoughts for Walmart and Suppliers

(1) Companies that invest in R & D (research and development) for emerging technologies or new innovative products typically try to recoup their upfront expenses in the initial price of the merchandise. I'm certainly not a product guy or an MBA, but I believe R & D should be an investment in the business, not built into the cost of a product. I'm sure "experts" will laugh at me for making that statement, but I refer to a good book, *Crossing the Chasm*, by Geoffrey A. Moore. Mr. Moore describes the challenge of bringing products to the marketplace which appeal to the "early adopters" (customers who want the latest, greatest), then making the products affordable for the masses, and crossing the chasm to reach them. He points out how many products fail to reach the masses from the companies that actually created ·them. Often, lower-priced competitors pick up the mantle. I believe companies and brands that have truly invested in innova-

tions and/or better quality, but have priced the products artificially high, leave themselves vulnerable to lower-priced competitors and decreased market share.

Today, flat-panel televisions are the rage and have become affordable for most customers. But as far back as 1981, while attending the Consumer Electronics show in Las Vegas, I saw a demonstration of a flat-panel television hanging on the wall of a supplier's booth. It was being displayed only as "the future technology" that would take years to reach the public. When first introduced, the price was around $15,000. Of course, the companies had no chance of making a profit until a large segment of the buying public jumped on the bandwagon. Typically, each new electronic innovation is introduced to the public at an extremely high price, and then sold for less each year thereafter. I truly believe that priced lower in the beginning, a company could "own the market" for several years, keeping low-priced followers at bay. The industry has inadvertently trained most consumers to wait a couple of years to buy emerging electronic innovations, knowing the price will come down markedly. I equate it to buying a new car. I don't understand why people suffer the depreciation the minute they drive off the lot, when a year-old demo model is just as good and a much better "value."

(2) Globalization of the retail and consumer goods industries has resulted in no more secrets. Just as access to *Kelly Blue Book* pricing on automobiles by the consuming public has changed auto sales, the Internet has enabled competitors and suppliers access to myriad details of importing and pricing, plus financial details of public companies. Some of Walmart's successful suppliers have been able to build their businesses profitably because of their attention to supply-chain economics, new strategies in marketing expenditures, and cutting unnecessary costs from overhead. They've learned from the Walmart lesson. There will always be upscale brands, targeting upscale customers, but that's a different model and different world from that of the mass consumers. Walmart customers demand value. Whether a name brand product company or a producer of a low-cost alternative product, questions must be asked: What customer are you targeting? Does the cus-

tomer perceive your product as a value? Does your product truly command premium pricing, and if so, why? Are you satisfied with your market share or do you want more?

(3) There is a large base of consumers who have no choice but to buy the lowest-priced products they can find. This group is larger than the economic gurus or marketing executives seemingly want to admit. I don't believe any major brand targets them. This group has been a large segment of Walmart's core customer base from the beginning. They shop there with the confidence they will save money. If they truly believe a $3.00 private label laundry detergent will get the job done, they will buy it as opposed to the leading brand ... not because they want to, but because they *have* to. They must stretch their dollars as far as possible to pay the rent, buy clothing for their children, and/or simply make ends meet. Walmart has an obligation to this core customer, and historically has met their needs as well as any retailer. At the same time, they must also appeal to the consumers who demand higher-quality products and top name brands. In many small communities, Walmart is the major retailer in town, and customers expect to find the assortment and prices for which the company has always been noted. Both Walmart and their suppliers must continue to work together to offer these customers what they want and need. I speak to this issue because I lived the experience. As a young couple with two small children, barely living paycheck-to-paycheck, we were forced to look for the cheapest price on most of our everyday needs ... and the brand mattered very little. Even before that, growing up in Hiwassee on welfare subsistence, my mom bought only the bare necessities to exist — and that was long before the first Walmart opened its doors. Walmart has an obligation to consumers such as my family in those lean years. And suppliers can benefit by recognizing this fact.

(4) A broad assortment of merchandise fulfilling the everyday needs of consumers is the life-blood of general merchandise discount retailers. However, growth and comparable store sales increases are generally a result of finding more volume in promotional, new, and "impulse" merchandising. Common sense tells us that

there are only five factors which can contribute to higher sales in a typical store from year-to-year: (1) population growth, (2) inflationary pricing, (3) higher average purchases per consumer, (4) impulse purchase of items not on their shopping list, and/or (5) new products not previously offered. Actually, a combination of these factors should be given ongoing attention.

Walmart historically has excelled in the offering of special promotional purchases and new, exciting products. Through their use of Action Alley (the promotional tables and stacks running down the main aisles), cross-merchandising of impulse merchandise on "clip-strips" and "side-kick" displays on end caps, and an extensive assortment of "pick-up" items on or around the checkouts, I believe the company led the industry in reaping "extra" sales from their shoppers. I recall when upper management considered these "impulse" purchases to be such an important part of the overall sales increases that the company actually separated them into a new departmental category with its own buyers. Clifford Young, a friend of mine, led this category for quite some time, achieving billions in sales.

In an effort to improve the shopping environment for the customers, much of this emphasis has been recently curtailed, and the comparable store sales reflect the negative impact of the change. The size of the company today makes it difficult to buy truly new, innovative products from small suppliers. This challenge warrants further discussion, because Walmart needs to find ways to aggressively offer impulse and new items.

(5) Without question, Walmart outperformed most of their competitors because of Sam Walton's insistence that *everyone* in the company be involved with merchandising. To that end, he created programs designed to enthuse everyone about being a "merchant." Admittedly, certain company positions have little to do with directly buying or promoting merchandise. But whether it's IT, distribution, transportation, PR, finance, or insurance, the more awareness managers have in this area, the better overall decisions they can make.

On a couple of occasions, Sam Walton shared with us a statement made by Bob Kahn, a former Walmart director and close friend. In a newsletter he wrote in 1968, Bob made this statement:

> The introduction of the computer in retailing is tending to produce the myopic merchant of the future who in the long run must lose out to the fundamental merchant of the past and his progeny.

Mr. Sam then went on to say, "Let all of us in Walmart continue to think and believe we're merchants, even if we choose some occasional losers, such as our outstanding President Dave Glass with his key chains and our head merchandiser, Exec. VP Bill Fields and his Crackling Oat Bran Cereal. I'm being facetious and jealous, probably because as of now, David and his key chains are ahead of my $1.00 can of peanuts. But the race isn't over. The truth is, if we're aggressive and merchandise-driven with all our associates throughout Walmart, we'll make mistakes, but on balance, we'll win because we learn and correct."

Yes, Sam Walton was first and forever a merchant. He wanted everyone in Walmart to be merchants. We were in the merchandise business, so what else should we be? He always reminded us in the G.O. that the store folks knew better what the customer was asking for and needed than any of us. And he was right.

CHAPTER 21

The Third Party Issue

Within both Walmart and the supplier community, the issue of dealing with and through "third-parties" has been a constant point of discussion and confusion. The term third-party can represent a number of different relationships: manufacturer's representatives (reps), brokers, in-store service companies, agents, distributors, and rack jobbers. All are, in one form or another, third-parties.

The issue I wish to discuss here is the one involving manufacturer's reps. I touched on the subject in an earlier chapter. In explanation, manufacturer's reps work as middlemen. They attempt to sell products to various companies for the manufacturers they represent. Many reps still call on Walmart today. They continue to serve a key role in bringing products to the marketplace. A large number of manufacturers develop products, but have no corporate structure for selling and managing their business with retailers. That's where reps come in. However, selling to and managing the business with the mega-retailers of today requires a level of expertise and structure that most reps cannot offer. Successful reps have developed their own organizations to manage the details required. They literally provide their manufacturers the expertise and processes necessary in selling to mega-retailers.

Most suppliers and reps don't understand why and when the rep quandary became an issue for Walmart. Because of my direct involvement when this issue initially came to a head in 1980, I'd like to share the story and help all to better understand both sides of the equation.

283

The Lawn Mower Rep Problem

In 1980, while serving as GMM, our merchandising division was planning for the spring lawn and garden sale circular. We decided to make an impact with consumers by putting a twenty-inch, 3 1/2 horsepower lawn mower on the front page priced at $39.99, a tremendously low price for this item at the time. We ran into a problem when our suppliers, MTD and Murray, could not offer the price necessary for us to sell a mower for under $40.00. However, a rep had called on one of our buyers representing Air Capitol Mfg., a lawn mower manufacturer in Memphis. AirCap could give us the price we needed, but the lawn mowers were powered by Tecumseh engines. Consumers generally perceived the Tecumseh engine as of lesser quality than Briggs & Stratton, but we felt the tradeoff would be worth it for the excitement we would generate with the price point.

From the beginning days of Walmart's rapid growth until the early '80s, many orders and most communication with reps was mailed to the rep's home or office address, rather than directly to the manufacturers. It was simply the way we operated in those days. We ordered thousands of the AirCap lawn mowers featured in our circular, with the understanding they were to be delivered in stages to our warehouses. When the first ship date arrived, the lawn mowers didn't. Our buyer contacted AirCap — they were not aware of any orders for Walmart. We couldn't believe it. When we told AirCap how many mowers we had ordered, it was their turn not to believe it. They informed us there was "no way" they could provide the quantity we needed at this late date. We had ordered 50,000 mowers and they could provide only 10,000. We scrambled, begged, and pleaded to get more mowers from our current suppliers, MTD and Murray, to make up the difference. They sold us the mowers, but at the $39.99 price point we lost $10.00 on every mower sold.

As we began to research what happened to the AirCap order, we found that the orders had been mailed to the rep's home in Mississippi. Although inconceivable that an order of that size could have been mishandled, it turned out that the manufacturer had never received the order from the rep. It also meant the rep hadn't bothered to follow up on the order from the time we placed it until the ship date. A lot of things had to go wrong to wind up in this predicament, kind of a "perfect storm" of ordering.

I was irate. Our buyer tried to reach the rep at his home, only to learn that he was "in the Bahamas" for two weeks and could not be reached. Upon his return, he was immediately summoned to Bentonville for a meeting. That meeting took place in Sam Walton's office. I suppose the fact that Sam Walton himself wanted to be in on this meeting is indicative of how serious the company considered the problem. For the protection of readers with delicate sensibilities, I will not repeat what was said. Suffice it to say it wasn't pretty. In the end, we "asked" the rep to never darken Walmart's door again.

In addition to losing money on the sale of the mowers that spring, we also received many customer complaints because the mowers we carried weren't the same ones we advertised. Although customers got a higher-priced mower with a Briggs & Stratton engine, some felt we had misled them. The 10,000 mowers that AirCap shipped didn't last one day of the sale, so we gave rainchecks that could be redeemed for the higher-priced mowers over the next several weeks. What a nightmare!

As a result of this fiasco, Walmart decided that we would no longer mail orders to a rep's home address. We would always send them directly to the manufacturer. Additionally, I received instructions to meet with our top suppliers who used reps to call on our company. My mission? To explain that we desired a "direct relationship" with manufacturers, thereby eliminating reps. In light of recent occurrences, I understood and agreed with this position.

Vendor/Rep Meetings

Throughout the next few months, I held a constant series of meetings with the key suppliers who utilized reps. I explained to the principals that Walmart desired to have a direct relationship with them in order to improve communication and ensure a "decision-maker" participated in every meeting. Often, when calling on a buyer, reps could not make the necessary decisions for the manufacturers regarding price, dating, ship dates, and many other details key to the transaction. They usually had to "get back with you on that."

Manufacturer's reps are paid a commission on sales to retailers. Some earn these commissions and some don't. In my opinion, the reps involved with Walmart at this time fell into one of two categories. The best ones represented only one or very few companies, in which case they were often authorized to act in lieu of the manufacturer as a "principal." These reps were fully authorized to make decisions for the manufacturers they represented. A "direct" relationship could actually become a negative for us because the company had no one who better understood the supplier/retailer relationship and negotiating factors. Other reps represented any company they felt could help them sell items to Walmart. In many cases they didn't know any more about their manufacturer than we did; they were more of a bother than anything else. I called them "lobby-loungers," because they hung around the lobby every day in the hope of making a sale.

The meetings with the suppliers taught me a lot. Many of them had a good, long-standing relationship with their rep firms, and completely trusted them to represent their companies. These suppliers informed me that regardless of our company's position, they would need to retain their reps to call on other clients within our trade territory. Others told us they would hire the rep as a "national accounts manager," who would continue calling on us. In this way, he could represent the company as a principal, but one who understood Walmart's needs better than anyone within their organization.

Many suppliers explained that their reps were under contract, so it would be illegal to fire them outright — according to obscure laws that protected their right to make a living. (I never understood this or found if it was true, but I quickly decided not to force the issue.)

After all the meetings, I found there was no clear-cut answer to the rep issue. I made the decision to leave it up to the suppliers to handle their particular situations and rep relationships. Walmart had grown large enough to become an important customer to suppliers. Many simply decided to assign a "national accounts manager" to the Walmart account.

Good Reps

Throughout my career at Walmart, I came to know a number of reps personally. I can attest that many of them actually fought with their factories to secure the best deals possible for us (often at the expense of their own sales commissions). Three individuals come quickly to mind: Dick Berryman, who sold Zebco; Don Brown, who sold Emerson Electronics; and Frank Fletcher, who sold Decorel picture frames and lamps. I dealt with other high-quality reps as well. As large as Walmart is today, reps can still serve a vital role in bringing new, innovative products to the company. But to do so, their association with the manufacturers must be structured properly and their role must be much broader than "just making the sale." They must manage the account and offer the services required by Walmart for data analysis.

Reps serve a legitimate function in assigned geographical areas by calling on smaller customers for whom it is not financially feasible to assign account executives. These smaller accounts, in the aggregate, continue to represent a large percentage of a supplier's total business. To adequately compensate these regional reps, most suppliers will pay them a small commission on the sales to large national accounts in their territory, utilizing them to handle some of the mundane details associated with the large clients.

Some rep firms and brokers across the country have chosen to concentrate on specific product categories such as housewares, appliances, sporting goods, lawn and garden, and more. These firms often employ people much more knowledgeable in dealing with retailers than the manufacturers themselves. Smart buyers will recognize and utilize that expertise to their advantage. The challenge for retailers is identifying these firms. Sales commissions should be a nonissue, because in many cases it costs a supplier more to hire and maintain a direct sales force than to work with third parties, who already live in the territory of the account.

The Walmart organization has changed significantly since I left. The lessons I learned were in the era before the company became a large purveyor of groceries. The grocery business necessitates the use of in-store services and brokers much more than my experience in general merchandise (non-foods). In-store item delivery, maintenance, and sampling, for example, are all handled by third-party service providers. Brokers are typically involved with many of the smaller brand manufacturers in selling into the myriad of grocery distributors and retailers. The lesson I learned in 1980 is still true today — it would be a mistake for any retailer to take an inflexible position in eliminating reps who facilitate the process of sourcing and buying merchandise.

The third-party issue continues to exist and seems to be an ongoing bone of contention with some retail executives and buyers. In my opinion, creating a steadfast policy for or against third-parties is not a viable solution. Establishing guidelines for identifying the "right" third parties would be more appropriate and beneficial.

CHAPTER 22

Top Ten List of Advice for Success in the Workplace (with Apologies to David Letterman)

As I reflect on my career and think about the highs and lows, I hope the lessons I share are of benefit to others. You are now familiar with my personal story, which runs the gamut from struggling stock boy to senior officer's position. The lessons I learned in that progression are multifold. Students entertaining the idea of a career in retailing, folks currently working in the stores with the goal of advancement, or middle-management personnel climbing their way up the corporate ladder will hopefully benefit from my comments. Here are the top ten areas I feel are important for a successful career in the retail and the corporate world:

1) Is Retail What You Want To Do?

When I started as a stock boy, I simply needed a job, any job. I had no designs on a retail career, but once I started working in the stores I quickly grew to like what I was doing. Although it involved long hours, low pay, and hard work, I took pride in my job. I enjoyed checking in freight, building a nice display of merchandise on an end cap, and watching it sell. I honestly can't explain why. Perhaps it was just "in my blood."

Whether you're currently working in a store, considering working in one, or graduating college and contemplating a job in retail, the first step is to determine whether retailing is something you'll enjoy. You must determine if you're willing to do the hard work necessary for long-term success. People work in retail stores for many reasons. Some need a secondary income to help support the family. Some need to earn extra money while going to school. Others need additional income to support retirement or maybe it's the only job available to them. In all these cases, progression into management is not necessarily their goal. The guidance I offer here is meant for people who desire to pursue a career in retailing.

When choosing a career, you should not waste your time working at a job that doesn't appeal to you. If you don't enjoy the work and can't be passionate about your chosen path, you won't be successful. Simple as that. My first piece of advice is: "Be convinced this is what you want to do."

2) Be the Best You Can Be

Whether you're an hourly associate shagging carts from the lot, a janitor cleaning toilets, or a college grad assigned an intern position, you must temporarily put your ambition and aspirations on hold, and determine to be the very best at your assigned task. In other words, like the older folks used to say, "Be where you're at, boy." (Or girl.) I know I possessed an inherent desire to be the best at whatever I did. I'm not sure this trait can be taught. But I do know that without this passion to excel, you more than likely will not succeed in retailing. I once heard that General Colin Powell, after a speaking engagement, stood in a "meet-and-greet" line when a young officer asked him, "General Powell, what advice would you give me to further my advancement in the officer's ranks?" The General replied, "It's real simple, Lieutenant; be the best damn lieutenant you can be." This puts what I'm saying in simple terms.

Throughout my career, I watched ambitious people push to be promoted. When department managers, assistant managers, store managers, or buyers felt they deserved to be promoted, but the promotion didn't come as soon as they felt it should, their ambitions affected their attitudes. Ultimately, they became negative and worried — more concerned about the promotion than doing their jobs well. They often grew bitter, looking for reasons they were being passed over. They spurned the constructive guidance shared with them during evaluations. I can honestly say that I never put my desire for promotion ahead of doing my job to the best of my ability. I took on everything as a challenge. I guess I had an "I'll show them" attitude. Regardless of the circumstances, superiors recognize when a job is being done well and by whom. I was never jealous of or worried about someone getting promoted around me. That was their business. So my second piece of advice is: "Strive to do the best you possibly can at whatever job you're assigned, for however long you must. The promotions come as a result of a job well-done."

3) Be a Self-Starter

Regardless of how you get your foot in the door — even though you are being the best you can be — you'll realize there is much you don't know. Rather than wait for someone to take them under their wing or become a "mentor," successful people aggressively set about educating themselves. Although we weren't so sophisticated in the early years at Walmart, I'm sure today there are numerous training and educational materials available to associates within the organization. Actively seek out these tools and information. Volunteer for assignments to further your knowledge, even though it will require more of your time. Ask questions. Become informed. Management recognizes the proactive people in their ranks. The old-fashioned term for this is "self-starter." They will achieve success far more quickly than folks who do just enough to get by. They stand out. Without question, every hourly associate who ultimately rose to the position of store manager (or higher) would tell you one or more mentors helped with their careers. But how does one gain a "mentor"? Because that mentor noticed them at some point. They were noticed because they were self-starters, worked harder than others, and educated themselves to become better. My third piece of advice is: "Be a self-starter. Don't wait for others to tell you what to do. Be proactive in educating yourself about the business."

4) Learn From All Types of Bosses

One of the most common mistakes I repeatedly saw associates make was quitting or developing a bad attitude, because they couldn't get along with or didn't like a particular boss. As you've read in the preceding pages, I came very close to doing the same thing many times myself. What a shame it is to see a person throw away a career because of one individual. You will work for all types of supervisors. Some you'll like and admire; they may serve as mentors in your career. Others may be poor people managers — managing through intimidation, fear, or a lack of simple management skills. (They may have been put into their positions through politics or favoritism.) No matter the reason, if you deem your boss to be weak or difficult to work for, keep in mind that he or she is not permanent. Supervisors and management positions constantly change. You should not sacrifice your career because of a problem with a particular individual. You can learn things from good supervisors as well as bad. Later, when facing the responsibilities of people management, you'll remember how and why you felt resentment for that bad boss and can avoid making the same mistakes with your people. My fourth piece of advice is: "Don't let a bad boss end your career. Learn both good and bad management techniques from your supervisors — for future use when you take on management responsibilities of your own."

5) Communication and Evaluation

One of the hardest things in life is to accept constructive criticism. (I include myself in this challenge.) However, done properly, the evaluation process can be the most helpful tool for anyone desiring a successful career. The first important step is communicating to your supervisor the desire to advance. The second important step is to objectively and actively ask your supervisors about areas in which you need to improve. There's an undeniable truth in the workplace that not everyone is cut out for a management position. The intrinsic qualities necessary for management level positions simply don't exist in some people. It's difficult for individuals to accept they are members of this group. Many people who reported to me over the years desired promotions, but were incapable of advancing. It was my unenviable job to point out why they would not receive a promotion, or through the evaluation process, outline improvements they needed to make to be considered for advancement. In the latter instance, they would eventually come to the realization that promotion wasn't in the cards. At that point, they would either resign or become satisfied with their current position. I actually held in high esteem people who, twenty years later, were still positive and happy doing the same job they had from the beginning.

But if your goal is to progress through the ranks, accept constructive criticism positively. See it as a challenge. Whether you agree or not, if your supervisor perceives shortcomings, set about to change his mind by making an effort to improve. My fifth piece of advice is: "Let your supervisor know you want to advance with the company, but be open and willing to accept constructive criticism. Be proactive toward self-improvement."

6) Store Level Experience

To advance in a retail organization, it should be mandatory to work a certain period of time in the stores. This should be required of hourly associates already in the stores, as well as college graduates with degrees in marketing, business, finance, law, information systems, or any other specialty area. During my career, we spent considerable time studying the causes of failure of many successful companies. Far too often, failure resulted when companies grew so large they felt it necessary to fill the management ranks with MBAs or other highly-educated individuals. Certain positions do require formal education. However, experience at the store level leads to knowledge regarding where and how the numbers are generated. This is far more important than just the ability to read numbers when challenged to make the right decisions for long-term success. In my opinion, the ideal future management talent is one who has a good education, combined with some store level experience and management background.

A friend and old colleague of mine eventually became head of IS (Information Systems) at Walmart. He once told me that their division had, at any given time, more than 400 projects on their "wish list" from various management folks. They needed to set priorities for getting them all done. Without a detailed knowledge of what was important to their core business of buying and selling merchandise for a profit, they would be managing these projects "blindly," not knowing how one decision might affect the overall company.

Being the CFO of a company the size of Walmart is a tremendous challenge. One of the primary responsibilities is to communicate with and appease the Wall Street retail analysts and keep the shareholders happy. They are also responsible for participating in the decisions and strategic directions to help meet monthly, quarterly, and annual financial goals. In this process, many companies make short-term decisions that help achieve the immediate goals, but might negatively affect over-all long-term performance. Continually successful companies always keep the long-term health of their business in mind, sometimes at the expense of short-term achievement. This is generally true of organizations that require management to have at least some hands-on experience in their core business. It's easy to say, "cut the inventory," but what effect will that have on sales? It's easy to say "cut the payroll," but what effect will that have on customer service? My sixth piece of advice is: "When applying for a job with a retailer, ask about the opportunity to gain store-level experience as an intern or as part of the training process."

7) So You're a Minority Associate

With companies that are proactive in their diversity hiring process, a person in one of the recognized minority groups (women, African-Americans, Hispanics, etc.) may be granted opportunities over other applicants. If you're in one of those groups and given the opportunity, the day you go to work, forget why they hired you. From this point on, you're just another of a large group of associates on the payroll. Your attitude, goals, and advancement opportunities require the same effort and approach as that of your fellow associates. I've observed many associates who believed they deserved special attention because of their minority status. Believe me, they don't. Everyone is equal in the workplace. Job performance is the key to success in any career. My seventh piece of advice is: "Everyone is equal in the workplace. Job performance gets you ahead."

8) Neatness Counts

Now, this little section may be somewhat controversial. (I might be considered old school or a fuddy-duddy, but remember I was a maverick in my younger days.) Experts say companies should adjust to change in the workforce. They say Gen Xers, for example, are simply different from the baby boomers and older workers, so companies must adapt accordingly. To some degree that may be true. But in retailing, associates in the stores represent the corporate image to the shopping public. I completely resent it (as do most people I know, both young and old) when I'm served by young people with tattoos, nose rings, bandannas on their heads, and chains dangling from every pocket of their clothing. Perhaps employment discrimination laws address the hiring of folks today, but I believe that could legally be avoided by establishing a dress code. Rather than criticize any company's hiring practices, I will just state that I have never seen management-level people present themselves in this manner. If your personal freedom of expression is so important, look for a different career path. That should be reason enough to give you my eighth piece of advice, which is: "Your personal appearance is meaningful when you wish to progress in management." (By the way, shortly after my hiring, I cut off my ducktails and took the cigarettes out of my T-shirt sleeve.)

9) What They Don't Tell You in College

Retailing can be an exciting and lucrative career; however, entry-level salaries can't be compared with that of many other specialty career paths. I never went to college, so I couldn't tell you what I didn't learn. But I supervised many college graduates, and I can tell you some things they never learned in school. In my opinion, there are two types of college graduates. First, there are those whose parents paid for everything; perhaps they joined sororities or fraternities, or acted like big shots on campus. These graduates often enter the business world and continue to expect everything on a silver platter. They are usually shell-shocked by the reality of working long, hard hours to be successful. They are in for a rude awakening.

The second category of college graduates includes the students who relied on scholarships and/or student loans and worked their way through school — the hard way. After earning their diplomas, these grads are prepared to work their way through the business world in the same manner. Would you venture to guess which type is more likely to succeed? A college degree is more crucial today than ever before in getting your foot in the door, but does not ensure a good salary or advancement. You should be willing to enter the workforce at entry-level compensation, and follow the guidance I've already given. My ninth piece of advice is: "Upon graduation from college, you must be prepared to start at the bottom, accept an entry-level salary, and set about to work your way up the corporate ladder."

10) Playing Politics versus Personalities

Workplace politics are a fact of life in the business world. Success depends on your ability to identify and understand the problem, and operate within those parameters. You'll recall my story of Tom Jefferson. My strategy of "telling him what he wanted to hear" could have been construed as "playing politics," but I determined it was "playing personalities." There's a huge difference. Kathleen Kelley Reardon, in a best practice narrative, *Managing Internal Politics,* points out that there are generally four types of political arenas possible in any given corporate environment:

▸ The minimally politicized, where the atmosphere is amicable. Conflicts rarely occur and don't usually last long. Rules may be bent and favors granted, but people treat each other with regard.

▸ The moderately politicized, focused on organizational agility, but operate on commonly understood and formally sanctioned rules.

When conflicts get out of hand, managers will invoke sanctioned rules or shared morés for resolution.

▸ The highly politicized culture, where conflict is pervasive. "Who" is more important than "what" you know, and work is often highly stressful, especially for those not in the "in" group.

▸ The pathologically politicized organization, which is often on the verge of self-destruction. People distrust each other, interactions are often fractious, and conflict is long-lasting and pervasive. You must spend much time covering your back. Subordinates are seen as stubborn, willful — even stupid. Signs of political pathology include frequent flattery of persons in power, massaging information to avoid rocking the boat, malicious gossip (getting others before they get you), and "fake left, go right" (purposely misleading others to look good when others fail). Managers sacrifice subordinates' careers to avoid looking bad.

When you enter the workplace, you may face any form of these political levels within any organization. Recognizing the level and avoiding getting wrapped up in it are important elements of success. During my career, I identified all four levels at work in any given position. I can say that Walmart was never a highly or pathologically politicized organization during my time there. Most management folks went out of their way to avoid it, but there was always a smattering of political players and politically-inclined supervisors. The long-term successful associates were those who tried to "play the middle-ground" and avoided taking sides in obvious power alignment disputes. I tried never to align myself with any particular power group or become involved in the politics of the workplace. But I did learn I needed to "play personalities." It's a smart thing to do and essential to achieving success. I describe the difference as follows:

Playing politics is when you blindly obey orders that you know are wrong at the expense of the company or the people who work for you; people whose livelihoods depend on you doing the right thing. This also can involve aligning yourself and endearing yourself to some particular person or group whom you perceive as "the future power" within an organization, even though they're wrong. If they are ultimately removed from the organization, you may be right behind them.

Playing personalities, on the other hand, is when you must kiss someone's rear (so to speak), carry a briefcase, say what he/she wants to hear, and/or massage his/her ego to do what is right by your people and the company without harassment. This approach is often challenging but necessary. It means swallowing your pride or "going along" with things you may not agree with.

I saw many folks throughout my career who received promotions and advancement by playing politics, not because they were the most capable. There's something I also noted. The people who engaged in politics didn't last long, because their lack of talent became apparent as they progressed. When they lost the support of their political backers, they disappeared quickly. My tenth piece of advice is: "Learn to play personalities, but avoid playing politics in the process of getting ahead. Learn to recognize the difference."

> You can play too much at corporate politics. Just say, I may lose my job, but I will try to do the best I can.
> — DENNIS STEVENSON

> Managers should work for their people, and not the reverse.
> — KENNETH BLANCHARD

CHAPTER 23

Lessons for Life — Regrets

L ooking back on my career and life, I have a number of regrets and have learned many lessons. I hope by sharing some of my personal trials and tribulations, perhaps I can help someone else avoid a few pitfalls along the way. I know I've been fortunate to have been given opportunities that people just as capable as me have never received. But how many folks have you heard say, "If only I had it to do over again?" I suppose every person, if honest, wishes some of his or her actions could be "do-overs." I certainly do. We would all like a "Mulligan" now and then. Following are examples and lessons I learned the hard way:

Planning for the Future

I've told people throughout my life that I could manage the company's money better than my own. For the first twelve years of my career, I barely eked out a living on my salary, what with two young children and moving from town to town. But finally, when I began making "good money," I became mostly interested in acquiring stuff I'd always wanted. That may be the norm, but looking back, I observed many of my colleagues buying up all the Walmart stock they could. These folks lived frugally and saved a portion of their salaries. They planned for their children's education; they were careful with their investments, and averse to risks. I, on the other hand, had a tendency to "live for today." Although I built up a nice retirement fund and invested in solid long-term annuities and the like, I look back on so many dollars that I spent unwisely, which would surely be welcome today. My advice is to think about the future at a young age. Whenever feasible, take any amount possible out of each paycheck and deposit it in a savings account that you can't access for many years. Businesses go bankrupt, jobs get eliminated, and the economy experiences ups and downs. You never know what the future holds. It's wise to plan for the unknown and have something to fall back on.

Importance of Family

I mentioned earlier that I went through a divorce in 1984, the result of an affair. It's by no means easy to share this story with strangers. Cindy and I were married for eighteen years. We were blessed with two wonderful children who suffered a great deal from the breakup. Although I've now been happily married again for nineteen years, the effects of a divorce never leave you or your family. From the moment the ink dries on the divorce papers, you feel as if something is missing from your life. That pain never really goes away, especially when you consider the vows taken at your wedding ceremony — "under God." When I see an older couple still together through thick and thin — celebrating forty, fifty, or even sixty years of marriage — I find myself feeling a special sense of pride for them. We all know that marriage is tough. Folks who can keep their love alive through the good times and bad, as God intended, deserve special recognition.

At one time, I tried to convince myself that retailing caused my family problems. I made plenty of excuses: I traveled a lot; I hardly remember my kids growing up; if I had only spent more time with them; it takes a special woman to put up with husbands who are devoted to their work; etc. While some of this may be true, most of my colleagues remained happily married throughout their careers. So I can't use that as a justification for my failed marriage. I can only blame myself for being weak and susceptible to the temptations that face all of us at one time or another. My advice is to: (1) be sure you are ready and don't rush to get married, (2) do whatever you can to ensure you and your partner are right for each other, and (3) once you take your vows, do everything in your power to make the marriage work. I assure you, things aren't "greener on the other side." Your problems don't go away with divorce. They generally get worse. Why? In my opinion, it's because God intended a marriage to last "until death do us part."

An Addictive Personality

I'm certainly not a psychology expert, but I've been told about the hereditary traits of parents being passed on to their children. I believe this is true. My father was an alcoholic, had a weakness for women, and struggled with many addictions. I've said many times that I always desired to be the best at whatever I did throughout my career. You could say that I became addicted to retailing. That may sound silly, but there's a lot of truth to it. In fact, I became addicted to practically everything I tried in my life. I shot pool at the pool hall growing up and remain hooked to this day. I took up golf in 1975 and have been obsessed with the game ever since. I played darts in a bar one time and kept at it until I became a very skilled player. When I play cards or board games, my competitive streak takes over and I stick with it until I'm as good as I can be. I took up smoking at seventeen-years-old and am sorry to say I still smoke today. I was never addicted to alcohol (in terms of drinking at home), but liked to go out for drinks with the guys. When I did, I found it difficult to stop until I had consumed far too much. So, my self-analysis tells me that I have an addictive personality. This in itself isn't necessarily bad, because we make our own choices. But I believe people with a family history of addiction should be aware of it and be careful with their choices. If they find themselves trending toward harmful activity, they should seek help or find someone to talk to. I believe addiction to anything is potentially damaging. Although I never sought nor received "professional" help for any of my addictions, I certainly was blessed with mentors, pastors, and family members who were there when I felt I was hitting bottom and guided me toward improving my life and circumstances.

Trusting Others with Your Money

One of the biggest disappointments in my life has been that I trusted others with my finances. I've always loved people and enjoyed having the ability to help others in need. Perhaps that was because I knew what it was like to have nothing. I can't remember all the people I've loaned money to (or invested with) over the years. But I can tell you that only two of those folks ever paid me back.

D. J. Coyle, whom I first met in 1976 when he worked as a route salesman for Proctor & Gamble in Kansas City, has remained one of my very best friends ever since. D.J. is a Viet Nam "tunnel rat" veteran. He served in the 173rd Airborne. He hails from Sulphur Springs, Arkansas, and knew my dad and the Loveless family better than I ever did. My dad, his siblings, and my grandparents lived in Sulphur Springs when D. J. was growing up there. At one point, D.J. and his wonderful wife, Sue, found themselves in financial trouble. I helped them out. It wasn't a lot of money to me at the time, but D.J. is quick to point out that it was a lot to him. As soon as he got back on his feet, he repaid me by giving me the only thing he owned — a car. That vehicle was worth much more than I had loaned him, but he was determined to settle up as soon as he could. The car, which I still own, was a 1984 McClaren — one of only fifty ever built, and therefore a true "collectible." As much as D. J. loved that car, our friendship was more important to him. Since then, D.J. and his wife have done well. They currently live in a nice neighborhood in Parkville, a suburb of Kansas City.

A young man named Ron Watson, who lived in Rogers, was a good friend of my son, Ronnie. While in college at the University of Arkansas, Ron needed money to continue his education. Again, it wasn't a lot and I was more than happy to help him out. I had completely forgotten about this incident until many years later, when I received an envelope containing a check from Ron. Here was a young man who never forgot his debt, and today he's a successful insurance agent in the northwest Arkansas area. It speaks volumes about Ron's character.

I share these two examples, not to embarrass D. J. or Ron, but to compliment them. They are the only two people of the hundreds I've helped who made an attempt to pay me back. In many other cases, involving much more money, these people were "friends" up until the debt came due. At that point I never heard from them again. Maybe they were embarrassed.

After leaving Walmart with retirement funds to invest, my problem became worse. I trusted personal friends who were so-called "money managers" with the big brokerage houses, such as Merrill-Lynch and A.G. Edwards. You can guess what happened; my funds evaporated almost overnight. Again, the lesson I wish to leave you with is that you must be very careful in trusting others with your money. You should absolutely be willing to help others, but have a clear understanding, especially with close friends and family, as to how you will be repaid. (Or make it known that you don't even wish to be repaid.) I don't believe friends or family set out to intentionally take advantage, but when they can't repay their debts, it can drive a wedge between you. Money issues ruin friendships and in some cases, families. Giving and/or donating money to people is not the same as loaning money for personal or investment purposes.

Idle Time is Not Good

When I left Walmart in 1986, divorced and forty-two-years-old, I chased my dream of making movies. After losing a great deal of money on one particular Arkansas film project, I came down to earth hard. I became depressed. I had no idea what I wanted to do. I bought a Ferrari and started drinking too much. I once saw a movie called *Middle-Aged Crazy*. That was me. The plot mirrored my life during that embarrassing time. I share this with you in the hopes there are lessons you can learn.

I was sitting in a local club at 7:00 p.m. one evening; I'd been drinking since noon after going in for a hamburger. I'd been driving my Ferrari around without a driver's license for a few months (because of a DWI). I received a call from my ex-wife, who asked me to come to St. Mary's Hospital immediately. My sister, Pat, had just collapsed and died at home from a heart attack. In my drunken stupor, I rushed to the hospital, stumbled into a room, and viewed my sister's body through bloodshot eyes. Sad but true. I dropped to my knees beside her bed, and prayed to God for forgiveness for my drinking, for my deteriorating life, for falling away from Him, and for not being there for my sister. We loved each other very much and loved playing cards together. My mom later told me that Pat had mentioned a couple of weeks earlier that she "sure wished Ronnie would come over and play cards more often, instead of being out running around." That incident occurred seventeen years ago. I have not touched a single drink since. That night, God removed my desire to drink. I have faith that Pat is looking down on me and is pleased.

My Testimony

Religion is certainly a touchy subject and I'm far from proficient in its intricacies. But like everyone else, I have an opinion on the subject that I'd like to share. As I've said in this book, my grandmother insisted on taking my sisters and me to the Nazarene Church throughout our childhoods. In 1959, an incident occurred which changed my point of view. One Sunday, I took a girlfriend to church. She was wearing lipstick and one of the stern church ladies asked me to take her out to the lobby so she could remove it. They chose to believe at that time that wearing makeup was wrong. I left that day and told my mom that I would never go back to that church ... and I didn't. To be fair, I don't believe the Nazarene Church today is that rigid, and I certainly don't judge any church and their beliefs. People can find fault with any one of the denominations. I believe a person should choose and attend a church regularly, but one that feels right for them.

My first wife, Cindy, and her wonderful parents, Leonard and Doralee Stearns, had always attended the First Baptist Church in Mt. Vernon, Missouri. Once married, and through all the moves we made during my career, Cindy and I would join the First Baptist Church wherever we lived. While in Mountain Home, I had the "born again" experience and was "saved." We Baptists believe this is the only way to salvation ... accepting Jesus Christ as our Lord and Savior. Many people and some other religions question this, but I can attest that you are a truly changed person when this occurs, and a "saved" person never forgets the exact time of that experience. It changes you inside. It certainly changed me. I became very close to the church and God during that time. I adored the pastor who led me to Christ. I became very involved in the church and taught Sunday school to young people for two years. We tithed faithfully and our financial situation improved steadily.

In 1975, I was promoted to district manager and we moved to the Kansas City area. Shortly after that, the pastor of the Mountain Home church, the man who was instrumental in helping me accept Jesus, was fired for an indiscretion with a female church member. I was shocked and dismayed. I found it hard to believe a man of God, and especially one I so respected, could have done something like that. I realize now that he is a human being, and susceptible to the same temptations as the rest of us. Regardless of the reasons (on the road a lot, another new town, a questioning of faith, perhaps a lot of things), I began to fall away from the church and my close relationship with God. I knew He was there; I knew I was doing the wrong things, but I continued my bad habits — until the night of my sister's death.

The culmination of events that went wrong in my life resulted in a self-examination that opened my eyes and heart. I do not take my salvation for granted. I've heard all the opinions of others. I've heard them question the "once saved, always saved" belief. They argue that a "real" Christian doesn't go out and do the wrong things. If you are "saved," you don't sin. My response to those arguments is as follows: God does not want to lose any of His people. He sent his son, Jesus Christ, to die for our sins. If you truly accept Jesus as your Savior, you are saved and will go to heaven. Yet we are human beings, with all our shortcomings, failures, and sins. By sinning, or continuing to sin, we lose peace of mind, joy, rewards, and the full life we could have if we lived the way Jesus taught us. I call this creating our own "hell on earth." We suffer in many ways by not living the life we should. I surely did.

I look back at the periods of time when I was close to God, attending church regularly, tithing, and doing my best to live the life God teaches us, and my life was good. I was rewarded financially, the family was happy, and I was happy. In the times I was farther away from God and ignored Him, troubles found me and my family. So that is the lesson. And that is my testimony. We make the choices in our lives. We can choose the good or the bad — and will reap the consequences that go with those choices. My hope in writing this is that someone, somewhere, might benefit from it and avoid the mistakes I've made.

EPILOGUE

The Business

Twenty-three years have passed since I left the Walmart company. Yet I still find myself as attached as ever — perhaps not physically, but certainly mentally. I continue to be a student of retail and merchandising. I watch the competition, I read the analyst's reports, and I readily defend the company. When thinking of the past, I think of all the hard work, the long hours, and the dedication of the early managers and associates so instrumental in the building and success of Walmart. I know most of these people continue to take great pride in what we built. We still feel it is "our" company . . . and it is. We are shareholders.

We also recognize that it is a different company with different challenges today. That's why we are hesitant to criticize or interfere. My hope is that the company will continue to realize the value of the large retiree base here in northwest Arkansas, a core of experienced and devoted individuals who could assist them in many ways as needed.

Today, Walmart faces challenges from many different directions:

▸ Wall Street and shareholders demand increasing profits and return on capital to offset the slower pace of growth.

▸ With U.S. sales slowing, an increasing percentage of growth will come from opportunities in the company's international division. The company is now a truly global corporation, increasing the complexity of execution.

▸ An increasingly diverse and global work force requires new and innovative training and motivational programs.

▸ Competition is stronger and more diverse. The company is challenged by the "category killers" such as Best Buy, Cabela's, Bass Pro Shops, Academy Sports, Staples, Office Depot, and PetsMart; strong grocery competitors such as H.E.B., Publix. and Aldi's; savvy convenience pharmacy operators such as Walgreens and CVS; thriving dollar store leaders such as Dollar General and Family Dollar; and formidable club contenders such as Costco and B.J.'s.

▸ Continued pressure and scrutiny by the anti-Walmart union and environmental groups.

▸ The sheer scope of managing a company the size of Walmart today boggles my mind. That the company has continued to perform well is a credit to its management capabilities.

▸ As I completed this book and pondered writing the epilogue, I thought again of my Building Blocks of (Walmart's) Success. I thought of the competition we faced and defeated through the early years. I thought of the daily comments from my neighbors, friends, colleagues, and the suppliers. But primarily and lastly, I thought of my mentor and the founder, Sam Walton. For better or worse, the standard question is WWST ("What Would Sam Think?")

▸ I believe Mr. Sam would be proud of the company today: the size, the profits, the initiatives undertaken to become a better corporate citizen, the philanthropic activity, efforts in diversity, and the proactive stance in dealing with the critics.

▸ But I also know that he would be challenging the company on a daily basis, in no uncertain terms, regarding some issues. Not because anything is necessarily broken, but because that was his nature, from day one until the day he died.

▸ He would challenge us to listen to the folks in the stores, take care of them, and motivate them. They are the key to success.

▸ He would challenge us to be "merchants" — all of us. He would ask how everyone's VPI items were performing.

▸ He would make sure that everyone in the Home Office was out in the stores as much as possible, right beside Mr. Sam himself.

▸ He would harp on whether the stores were in-stock and carried exciting new merchandise. He would want to see eye-catching displays in Action Alley.

▸ He would still be trying to enforce the "Ten-foot Rule," to make the customers feel appreciated and taken care of in the stores

▸ He would insist on MBWA (Management by Wandering Around) in the Home Office . . . saying hello to the people and giving them support.

▸ He would insist on being firm but fair, and treating suppliers with respect.

▸ He would still be having fun while doing business.

▸ And lastly, he would question every single dollar spent by the company to ensure it would result in better sales and profits.

▸ These things represent Sam Walton's personal philosophy and the elements that made Walmart great. And even with all the pressures upon the company today, he would know that these things can still be done, and remain crucial to Walmart's continued success.

My Personal Life

I have now been married to my second wife, Robin, for nineteen years. April, my beautiful and sweet twenty-six-year-old stepdaughter, works for Octagon Global Events office in Rogers. We are raising my grandson, Nicholas Dakota Taylor, who is seventeen and a straight-A junior at Heritage High School. My son, Ronnie II, forty-two, played football, graduated from Rogers High School, received a bachelor's in marketing from the University of Arkansas, and now manages the Walmart business for Farleys and Sathers, a confectionary supplier to Walmart. He and his wife, Debby, have given me two beautiful grandchildren in Ronnie III (Tripp) and Morgan. My daughter, Kim, also graduated from Rogers High. She was a beautiful straight-A student, on the pom squad, but made bad choices right after high school.

Kim fell in love with a rock band artist in Kansas City and became involved with drugs. I asked Kim if I could share this with the readers, and she agreed in the hopes it might help someone else avoid the problem.

I wanted to mention this story because it became a significant issue in our family's lives. After a number of failed attempts at rehab, and after having a baby, Kim gave Cindy and me guardianship of Nicholas (Kody) when he was five-years-old. He is a fine young man and a good student. Today, Kim lives in Bentonville and has turned her life around. She has conquered the addiction problems. Going through this, I've asked myself many times what I might have done differently that could have changed things for her. I've never found any definitive answers. We raised our kids in the same manner . . . they were both exposed to church, cared for, and loved equally. But at some point, all people must make their own choices. Some choose better than others. All we can do is support, love, and help them as much as possible.

Kim is a great girl and I love her dearly. She has a great personality, is one of the hardest workers I've ever known, and I am proud of her. I am pleased she agreed to share her experience with drugs, because it is one all too familiar to far too many families.

My mom, Angie, passed away last year, and I miss her terribly. She was always proud of what I accomplished in my life, while quick to let me know when I disappointed her — a typical good mother. She struggled much of her life, and worked so hard to support our family and give us what she could.

My sister, Connie, and her husband, Frank, live in Joplin, Missouri, and she is one of the sweetest and most giving people you could ever meet. We're currently closer than ever before.

The last family story, one that taught me an important lesson, has to do with my father, Clifford Loveless. As I shared earlier, he was an alcoholic who never played a role in my life. He left Mom when I was two-years-old, and I never met the man until 1964, when Mom arranged a meeting at the airport in Seattle — I was on my way to Alaska for my Air Force assignment. The experience was like meeting a stranger; I had no positive feelings for him. I've been told by many people and members of the clergy that we should forgive and reconcile in these situations. Two years ago my sister, Mom, and I decided we should attend a Loveless family reunion that is held in Bellingham, Washington every summer — just to say hello to my dad's side of the family, many of whom stayed in touch with us over the years. We traveled to Washington and spent a wonderful weekend with my dad and his family in that beautiful part of our country. My dad and I had ample time to discuss our lives and regrets. I found him to be apologetic and humble about how our lives turned out and his failure to stay close to his children. I felt good about having gone there, telling him that I no longer harbored any animosity toward him. I recognized that he was a nineteen-year-old young man when the family problems occurred, and that we all make mistakes in our lives. My dad passed away six months after this reunion. I am thankful for that visit and the sense of closure it gave me.

Our Country and Business

I will not expound further on my concern for our country and the free enterprise system. I've already addressed that issue in the book, and recognize that a discussion of politics in this venue would be futile and controversial. But perhaps a little story I read many years ago might be a good way to say what I am thinking and to leave you with some thoughts.

The Little Red Hen

Once upon a time, there was a little red hen who scratched about the barnyard until she uncovered some grains of wheat. She called her neighbors and said, "If we plant this wheat, we shall have bread to eat. Who will help me plant it?"

"Not I," said the cow.

"Not I," said the duck.

"Not I," said the pig.

"Not I," said the goose.

"Then I will," said the little red hen. And she did. The wheat grew tall and ripened into golden grain. "Who will help me reap my wheat?" asked the little red hen.

"Not I," said the duck.

"Out of my classification," said the pig.

"I'd lose my seniority," said the cow.

"I'd lose my unemployment compensation," said the goose.

"Then I will," said the little red hen, and she did.

At last it came time to bake the bread. "Who will help me bake the bread?" asked the little red hen.

"That would be overtime for me," said the cow.

"I'd lose my welfare benefits," said the duck.

"I'm a dropout and never learned how," said the pig.

"If I'm to be the only helper, that's discrimination," said the goose.

"Then I will," said the little red hen.

She baked five loaves and held them up for the neighbors to see.

They all wanted some, and in fact, demanded a share. But the little red hen said, "No, I can eat the five loaves myself."

"Excess profits!" cried the cow.

"Capitalist leech!" screamed the duck.

"I demand equal rights!" yelled the goose.

And the pig just grunted.

And they painted "unfair" picket signs and marched round and round the little red hen, shouting obscenities.

When the government agent came, he said to the little red hen, "You must not be greedy."

"But I earned the bread," said the little red hen.

"Exactly," said the agent. "That is the wonderful free enterprise system. Anyone in the barnyard can earn as much as he wants. But under our modern government regulations, the productive workers must divide their product with the idle."

And they lived happily ever after, including the little red hen, who smiled and clucked, "I am grateful. I am grateful."

But her neighbors wondered why she never again baked any more bread.

Ronald Leroy Loveless graduated from Bentonville High School in 1960, served four years in the U.S. Air Force and accepted a job with Walmart as a stock boy in 1964.

He rose steadily through the Walmart operations ranks, achieving senior vice president status in 1983. Along the way, he was appointed general manager of the Sam's Club operations. Ron left the company in 1986 to pursue interests in the entertainment industry.

Ron is married to Robin Loveless, has three grown children and is raising one of three grandchildren, Kody Taylor. He and his family reside in Rogers, Arkansas, home of the first Walmart.

Anna Morter lives in Rogers, Arkansas with her husband Dr. Tom Morter. She has two grown children, Dr. Sarah Rowden and Russ Morter. She graduated from the University of Arkansas with a M.Ed. in 1981. After working in the education field for many years, she turned to her first love: writing. Her previous works, published as ghost writer for Morter HealthSystem, include: one book (*The Soul Purpose*), numerous newsletters, trade journal articles and educational materials. This is her first published work as co-author.